FOUNDATIONS OF ETHICS

BOSTON UNIVERSITY STUDIES IN PHILOSOPHY AND RELIGION

General Editor: Leroy S. Rouner

Volume Four

Volume Three
Meaning, Truth, and God
Leroy S. Rouner, Editor

Volume Two
Transcendence and the Sacred
Alan M. Olson and Leroy S. Rouner, Editors

Volume One
Myth, Symbol, and Reality
Alan M. Olson, Editor

Foundations of Ethics

Edited by

Leroy S. Rouner

UNIVERSITY OF NOTRE DAME PRESS
Notre Dame & London

Library of Congress Cataloging in Publication Data

Main entry under title:

Foundations of ethics.

(Boston University studies in philosophy and
religion; v. 4)
  Includes index.
  Contents: Kant and the mythic roots of morality /
John R. Silber — Reason, tradition, community / Charles
Davis — "But we do see Jesus" / John Howard Yoder —
[etc.]
  1. Ethics—Addresses, essays, lectures. 2. Social
ethics—Addresses, essays, lectures. I. Rouner,
Leroy S. II. Series.
BJ1012.F637 1983   170   83-10280
ISBN 0-268-00963-5

Manufactured in the United States of America

Contents

Preface

Boston University Studies in Philosophy and Religion is a joint project of the Boston University Institute for Philosophy and Religion and the University of Notre Dame Press. While these Studies may eventually include occasional volumes by individual authors dealing with critical issues in the philosophy of religion, it is presently focused on an annual volume edited from the previous year's Institute lecture program. The Director of the Institute, who also serves as editor of these Studies, chooses a theme and invites participants to lecture at Boston University in the course of the academic year. These public lectures are on Wednesday evenings, chaired by faculty from the various schools and departments within the university which jointly sponsor the Institute. There is a critical respondent to each paper and general discussion by the audience. The papers are then revised by their authors, and the editor selects and edits the papers to be included in these Studies. In preparation are volumes on religious and cultural pluralism and on problems of religious epistemology.

The Boston University Institute for Philosophy and Religion is sponsored jointly by the Graduate School, the School of Theology, the Department of Philosophy, and the Department of Religion at Boston University. As an interdisciplinary and ecumenical forum it does not represent any philosophical school or religious tradition. Within the academic community it is committed to open interchange on questions of value, truth, reality, and meaning which transcend the narrow specializations of academic life. Outside the university community it seeks to recover the public tradition of philosophical discourse which was a lively part of American intellectual life in the early years of this century before the professionalization of both philosophy and religious studies.

Our themes are intentionally broad and inclusive in order to provide a home for a variety of views and projects. Our essays focus on the analysis of quite specific issues within the theme, however, and we encourage our authors to make an autobiographical connection with their analysis. We also emphasize the need for comparative studies. What William Ernest Hocking once called "The Coming World Civilization" is now the inescapable context for all serious work in philosophy and religious studies.

The Institute receives support from various sources and we have too few occasions to express our appreciation. Our primary budget is provided by the Graduate School of Boston University. Dean Geoffrey Bannister and Associate Dean Michael Mendillo have been generous and imaginative in a period of increasingly tight budgets, as has Dean Richard Nesmith of the School of Theology, who supplements our budget. And the Institute's growth from an informal faculty seminar only a few short years ago is due in no small part to the encouragement and help of various sorts given us by Provost Robert Mayfield, and especially by President John Silber. These friends and colleagues have also participated in our program by chairing meetings and, in John Silber's case, acting as respondent and as lecturer. We are grateful to them all.

We also receive occasional funding from sources outside the university, most notably the United Methodist Board of Higher Education and Ministry, which, for three successive years, has made a very substantial contribution to our work. We have also received help from the Lilly Endowment and the Hazen Foundation that has enabled us to expand our lecture program and to fund a Consultation on World Religions. The Consultation is a seminar of a dozen scholars from Amherst, Boston University, Brandeis, Fordham, Harvard, Smith, Syracuse, Temple, and the University of Pennsylvania who represent various world religious communities and meet six times a year. The current theme is the meaning of selfhood and person in the various world religious traditions. These papers may eventually become a volume of the Studies. Our thanks go to Julius Scott of the United Methodist Board, Robert Lynn of the Lilly Endowment, and William Bradley of the Hazen Foundation for this additional support and the confidence in our work which it expresses.

It is our hope that these volumes will provide a resource for critical reflection on fundamental human issues both within the academic community and beyond.

For CHARLES HARTSHORNE,
Dean of American philosophers and articulate defender of the
logic of belief. His lectures to the Institute for Philosophy and
Religion have renewed and enhanced the ancient alliance between
the rigor of reason and the profundity of faith.

Acknowledgments

The editor wishes to express his thanks to the authors of these essays, the members of the Institute staff, and our publishers at the University of Notre Dame Press. Because editorial revision of these essays was more than usually intrusive, I am both relieved and grateful that our authors responded with such goodhearted acquiescence. Irena Makarushka is responsible for the Institute's initial technical editing and preparation of the index, but she has made substantive editorial suggestions as well. Barbara Darling Smith, my omnicompetent Assistant, not only supervises the Institute's lecture program but schedules and oversees manuscript preparation with easy expertise and infectious enthusiasm. Without her, *Boston University Studies in Philosophy and Religion* would not be possible. A manuscript becomes a book, however, only in the hands of the publishers, and our friends at the University of Notre Dame Press effect this transformation with a sensitivity to our best hopes and a graceful professionalism that is unrivaled. Ann Rice, Executive Editor of the Press, has once again put us in her debt by knowing just what needed to be done and seeing to it that it was done expeditiously and well. Our most profound gratitude, however, goes to Jim Langford, Director of the Press. It was he who first suggested that Notre Dame might publish the Institute's lectures, and his openness to new ideas provides constant encouragement and a continuing challenge.

Contributors

SISSELA BOK was born in Sweden and educated in Switzerland, France, and the United States. She received her B.A. and M.A. degrees in psychology from George Washington University and her Ph.D. in philosophy from Harvard University. She has taught ethics and decision-making at the Harvard Medical School and the John F. Kennedy School of Government and has been a member of the Ethics Advisory Board to the Secretary of Health, Education, and Welfare. In addition to numerous articles on medical ethics, Sissela Bok is the author of *Lying: Moral Choice in Public and Private Life* (1978) and *Secrets: On the Ethics of Concealment and Revelation* (1982).

JOHN B. CARMAN is Professor of Comparative Religion at the Harvard University Divinity School and Director of the Center for the Study of World Religions. Born in India of Christian missionary parents, he studied at Haverford College, Yale University, and the University of Leiden. He has also been a Research Fellow of the Christian Institute for the Study of Religion and Society in Bangalore, India. In addition to many articles, his publications include the translation of W. Brede Kristensen's lectures in phenomenology of religion, *The Meaning of Religion* (1960). He is the author of *The Theology of Rāmānuja* (1974) and (with P. Y. Luke) of *Village Christians and Hindu Culture* (1968).

ROBERT S. COHEN is Professor of Physics and Philosophy at Boston University and chairs the Center for the Philosophy

and History of Science and the Boston Colloquium for the
Philosophy of Science. He received his doctorate in theoretical physics from Yale University in 1948. He has been visiting
professor at a number of American universities and has lectured widely in this country, Europe, and the Soviet Union.
Professor Cohen is the author of many scholarly papers and
is general editor, with Marx Wartofsky, of *Boston Studies in
the Philosophy of Science.*

CHARLES A. DAVIS was educated at St. Edmund's College, Ware,
England, and at the Gregorian University in Rome. From
1949 to 1965 he was Professor of Theology at St. Edmund's.
Currently he is Professor of Religion at Concordia University in Montreal. Professor Davis has lectured in Europe, Can-
ada, and the United States, and has appeared on numerous
radio and television programs. He is the editor of *Studies
in Religion, Sciences Religieuses,* as well as several other
publications. Professor Davis has written many articles and
reviews in scholarly journals, and his books have been translated into several languages. Among his more recent works
are *The Concept of God* (1981), *Theology and Political Society* (1980), and *Body as Spirit: The Nature of Religious Feeling* (1976).

DANIEL R. DeNICOLA received his B.A. in 1967 from Ohio University, where he was a National Merit Scholar. He took the
M.Ed. degree at Harvard University in 1968 and the Ed.D.
degree in philosophy of education from Harvard in 1973. He
is Associate Professor of Philosophy and Dean of the Faculty
at Rollins College, Winter Park, Florida. Professor DeNicola
is a member of Phi Beta Kappa and has received the Hugh F.
McKean Award at Rollins, as well as the Arthur Vining Davis
Fellowship. His recent articles include "Sociobiology and Religion" (*Zygon, Journal of Religion and Science,* 1980). He
serves on the Editorial Advisory Board of *Zygon* and was editor of *Philosophy of Education 1981: Proceedings of the
Thirty-Seventh Annual Meeting of the Philosophy of Education Society.*

ROGER S. GOTTLIEB is Assistant Professor of Philosophy at Worcester Polytechnic Institute. He received his B.A. in 1968 and his Ph.D. in 1975 from Brandeis University. In 1980–81, he was a National Endowment for the Humanities Fellow. Professor Gottlieb has taught at Tufts University and at the University of Connecticut. His many articles include "The Contemporary Critical Theory of Jürgen Habermas" (*Ethics*, 1981), and "Kierkegaard's Ethical Individualism" (*The Monist*, 1979). In 1979–80 he participated in the Nietzsche Colloquium of the Boston University Institute for Philosophy and Religion and was a respondent to Alasdair MacIntyre in the program of the Boston Colloquium for the Philosophy of Science.

EDWARD W. JAMES is Associate Professor of Philosophy and Religious Studies and chairs that department at Bridgewater State College in Massachusetts. Previously he was Assistant Professor of Philosophy at Bates College in Lewiston, Maine. Professor James received his A.B. (*magna cum laude*) from Tufts University in 1964 and his Ph.D. from the University of Southern California in 1970. He is a member of Phi Beta Kappa and has served as Secretary of the Maine Philosophical Institute. Among his more recent essays are "A Reasoned Ethical Incoherence?" (*Ethics*, 1979), and "On Dismissing Astrology and Other Irrationalities" (in *Philosophy of Science and the Occult*, ed. P. Grim, 1982). His concern for the problem of privacy was set forth initially in a lecture to the Maine Philosophical Institute in 1978 on "Privacy and Self-Criticism."

STEVEN T. KATZ received his Ph.D. from Cambridge University. He has lectured at Hebrew University, Jerusalem; the University of London; the University of Lancaster, England; the University of Toronto; and Yale University. He is Professor of Religion at Dartmouth College, currently on leave as Fellow of the Center for Jewish Studies and Visiting Scholar at the Center for the Study of World Religions at Harvard

University. Professor Katz has written extensively on Jewish philosophy. His books include *Jewish Philosophers* (1975), *Jewish Ideas and Concepts* (1977), *Mysticism and Philosophical Analysis (1978), Martin Buber and Hasidism* (1982), *Mysticism and Religious Traditions* (1983) and *Post-Holocaust Dialogues* (1983). He is editor of *Modern Judaism* as well as of *Continental Judaica.*

WALTER G. MUELDER is Professor Emeritus and Dean Emeritus of the Boston University School of Theology. He is a member of Phi Beta Kappa and a Fellow of the American Academy of Arts and Sciences. Educated at Knox College and Boston University, he received his Ph.D. in 1933 and was a postgraduate Fellow at the University of Frankfurt in 1930–31. He holds honorary degrees from Claflin College, West Virginia Wesleyan University, Colby College, Boston College, and Boston University. He was a member of the Faith and Order Commission of the World Council of Churches 1952–75. Professor Muelder has written several hundred articles, essays, and reviews. His books include *Moral Law in Christian Social Ethics* (1966), *Foundations of the Responsible Society* (1960), and *Religion and Economic Responsibility* (1953).

LYNDA SHARP PAINE is an Associate Attorney at the firm of Hill and Barlow in Boston. She holds a J.D. from the Harvard Law School (1979) and a D.Phil. in moral philosophy from Oxford University (1976), where she wrote her thesis on "Forms and Criticisms of Utilitarianism" under Professor R. M. Hare. She received her undergraduate education at Smith College and Duke University. Dr. Paine was awarded the Henry Luce Foundation Fellowship (1976–77), the Leopold Schepp Foundation Fellowship (1972–74), and the Smith College Art Seminar Fellowship (1971). She was Associate Professor of Philosophy at the National Cheng Chi University in Taiwan (1976–77) before returning to this country to study law. She is the author of "Instrumentalism v. Formalism: Dissolving the Dichotomy" (*Wisconsin Law Review*, 1978).

LEROY S. ROUNER is Professor of Philosophical Theology at Boston University, Director of the Institute for Philosophy and Religion, and general editor of Boston University Studies in Philosophy and Religion. He graduated from Harvard College (A.B., 1953), Union Theological Seminary (B.D., *summa cum laude*, 1958), and Columbia University (Ph.D., 1961). He was Assistant Professor of Philosophy and Theology at the United Theological College, Bangalore, India, from 1961 to 1966. He is editor of the Hocking Festschrift, *Philosophy, Religion, and the Coming World Civilization* (1969), and (with John Howie) of *The Wisdom of William Ernest Hocking* (1978), as well as author of *Within Human Experience: The Philosophy of William Ernest Hocking* (1969). A member of Phi Beta Kappa, he has lectured widely in this country and in India and has published a number of papers on philosophy of religion and theology in scholarly journals. He was Visiting Professor of Philosophy at the University of Hawaii in 1982.

JOHN R. SILBER is President of Boston University and University Professor of Philosophy and Law. He received his B.A. (*summa cum laude*) in 1947 from Trinity University in San Antonio, his M.A. in 1952 and Ph.D. in 1956 from Yale University. He has been Professor of Philosophy and University Professor of Arts and Letters at the University of Texas at Austin and has been awarded a Fulbright Research Grant (1959–60) and a Guggenheim Research Grant (1963–64). He holds a number of honorary degrees from institutions in the United States and abroad. Dr. Silber has numerous publications on ethics and philosophy of law, and he is internationally known for his work on Kant's philosophy. He is the editor of *Works in Continental Philosophy* and an associate editor of *Kant-Studien*. He has received four awards for distinguished teaching, including the Danforth Foundation's E. Harris Harbison Award.

JOHN HOWARD YODER studied at the College of Wooster, Ohio, and at Goshen College. After serving on the Mennonite Cen-

tral Committee, where he administered relief and welfare
services in France, he received his doctorate in theology from
the University of Basel with a dissertation on the history of
the Radical Reformation. Since 1965 Professor Yoder has
taught theology and ethics at Goshen Biblical Seminary, and,
in addition, since 1967 he has also been on the faculty of
the Department of Theology at the University of Notre Dame.
He has been guest lecturer in Buenos Aires (1970–71), in Stras-
bourg (1974–75), and in Jerusalem (1975–76). His best known
work is *The Politics of Jesus* (1972).

Introduction

LEROY S. ROUNER

A BEMUSED JAPANESE GENTLEMAN noted that he could publicly bathe with a nude lady but could not properly have a nude lady's picture on his wall, whereas for his Western counterparts the moral situation was quite the reverse. His reported conclusion was that pornography is a question of geography.

It is true, of course, that some of our present ethical uncertainty is rooted in the fact that our geography is so much better than it was even a generation ago. It turns out that foreigners do things differently, and somehow it seems to work for them. But cultural pluralism and the resulting ethical relativism are the context for a more significant moral threat: nuclear destruction.

So just when we need them most, our ethical resources seem least clear and reliable. Hence our search for foundations of ethics. Our intent in this volume has not been to solve any specific moral problem, but to explore basic issues: the prospects for a rational ethic; the relation between ethics and a religious mythos; the challenge of non-Western ethical values; problems raised by the practice of confession, the evaluation of privacy, the ubiquity of science, and more. We obviously have not explored all the foundation issues. We cannot even claim that the ones we have explored are always the most significant. We do claim, however, that these explorations give a vivid picture of our ethical dilemma, and present some of the best thinking currently being done.

We begin with John Silber's essay on "Kant and the Mythic Roots of Morality" because it raises a fundamental question about the possibility of a rational secular ethic. Can such an ethic have sufficient motivating power? Kant was persuaded that a good will

1

is the only thing which is good without qualification, and that it alone makes us worthy to be happy. Silber makes it clear that Kant therefore had to protect the freedom of the will if morality was to be genuine. The Christian piety in which Kant himself had been reared, and which was still an influence in eighteenth-century Europe, clearly provided sources of strong moral motivation, but they were authoritarian sources. To ground morality in the theological myths of immortality and a personal God is to compel moral behavior through fear of punishment or hope of reward. But since genuine morality is the free recognition and fulfillment of one's duty for its own sake, Kant sought to establish it on the basis of a demythologized rational ethic. The primary concern of Silber's paper is to examine Kant's problem and evaluate his success in dealing with it. Sorting out the issues with considerable care, Silber concludes that Kant paid a price for eschewing the mythic roots of morality, and that, indeed, the force of moral feeling provided by reason is relatively weak. Silber puts his conclusion in historical context, however, pointing out that Kant stood between two worlds: a civilization based on mythic Christianity which was rapidly dissolving in the solvent of the scientific world view, and the newly emerging neo-religions of socialism. Kant was mindful of Plato's proposal that the state invent its own mythic roots. Silber shows how this possibility was unacceptable to Kant, however, because of its totalitarian curtailment of human freedom. Silber argues that Lenin, Stalin, and Mao have all shown the dangers of Plato's proposal, and that Kant's rational ethic can at least immunize us against totalitarian schemes for human betterment without freedom.

Charles Davis also explores the relation between a rational ethic and the motivation of a moral agent. He is more optimistic than Silber. His "Reason, Tradition, Community: The Search for Ethical Foundations" argues that there can indeed be a purely rational ethic with strong motivating power. His interpretation of reason follows Eric Voegelin's, however, and differs from Kant's. Davis points out that, while Kant's notion of reason is not purely calculative or instrumental, it is entirely autonomous. Kantian reason is the expression of the human person as a self-defining subject, and the rational will is therefore the ground of obligation and the criterion of moral action. As Davis reads him, Kant refuses any appeal to a transcendent rational order which is not of human making. Voegelin, on the other hand, is persuaded that the depth of reason, as Tillich would say, is substantive. Following Voegelin, Davis argues that reason as substance is the seat of a fundamental experience of reality which gives rise to tradition and community in the authentic sense. For Voegelin there is a noetic experience which is the same in classical Greek philosophy and in the Christian gospel movement. Davis interprets Voegelin's argument boldly: "The gospel is not an alternative to philosophy, but the same noetic experience in a perfected state."

Recognizing the need to take seriously more recent attempts at the Kantian project of grounding reason in autonomy, Davis presents a very thorough analysis of the views of Jürgen Habermas and his younger collaborator Rainer Döbert. Habermas and Döbert are persuaded that rational discourse can lead to common ground among participants seeking agreement, as long as freedom, justice, and equality are established as preconditions of rational discourse. Again, however, the motivation of the moral agent proves to be weak, and Davis finally sides with Voegelin. The emphasis on noetic experience gives the impression that Davis has avoided Silber's historic concern with mythic roots and ethical education by grounding rationality in a mystical experience. In concluding his essay, however, Davis notes that the order of reality which substantive reason grounds is not just the autonomous world of the individual, but the life of a community where tradition represents the accumulation of originative experiences. Morality, he argues, can be completely realized and expressed only in a community with its traditions.

In defense of Kant's rational ethic, however weak its motivating powers might be, John Silber argued that it was the best option among three alternatives. The new myths of Lenin, Stalin, and Mao were unacceptable because of the defective freedom which they offered; and the old myths of Christianity were unacceptable because, while they might still motivate individuals like Kant himself, they were rapidly losing their cultural power to shape a civilization. Charles Davis's argument claimed continuing power for the Christian mythos because it was identical with the noetic experience at the heart of classical or substantive reason. Davis's comments about the religious community and its tradition were brief, however, and posed in general terms. John Howard Yoder, on the contrary, is quite specific. His essay "But We Do See Jesus: The Particularity of Incarnation and the Universality of Truth" deals with the question of whether, indeed, the wider world of modern pluralistic and relativistic secularism has really made a compelling case against the narrower world of mythic biblical Christianity, so that Christianity should adapt itself to this wider world in which it now lives.

Beginning with a review of major critiques of Christian particularism, and a number of adaptive strategies which have been used by Christians to meet these criticisms, Yoder turns to the experience of early Christianity as a paradigm case of relationship between the narrow mythic world of Jesus' followers and the wider world of Roman power and hellenistic culture. Examining five different New Testament texts, he discovers that each Christian writer takes the same fundamental approach. They use the language and face the questions of the wider world's culture but do not try to integrate the Christian vision of salvation into Hellenism's cosmic visions. Rather, each presupposes the power of Jesus over the hellenistic cosmos, and proceeds to restructure the cosmic vision in terms of Christ's lordship.

Yoder's evangelical strategy is noncoercive and argues that Christians can appropriately claim the wider world of contemporary pluralism. "This land," he says, "is our land." The task of Christian ethics is precisely to meet the critical issues posed by this land. To claim Christ's sovereignty over the cosmology and culture of the modern world is not to destroy the present principalities and powers. It is to deny their claim to rule, and to reenlist them in the service of the rightful Ruler.

Walter Muelder concludes this first section on Christianity and modern culture with "Pilgrimage to Communitarian Personalism," an account of his development as a communitarian personalist. He shares Silber's philosophical concern for a rational ethic, but Muelder's rationality subscribes to a coherence theory of truth. In integrating philosophy, theology, and ethics he stands between Davis's view that the fundamental insights of Christianity and classical culture are identical, and Yoder's view that they are radically different. Muelder's concern is for a Christian ethic which is coherent within a modern ideological context shaped by philosophy, theology, science, and modern technology. His essay is a conspectus of his thought, beginning with his views on the moral experient as person-in-community, and the centrality of the person as subject and agent. He then deals with the dialogue between theology and philosophy, the regulative notion of moral law, and the role of science in ethics. He relates his personal history to the development of his thought, his rejection of both naturalism and neo-orthodoxy, and his growing identification with personalistic idealism. For Muelder the principle of coherence not only tests philosophic truth, it also sets Christian ethical reflection in an ecumenical context. An ecumenical ethic must be more specific than the natural moral law in general, but it can embrace common ground among churches and among various philosophies and ideologies in world society. He concludes that "the believer needs the philosopher and the scientist, as these need the radical faith, hope, and love of the ecumenical disciple. Emerging coherence encourages the pilgrimage to communitarian personalism wherein the moral experient finds Christian love in partnership with reason."

To balance these broad-gauged discussions of religion, our second set of essays deals specifically with various issues in contemporary philosophical ethics, beginning with Lynda Sharp Paine's "Utilitarianism and the Goodness of Persons." Utilitarianism is the dominant ethic of modern culture, and Charles Davis pointed out that it presupposes a calculative and instrumental view of reason. Paine's concern for an ethics of character tests the sufficiency of that view. She begins with a question: "Does utilitarianism sometimes require an act which a morally good person would not do?" Since utilitarian theories focus on the effects of conduct, the question of moral character is usually either ignored, or presupposed as the disposition of one who regularly acts in ways which produce the best results. Paine argues, on the contrary, that moral evaluations of persons must occupy a fundamental place in any acceptable moral theory. Her question then is whether utilitarianism can grant that place and remain genuinely utilitarian. Paine's conclusion is qualified, and reached only after a close examination of the problem as it affects both act and rule utilitarianism. She is persuaded that utilitarian theories which allow a primary place to the moral evaluation of persons will, on that basis, be able to cope with conflicts between personal values and the utilitarian moral calculus. Such a theory remains consequentialist, and therefore utilitarian in spirit. It is clear, however, that the moral reasoning she requires will involve more than the instrumental calculations usually associated with utilitarian theory.

Edward James's essay on "Rights, Privacy, and Tainted Ideals" reverses a common assumption about rights. Whereas Rawls, Gewirth, and Dworkin all speak positively of rights as constituting our personhood, James suggests that rights are essentially negative ways of protecting our moral and political systems from their own shortcomings. The right of privacy is his paradigm case. In a metaphor reminiscent of William James, our James refers to the dilemma of the "tight tie" of privacy to any fundamental value like friendship. "Make the value fundamental and its very richness rules out any necessary connection to privacy; yet make the tie tight and the value is so narrowed in meaning that it is no longer fundamental." Our dilemma, he argues, is somewhat similar to those who return to Plato's cave. The light of our ideals shines so sharply that it deforms what it illuminates. In short, all utopias are defective, and utopians regularly criticize and dismiss one another for the logically analogous reason that they are tainted by their failure to meet the demands of the real. "Like light, they serve as a beacon but not as a road." In the failure of our ideals we find the need for rights in general and privacy in particular.

John Silber defended Kant's rational ethic, in spite of its lacking "motive power to move a ship to harbor," because "it may yet prevent its foundering on the rocks." James uses the same metaphor in defense of rights like privacy. They do not "light the way to the promised land," but they serve to keep us "steady and off the rocks." Individual rights, then, emerge from the essential failures, or taints, of our ideals. One type of failure calls for "roadblock" rights like privacy, however, while another calls for "springboard" rights which do not stop the system's encroachments, but push the system to do more. Liberalism unites the roadblock rights of libertarianism, such as privacy, with the springboard rights of socialism, such as demands for health care and education. James defines liberalism as the general and insistent demand for rights of both kinds. Liberalism is that openness to a variety of ideal-clusters which recognizes that rights are simply ad hoc adjustments aimed at preventing any system from gaining too much power.

Sissela Bok turns to a moral practice which eludes the utilitarian calculus and is in no sense a right, but which performs the indispensable function of setting right those negative elements in an individual's moral life which need to be accounted for, squared away, forgiven, healed, or punished. The practice is confession, whether it be legal, political, religious, or therapeutic. Her essay on "Confession and Moral Choice" focuses on the moral problems raised by the practice and traces two clusters of moral distinctions: first, openness and concealment in communication; and secondly, the freedom or subjugation of participants in confessions. Confessors like Rousseau or Clamence in Camus's book *The Fall* illustrate the problem. They blend disguise and concealment with candor in their confessions. And torture has subjugated so many in producing confessions, past and present, that the practice needs no illustration. Confession, as Bok uses the term, is more than confiding. She is concerned with the institutionalized, often ritualized practice. Her paper is a careful phenomenology of institutionalized confession, from the perspectives of both the confessor and those to whom confession is rendered. She is particularly interested in the ethics of psychotherapy. Her emphasis is on the moral problems raised by confession, and she warns that when confessions transgress the basic norms for what is right they do no good for those who take part in them or for the institutions sponsoring them. What is needed, she argues, is a moral casuistry of confession which compares cases and arguments used in a wide variety of confessional practices, thereby questioning the fundamental premises regarding guilt, penance, and social need in any one tradition. In so doing she echoes the values which Edward James claimed for liberalism, and which Walter Muelder argued for in a personalistic communitarianism based on a coherence theory of truth. Mindful of the extent to which confession is subject to the moral weaknesses of those involved, she calls for an interdisciplinary study of the casuistry of speaking and listening in self-revelation.

John Yoder argued that the powers of modern pluralism/relativism must be defeated, if not totally destroyed, before they can be reenlisted in the service of the cosmos's rightful Ruler. He said little about the values which pluralism/relativism contributes to the good life. Most of our other essayists, however, join with Bok in attributing a negative and weak but important contribution to pluralism/relativism: it provides a form of moral protection. They do not look for a new ruling authority for ethics, but they trust that rational discourse among diverse folk will at least safeguard against immoral excess.

Edward James proposed a reversal of the common wisdom concerning rights, and Daniel DeNicola, not to be outdone, reverses the common wisdom regarding the nature of morality itself in his "Supererogation: Artistry in Conduct." Morality, he argues, is not primarily a matter of duty or obligation. Morality is an art. Works of supererogation, which are always inexplicable for an ethics of duty, are normative for the genuine creativity which, DeNicola argues, is at the heart of all morality. After a brief review of the current discussion on supererogation, DeNicola turns to the clarifying question, "What does it mean to say that an act is above and beyond one's moral duties?" Following Joel Feinberg, he distinguishes between acts which are merely quantitative oversubscriptions — like working five hours when one only promised four hours — and meritorious nonduties, as when a physician volunteers to help in a plague-infested city. But supererogation is not only giving an excess; it may also be permitting a deficiency, as in acts of forgiveness, grace, and mercy. Since the notion of supererogation is obviously defined by the notion of duty, DeNicola pays particular attention to the qualities of supererogatory acts which distinguish them from duties and give them their special moral worth. Style, grace, sensitivity, and imagination are the aesthetic hallmarks of such actions. They are primary evidence that the moral spirit cannot be confined to obligations. Duty is the controlled aspect of ethics; supererogation is the spontaneous and gratuitous expression of moral skill, and leads to the development of a distinctive moral style. Duty is not a lesser form of moral activity; it is only the ordinary form. But the regular form of moral practice is not the most revealing form of the moral spirit. For DeNicola, the reality of the moral life is expressed most vividly and most profoundly in those acts which are beyond duty, not as a mere quantitative extension of dutiful behavior, but in those graceful and imaginative moments associated with the lives of saints and heroes.

Thus far our exploration of foundation issues in ethics has focused on Western traditions, although issues like the possibility of a rational ethic are not entirely culture-bound. Indeed, while pluralism/relativism began as a description of technological society in the modern West, it is now the name of an emerging world civilization. Our final group of essays has an intentionally global perspective. John Carman's essay, "The Ethics of the Auspicious: Western Encounter with Hindu Values," deals with a category of moral worth which has no direct counterpart in the West, but has much in common with DeNicola's works of supererogation. Certain acts, places, and persons in Hindu culture are regarded as being *auspicious*. Since the term virtually defies concise definition, Carman begins with a dramatic description of the immolation of a young widow on the funeral pyre of her dead husband. Here is an act which was widely regarded as morally outrageous by both Westerners and enlightened Hindus in nineteenth-century India. Yet, from the point of view of an element of Hindu tradition, this event of *satī* ("suttee" or "widow burning"), and the widow who thus sacrifices herself, are both highly auspicious. (There has recently been a protest in India by a group of women's liberationists against the outlawing of suttee, on the grounds that they should be free to honor that aspect of their tradition if they choose.)

Carman's first project is to make the moral aspects of the notion comprehensible to his Western readers. He relates it to the practice, also problematic, of *devadāsīs* or Hindu temple dancers who had sexual intercourse with devotees of the temple's god. This requires an extensive discussion of the related notions of *mokṣa* and *dharma* in Hindu ethics. He then points out that the notion of auspiciousness is a formalized version of the informal Western notion of "luck," and he suggests that this idea plays a large role in the evaluation of the good life in the West but has never become a formal category of ethical reflection. The implication is that this Hindu notion may fill a void in Western ethical thinking. Carman argues that traditional Hindu society has been realistic in confronting the fact that life is not fair, and that the unfair allotment of good luck and bad luck is an issue which any serious moral theory ought to confront.

Steven Katz deals with "Ethics and Mysticism" as a cross-cultural issue, and he too counters the conventional wisdom. He opposes the view that mysticism is either anti-ethical or trans-ethical and in neither case a major source of ethical insight. Mystics, he insists, are fully situated in the metaphysical, theological, and social contexts of their traditions. Like DeNicola, Katz denies the strong Kantian position that limits ethical action to the performance of one's moral duty, based on the intention of an autonomous will. Katz argues that an act can be morally significant whatever its intentions. In dealing with both Buddhist and Christian mysticism Katz points out that virtuous action is the necessary preamble to the later stages of mystic enlightenment. The process is also reversed. Moral action later becomes evidence that the mystic vision was authentic. Katz points out that this is true of Christian mysticism, as it is of Buddhism and Hinduism, and he quotes extensively from Meister Eckhart and Saint Teresa to make his point. While there are varieties in religious traditions, Katz argues that there is little variety in the relation between ethical action and mystical insight. "There is no recognizable pattern that suggests that Christian mystics or Hindu mystics or any other mystics act in ways contrary to, or disapproved of by, the larger Christian or Hindu or other communities. Despite the common caricature, mystics tend to be good citizens, in nearly every sense, of the traditions out of which they emerge and on which they in turn have an impact."

Roger Gottlieb writes on "Tragic Choices: Ethics after the Holocaust," not as a study in Jewish ethics but regarding the Holocaust as a "decisive event for our time." While a great deal has been written about the Holocaust as such, relatively little notice has been given to it by philosophers. Like other writers on the Holocaust, Gottlieb is concerned that it not be forgotten; but unlike many, he makes a philosophical distinction between authentic and inauthentic ways of remembering. He is also concerned with problems posed by the Holocaust for a theory of human nature, for its relation to the positivist conception of rationality, and for our understanding of social justice. The implications of the Holocaust for liberalism and rationalism are particularly significant. We have already noted the hope expressed by several of our essayists that ethical problems in a pluralistic and relativistic culture could find at least a weak negative value in the limitation of immoral excess through open rational discourse. Gottlieb points out that it is precisely this rational discourse which broke down in German National Socialism and led to the Holocaust. "These are historical developments which, on liberalism's terms, can only be viewed as regressions. But liberalism has little room for regressions, since regressions are caused by the rejection of the accomplishments of reason." Gottlieb criticizes positivism's calculative and instrumental view of reason and is equally critical of Habermas's assumption that truth and justice are presupposed by the use of speech. He offers no easy solution. "Ethical theory will no longer presuppose that the accomplishment of moral values is possible. Rather, in a post-Holocaust age we need a moral theory which situates human actions within a history which compels us toward evil, where the meeting of the needs of one group inevitably leads it into conflict with another. For this moral theory, tragic choices are not the exception, but the rule of moral life."

Our concluding paper is from Robert Cohen, physicist and philosopher, whose "Reflections on the Ambiguity of Science" offers a meditation on comments by C. S. Lewis and Max Horkheimer. They suggest that the ideology of science actually hides the extent to which human power over nature is really power over other human beings, with nature as its instrument. Far from being one among several cultural activities, Cohen points out that science is now the only ideology with global legitimacy, cross-culturally characterizing entire societies. In spite of this universality, however, science is the object of massive fear, as well as profound trust. Science is determined by economic factors, social factors, and military needs; but it also represents a religious need to understand the cosmos, literary and artistic needs, the tacit needs for power and the satisfaction of curiosity. Prior to the First World War, science was a pervasive cultural influence in the West, but the explosion of technology and its domination by the military in the twentieth century have raised moral problems for the scientist vividly illustrated by the physicists who participated in the Manhattan Project to build the atom bomb. Cohen argues that the scientist of the earlier Little Science was a servant of power, whereas the scientists of our present Big Science have become soldiers of power. He finds this position morally repugnant, because science has increasingly become the instrument of ruling social elites. What science now knows is the possible doom of nature, and for that reason a new dimension has been added to the morality of science and the vocation of the scientist. Science, as "our only species-wide ideology, now gradually, awkwardly, but inevitably, becomes both a new humanism and a new naturalism. No longer either servant or soldier, the responsible scientist as natural humanist has been forced, often unwillingly, to speak for the values of a . . . [genuinely human] community."

Our participants were chosen for the diversity of their views and the expertise with which they expressed them, not because they represented a consensus. There are common themes, however, some articulated and others only implied. The strongest articulated theme is the criticism of reason as a purely technical and instrumental calculus. This leads in turn to the strongest implied one: a poignant search for some way to infuse reason with those values which make survival possible in a world threatened by new holocausts and the doom of nature itself.

Kantian rationality or minimal rights may keep us off the rocks; interdisciplinary casuistries and ecumenical conversations may keep us working on our problems together; an emphasis on moral character may humanize utilitarian theory; a new humanism may come from responsible scientists; we may become more tolerant of strange religious values and customs. But none of these are pathways to the light; they only keep us from stumbling in the dark. Roger Gottlieb's stark conclusion reminds us how serious our ethical search is; and John Yoder's triumphal affirmation reminds us how sorely we miss an acknowledged Ruler.

If I read these papers rightly, the message is that there are no widely acknowledged foundations of ethics. There is only a growing awareness of the seriousness of our dilemmas, and the beginnings of a consensus on needs and methods for meeting those needs. We are not without grounds for hope. We just have a long way to go, and not much time.

PART I

Christianity and Modern Culture

1

Kant and the Mythic Roots of Morality

JOHN R. SILBER

THE TRANSCENDENCE ON WHICH great philosophy depends, that ability to write and think, as Spinoza said, *sub specie aeternitatis,* can never be fully attained. Indeed, the finest philosophers may be those who, rather than withdrawing from the movements of their times, include all of them in their intellectual grasp and assign to each its proper weight and influence.

Immanuel Kant was such a philosopher: revolutionary thinker in the age of revolution, quintessential child of the eighteenth century. He caught the spirit of the Enlightenment in writing, "*Sapere aude!* 'Have courage to use your *own* reason!'—that is the motto of enlightenment,"[1] and in Kant most of the complex and often conflicting movements that gave the eighteenth century its distinctive character were present and held in a balance of extraordinary coherence.

A pietism that emphasized moral practice over abstract theology—a religious tradition that asserted the still powerful influence of the Christian *Weltanschauung*—was dominant in Kant's home and in his early schooling. Reflecting the intellectual balance of the eighteenth century, the influence of this powerful motivational force was checked in Kant by the rising influence of a new *Weltanschauung* based on Newtonian science, to which Kant was himself a significant contributor. Kant believed that "the heavens declare the glory of God," but those "starry heavens above" continued to fill Kant's mind "with ever new and increasing admiration and awe" not through revealed mystery but through Newton's revelation of a God of reason who had created a natural order, devoid of mystery and miracle and comprehensible through human reason. As Pope had written:

> Nature and Nature's laws lay hid in night;
> God said, "Let Newton be!" And all was light.

The balance of world views in the Enlightenment

The most significant intellectual work of the eighteenth century involved the assimilation of the Christian and Newtonian world views into some coherent or at least plausible synthesis.

Among the literate of the eighteenth century, the scientific world view gradually displaced the Christian world view as the dominant climate of opinion. Aristophanes' commentary on the collapse of Greek religion in the face of natural philosophy at the end of the fifth century B.C. was, as Carl Becker remarked, equally descriptive of the transition from the medieval to the scientific world view: "Whirl is king, having cast out Zeus."[2]

Newtonianism held forth the promise of understanding and ultimate control of nature, but it placed in doubt the spiritual and moral foundations on which the meaning of human existence depends. If nature is the expression of God, and moves in accordance with inexorable laws, then whatever evil exists in the world is the consequence of God's creation, the result of either incompetence or indifference (if not malevolence) on the part of God. This dilemma posed by the new philosophy drove many to reconsider the relationship of reason and religion, the very question that had preoccupied the great scholastic philosophers of the later Middle Ages. But now the apparent moral indifference of the universe, which seemed to many the inescapable consequence of the work of Newton and his followers, posed a terrible dilemma for thinkers who feared that Whirl might truly be king, and that, by a cruel irony, truth itself might overthrow virtue. Concerned about the effect that his *Dialogues* might have, Hume voluntarily withheld them from publication during his lifetime, and he revised his published work so that, as he said in 1737, "it shall give as little offense as possible."[3]

Diderot, like Hume, also wrote works he refused to publish. But unlike Hume he was personally distressed by his inability to find "any sufficient reason for virtuous conduct, his heart unable to renounce the conviction that nothing is better in this world than to be a good man."[4] Diderot could intellectually articulate, but could not finally follow, the moral indifference that appeared to result from the Newtonian philosophy. Diderot was profoundly troubled by his inability to establish morality on a rational foundation, and was not content to attack the Christian faith and doctrine without offering something positive and superior to take its place. He concluded, "it is not enough to know more than they [the theologians] do; it is necessary to show them that we are better, and that *philosophy makes more good men than sufficient or efficacious grace.*"[5]

Although Diderot devoted years of effort to the establishment of morality on rational foundations, he never wrote on the subject. He said, "I have not even dared to write the first line; I say to myself, if I do not come out of the attempt victorious, I become the apologist of wickedness; I will have betrayed the cause of virtue. . . . I do not feel equal to this sublime work; I have uselessly consecrated my whole life to it."[6]

Diderot may have been unusually honest in recognizing his inability to solve the problem he had framed, but he was right — and hardly alone — in his diagnosis: the eighteenth century lacked a comprehensive and coherent world view, and its construction was the central intellectual project of the age. In the opinion of the most sensitive of the *philosophes,* one could not abandon the mythic roots of Christianity until the problem of evil had been dealt with and a rational foundation for morality had been provided. Diderot framed the problem: a "sufficient reason for just conduct" must be found.

Kant's response to Diderot's dilemma

Clearly, it was in this spirit that Kant wrote his first *Critique* and established the limits of knowledge "in order to make room for faith."[7] In particular, it was in this spirit that Kant sought not to discover or invent morality, but to complete that "sublime work" which Diderot found beyond his powers — that is, "to seek out and establish the supreme principle of morality"[8] and the principles and doctrines of religion on the basis of reason, and to ensure that the laws of practical reason have "access to the human mind and an influence on its maxims."[9]

Kant recognized, perhaps more clearly than Diderot, that

there was no going back. No one, least of all Kant, could minimize the appeal of the new scientific *Weltanschauung.* As a contributor to the Newtonian philosophy, he recognized, like King Canute, that he could not hold back the tide, even though he was as concerned as Diderot to save morality and the essential tenets of the Christian religion.

Christianity proclaimed good news that could be understood by the most ordinary person. As Becker said,

> No interpretation of the life of mankind ever more exactly reflected the experience or more effectively responded to the hopes of average men. . . . The importance of the Christian story was that it announced with authority (whether truly or not matters little) that the life of man has significance, a universal significance transcending and including the temporal experience of the individual. This was the secret of its enduring strength, that it irradiated pessimism with hope: it liberated the mind of man from the cycles in which classical philosophy had enclosed it as in prison, and by transferring the golden age from the past to the future substituted an optimistic for a disillusioned view of human destiny.[10]

That Kant was concerned to preserve this good news for the average person through a rational interpretation of the Christian message is obvious, even from the most casual reading of Part 1, Book 2, and Part 2 of the *Critique of Practical Reason.* And though less obvious, this concern is still evident in his *Religion within the Limits of Reason Alone.* Where the Christian religion reassured all individuals, no matter how common, of their infinite worth as children of God—the hairs of whose heads were numbered and whose lives counted more than those of sparrows, no one of which fell without God's knowledge—Kant enunciated the secular good news of the moral worth of the individual personality that was beyond all price.

Thus he began the *Groundwork of the Metaphysic of Morals* with these words: "It is impossible to conceive of anything at all in the world, or even out of it, which can be taken as good without qualification, except a *good will.*" "A good will," he continued, "seems to constitute the indispensable condition of our very worthiness to be happy."[11] The human will is transcendentally free from determination by alien and antecedent influences (free, that is, according to Kant's negative definition of freedom) and also free in the positive sense of possessing the potentiality for freedom either in its fulfilled mode as autonomy or in its deficient mode as heteronomy. Because of its unconditioned and self-determining nature, the will possesses whatever moral qualities it might have (whether good or evil) without qualification. The moral law defines the conditions of personal fulfillment and those conditions are recognized as part of the given nature of any and every person. A being lacking either transcendental freedom or the potentiality of autonomy or heteronomy lacks these conditions essential to being a person, but those who have these characteristics are self-determining causes and totally responsible for whatever they make of themselves in the process of exercising freedom. Autonomy is achieved by acting in accordance with the moral law and for its sake, that is, by acting in accordance with the principle of universality which by virtue of its universality ensures the individuals' transcendence of particular motives for action. Individuals by their own volition establish a moral worth that becomes the basis for their right to happiness:

> Man *himself* must make or have made himself into whatever, in a moral sense, whether good or evil, he is or is to become. Either condition must be an effect of his free choice; for otherwise he could not be held responsible for it and could therefore be morally neither good nor evil.[12]

Observing society and history without distortion, Kant recognized that there was nothing to guarantee distribution of happiness in this world on the basis of moral deserts. And consequently, Kant argued that consistent volition requires that the free moral individual should *will* that there be a God and personal immortality.[13] Thus, having established the supreme principle of morality, Kant used that principle in its full development to establish religion on the basis of reason alone.[14] Under this interpretation, freedom of the moral agent is not determined by the introduction of God and immortality. There are no independent theoretical proofs for their existence; there is only a moral proof that follows as a condition of consistent volition from the recognition of one's duty.[15]

Since every person is possessed of freedom, the achievement of a good will is within the potentiality of each person. To this extent, there is good news for every person. But there is no guarantee of happiness. Persons of good will who have made a consistent effort to universalize the maxims of their acts, to put themselves in the place and point of view of another, to treat humanity, whether themselves or others, always as an end in itself and never as a means merely — that is, persons who have achieved "honesty, integrity, in the innermost depths of the self, both in relation to one's self and in actions towards others as the supreme maxim of one's life"— have established a worthiness to be happy. Such persons have established, Kant says, "the only proof in the consciousness of a man that he has character."[16] This is both the most and the least that can be demanded of persons. To do less than this is to fail morally; to do more is impossible.

In this context failure is not defined by the occurrence of specifically immoral acts but only by the loss of a genuinely moral disposition or that *Wahrhaftigkeit* in relation to one's self and in actions toward others as one's supreme rule of life. One who has achieved an essentially good will by making reason practical in one's life and by subordinating one's sensible interests to the achievement of rational action has clearly demonstrated a commitment to a universe that is also rational.

This does not prove theoretically the existence of God or the immortality of the soul, but it establishes God and immortality as part of a context of coherence and meaning in the life of the individual that becomes in itself, Kant believed, a powerful motive for moral conduct. Diderot asked for a sufficient reason for just conduct. He said it was necessary to demonstrate that philosophy makes more good persons than sufficient or efficacious grace. Kant's reply may be summarized as follows: If we reflect rationally on the presuppositions of our natures as persons, of our ability to function as responsible, accountable individuals, we become aware of our freedom and the law of its fulfillment. We recognize that through the fulfillment of our freedom in autonomy we establish our infinite worth, our ultimate significance, on the basis of which we can expect that whatever significance and fulfillment the universe has to offer will in fact be ours.

In Prelude 4 of *Fear and Trembling*, Kierkegaard was later

to observe, "When the child must be weaned, the mother has stronger food in readiness, lest the child should perish."[17] Was this the stronger food which Diderot had insisted upon before the Christian world view could safely be swept away? Had Kant succeeded in procuring for the categorical imperative and moral law "admittance to the will of man and influence over practice?"[18] Could one say of Kant's moral philosophy not only that it was true in theory but that it also worked in practice? That is, had Kant provided a sufficient motivation for moral conduct?

Although Kant made a place for religion, it is not at all clear that his religion had effective motivational force. For Kant's religion is devoid of mythic roots: all its doctrines are subjected to rational, essentially secular interpretations. The synthesis of Christian and Newtonian thought was genuine enough for Kant, and the motivational force that derived from Kant's religious upbringing continued to exert its influence on Kant long after he had completed his process of demythologizing Christianity. Kant continued, throughout his life, to speak at times with religious fervor, as in the passage quoted above on "the starry heavens above and the moral law within," or as in his moving apostrophes to Duty and Sincerity.[19]

Kant's religious fervor did not derive from his demythologized religion within the limits of reason alone. It came rather from the emotionally and mythically rich pietism of his parental home and from the religious training of the Collegium Fridericianum. Kant could hear the voice of duty as if it were the voice of God because he had heard the voice of God issue the categorical imperative: "Be ye therefore perfect, even as your Father which is in heaven is perfect" (Matt. 5:48). The refined stem of Kant's rational ethics had been grafted onto the hardy emotional root of Christianity. What effect would the demythologized religion of reason alone, itself derivative from a rational theory of ethics, exert on individuals devoid of childhood nurture in the mythic religious tradition?

No one can question the success of Kant's philosophical horticulture. His grafting of a secular interpretation onto mythic Christianity was brilliant. Those reared in a mythic religious tradition have, generation after generation, developed from childhood to adulthood along essentially Kantian lines.

The theological movement of the nineteenth and twentieth centuries from Schweitzer to Bultmann and Tillich illustrates the feasibility of Kant's program. But we must also note the inability of demythologized branches of Christianity to reproduce themselves. Whitehead, in *Adventures of Ideas*, pointed out that the Platonic idea of *psyche* had been without widespread influence until it was given motivational force through the Christian idea of soul. Had not Kant perhaps reduced the Christian idea of soul to an equally abstract and motivationally inept concept of personality?

This is the position taken by Reinhold Niebuhr. In *An Interpretation of Christian Ethics*, he wrote:

> No rational moral idealism can create moral conduct. It can provide principles of criticism and reasons; but such norms do not contain a dynamic for their realization. . . . Rationalism not only suppresses the emotional supports of moral action unduly, but it has failed dismally in encouraging men toward the realization of the ideals which it has projected.[20]

Moral incentive in Kant's ethics

Although Niebuhr may be correct in his conclusion, it is clear that Kant, no less than his critics, is aware of the insufficiency of the moral law and the categorical imperative as static formulae. For the purpose of moral life, Kant insists, they "require in addition a power of judgment sharpened by experience, partly in order to distinguish the cases to which they apply, partly to procure for them admittance to the will of man and influence over practice."[21] Judgment must provide the incentive which moves the will to do that which it knows it ought to do. Kant's recognition of the need to provide moral incentives is seen in his distinction between the moral law and the categorical imperative.

Kant observed that if human persons had holy wills, that is, if they were pure rational beings, they would act in accordance with the moral law without overcoming temptation. They would have neither obligations nor the need of incentives to follow the moral law because it would be the descriptive law of their behavior. Human persons are not pure, rational beings; the human will consists not merely of practical reason (*Wille*) but also of the faculty of desire (*Willkür*). *Willkür*, free and self-determining, confronts both the demands of reason and the desires of sensibility; it is tempted to act in accordance with the appeals of the latter, while it is obligated to act in accordance with the principle of the former. The moral law for pure, rational beings thus becomes the categorical imperative for human persons who, being both rational and sensible beings, require some sensible incentive for fulfilling the demands of reason.

In order to determine action in accordance with the categorical imperative, practical reason must gain control over the desires and inclinations that compete with it for determination of the will. And since reason cannot control nonrational desires and pleasures by means of argument, it must control them by means of pleasures and desires which the moral law itself can effect in the will. In order to fulfill the demands of the categorical imperative, the human will as a dynamic, unitary faculty must be able to find pleasure or delight in the fulfillment of duty. Thus, Kant argues:

> If we are to will actions for which reason by itself prescribes an "ought" to a rational, yet sensuously affected, being, it is admittedly necessary that reason should have a power of *infusing* a *feeling of pleasure* or satisfaction in the fulfillment of duty, and consequently that it should possess a kind of causality by which it can determine sensibility in accordance with rational principles.[22]

Reason must be able not merely to legislate the law for the human will; it must be able also to produce in the will a sensible incentive to fulfill the law.

It is here that judgment enters as the power of the mind to provide a priori principles for the feeling of pleasure and pain. It is that power or ability of reason to produce a feeling of pleasure in sensibility associated with the feeling of duty.[23] In providing for a moral incentive, Kant must show how judgment can win acceptance for the moral law in the human will. He must answer the question, How can judgment — as reason in its dynamic employment — be an efficient cause in the determination of an effect (a feeling) in sensibility? That is, he must answer the question, How can reason be practical?[24]

Before considering Kant's answer to this question, we must be sure the question is correctly interpreted. In the first place, it must not be understood as a question of whether or not reason can be practical. Freedom of the will — which involves the actual capacity of reason to be practical through the production of incentives — is presupposed in the experience of obligation from which Kantian ethics begins.[25] That reason is practical, that persons do take an interest in enacting the demands of the moral law, is a fact of human experience for which no additional proof is required.[26]

In the second place, granting that reason is practical, we must not suppose that a direct theoretical explanation of how it is practical is possible. In order to *explain* something theoretically, one must make it determinate by reference to the spatial and/or temporal conditions which necessitate it; the idea of freedom, however, presupposes an independence from all alien or antecedent causes and therefore the absence of the very factors which make possible a theoretical explanation.[27]

Thus, in asking how reason or judgment can provide an incentive for the will, we are not questioning that it can nor are we seeking a direct theoretical explanation of the conditions by which it does so. Rather we seek to show: (1) What kind of feeling is produced in the will by judgment whereby the will takes a sensible interest in the fulfillment of the moral law? (2) How can Kant introduce feeling into his ethical theory as an incentive of the will without destroying the categorical imperative and inheriting the difficulties of ethical empiricism? (3) Presuming that Kant can satisfy the previous issues, what practical means can judgment employ in providing moral incentives?

On the first question — what kind of feeling is produced by moral judgments? — Kant stresses that the feeling in question is different in kind from other feelings in that it is not aroused by material objects. In the *Critique of Judgment*, he enumerates three varieties of delight: delight in the agreeable, delight in the beautiful, and delight in the good. Delight in the good results from the activity of reason whereby the object (the morally good) is demanded and made attractive by reference to the moral law. Thus Kant's introduction of feeling into moral experience does not reduce his ethics to the empirical level. Feeling can be aroused not only by sensation in the judgment of something as agreeable, or by the play of imagination and understanding in the judgment of something as beautiful; it can be aroused also by a concept — the moral law — in the judgment of something as good. The moral law (as an expression of *Wille*) produces an incentive in *Willkür* that is moral feeling, the delight or sensible interest taken in an object that is good.

As to the second question, the introduction of this incentive does not undermine the theory of the categorical imperative. Moral feelings, the sensible incentive that moves the will (*Willkür*) to the fulfillment of duty, does not reduce Kant's theory to one of ethical empiricism, because moral feeling is rationally, not empirically, determined.[28]

Our central concern here is to understand Kant's answer to the third question: What practical means or devices can judgment employ in providing moral incentives, and are these incentives adequate? Recognizing its proper task as the cultivation rather than the creation of moral feeling, judgment may enlarge the moral incentive of each individual by directing the will's attention to any of the following: to the elegance of rational thought;[29] to the beauties of nature;[30] to the beauties of art;[31] to the sublime;[32] to the examination of the lives of good people;[33] and to practices in moral casuistry.[34]

The limits of moral incentive

These various means for the cultivation of moral feeling and the encouragement of moral conduct are ingenious and imaginative — but not convincing. Morality is ineluctably contingent upon the exercise of freedom and cannot be guaranteed by force or sufficient incentive. It was for this reason that Kant stressed the importance for morality of the fact that there is no theoretical proof of God and immortality. For if there were, human freedom would be destroyed and moral action would be determined simply by fear of hell or hope of heaven.[35] Consistent with his ethical theory, Kant recognized in *Über die Pädagogik* that "if we wish to establish morality, we must abolish punishment. Morality is something so sacred and sublime that we must not degrade it by placing it in the same rank as discipline."[36]

Kant is basically consistent in holding that no program of

education which accorded with his ethical theory could develop moral persons by means of social and psychological influences that would undermine the freedom of the students and destroy them as moral beings. Whatever humanity is in a moral sense, whether good or evil, must be a condition of free choice. The inscrutable and irreducible nature of freedom which we comprehend only to the extent that we recognize its incomprehensibility precludes Kant's development of sufficient moral incentives or a genuine theory of education that is determinative of personal character.

He proposes in lieu of a theory of education a two-stage educational process that first encourages legality of action by insisting that students act in accordance with the moral law and train their judgment in assessing their actions and those of others in terms of conformity to law. A second stage follows in which moral feeling is developed, in which the moral individuals' growing sense of their own worth as free moral persons becomes itself the dominant incentive to action.[37]

Kant does not have, strictly speaking, a pedagogy, but merely offers observations on training, cultivation, and education. Kant's educational program is better understood in Aristotelian terms as a natural process of entelechy in which individuals, after being subjected to a series of educational influences, are not *made* moral but simply become moral persons. Just as in puberty children suddenly and dramatically become sexually potent, so moral persons, attending the voice of conscience, naturally but inexplicably cease to be led by the inclinations that dominated infancy and answer to the voice of their own practical reason. Kant would hold that reason and freedom are immanent in the human being from birth and that the unfolding of moral capacity is no more remarkable, and no more comprehensible, than the capacity for rationality in any of its other employments.

On Kant's theory, the moral individual cannot be "programmed" by sociological or educational techniques. How, then, does one provide sufficient reason for moral conduct? If one accepts Kant's understanding of moral conduct, there is no way to *make* persons morally good and worthy of happiness. Strictly speaking, they make themselves morally good and worthy by their own acts. The teacher in a moral community provides, to use a metaphor, oxygen for the tiny spark of reason until it bursts spontaneously into fire. Freedom is potential from the start, and education is no more than guardian and encourager of the flame. Programs are developed, exercises are completed, and free moral persons emerge as if by a process of moral entelechy.

In his concern to provide an adequate foundation for moral conduct, Kant was occasionally swept away by the extravagance and utopianism of the eighteenth century. But for the most part Kant held his enthusiasm in check. His characteristic view of the limits of education was clearly stated in the *Anthropologie:*

> Man must . . . be *educated* to be good. But those who are supposed to educate him are again men who are themselves still involved in the crudity of nature and are supposed to bring about what they themselves are in need of . . . But since he needs, for his moral education, *good* men who must themselves have been educated for it, and since none of these are free from (innate or acquired) corruption, the problem of moral education for *our species* remains unsolved even in principle and not merely in degree.[38]

In the final analysis, Kant only partially succeeds in solving the problem framed by Diderot. Kant, like Pentheus, must refuse to acknowledge God except as an afterthought of consistent volition. Kant cannot but fail to offer adequate incentives for ethical conduct, for if they were adequate they would destroy the freedom of the moral person. Hence, he offers a limited educational curriculum incapable of reshaping history but capable in some cases of developing morally sound individuals.

Kant discovered that his theory of morality contained the implication that it is impossible to *make* persons morally good. Hence, while he was successful in meeting Diderot's concern to establish morality on a rational basis, he was unable to deal adequately with the other aspect of Diderot's concern: that philosophy make "more good men than sufficient or efficacious grace." This concern, Kant would argue, is mistaken. It is a consequence of Diderot's confusion. Do we wish to encourage moral conduct, that is, true morality? If so, virtue must be the free expression of the moral person. Or do we wish rather to encourage conformity to the moral law, that is, mere legality? The latter can be motivated through laws and social pressure; the former can only be nurtured.

Similarly, Kant can answer a part of Niebuhr's concern. The

moral law does in fact contain a mechanism for its realization: it produces moral feeling and thereby provides some emotional support for moral action. On the other hand, that support is so attenuated that Niebuhr might reasonably conclude that it "has failed dismally in encouraging men toward the realization of the ideals which it has projected."[39]

Ethical orthodoxy in religious education

But why did Kant reject a middle course? Why should we not rear the young child in a mythic tradition — as Kant himself had been reared — and after the mythic religion with its powerful motivational power had been established only then introduce the process of rational pruning and grafting? Kant did not reject the mythic religion of his childhood either from personal whim or from prejudice against religion as such. It is a logical condition of Kant's theory of ethics that morality be introduced without the threat of punishment or the inducement of reward. Thus, ethics and moral education must precede rather than follow religion and religious education. As Kant says,

> The religion which is founded merely on theology can never contain anything of morality; hence we derive no feelings from it but fear on the one hand, and hope of reward on the other, and this produces merely a superstitious cult.[40]

On ethical grounds, consistent with the implications of his moral theory, Kant would restrict the child's experience of God and participation in religious practices. When explained to children in eighteenth-century religion, God was presented on the same footing as any other fact and was characterized as a being who knows the human heart and who directly rewards and punishes it according to its intent. Presented thus, the presence of God in the consciousness of the child destroys the child's freedom. Consequently, Kant would recommend that children be reared in their earliest years in the absence of religious rites and without hearing the name of God. Instead, they should be given instruction about the ends and aims of humanity, about the order and beauty of nature; their judgment should be exercised, and they should be provided with a wider knowledge of the universe and its laws. "Then only might be revealed to them for the first time the idea of a supreme being — a law giver."[41]

Having established religion on the foundation of ethics, Kant is consistent in holding that education should progress from ethics to religion: "Morality must come first and theology follow; and that is religion."[42] "Religion is the law in us, in so far as it derives emphasis from a Law-giver and a Judge above us. It is morality applied to the knowledge of God."[43] "Religion without moral con-scientiousness is a service of superstition."[44]

In practice, nevertheless, Kant reluctantly recommends the introduction of religious education into early childhood educa-tion. This, however, is only because it is absolutely necessary in order to prevent the miseducation that children would receive in their daily lives through contact with morally corrupting religious ideas. The religious education Kant would offer to counteract this problem is not, of course, an education in Christianity or in any mythic religion. It would be education — even for the youngest child — in the demythologized religion of reason alone. Rejecting the advice of Saint Paul that a child be taught as a child and allowed to grow to adulthood before putting off childish things (1 Cor. 13:10), Kant proposes to teach the ethical religion of rea-son to the little child as if it were a little man or woman.

With an eighteenth-century confidence that nature does nothing without purpose and is organized to ensure the maximum efficiency of means, Kant concluded that the human race had not been created for happiness but for a moral pilgrimage that could establish dignity and a worthiness to be happy.

Kant could find no way to use historical Christianity as a foundation for ethics. Christianity was presented to the public in many varieties of religious orthodoxy, each of which contained elements inimical to Kant's moral orthodoxy. But Kant had no way of imposing his moral orthodoxy on any branch of the Chris-tian church. Unable to make over the culture of his day, Kant was forced to accept it as a limiting condition for his theory of moral education. He concluded that a sound moral education would have to proceed with the simultaneous introduction of a morally orthodox interpretation of Christianity that would be un-derstood as a derivative rather than as a foundation of morality.

The necessity of freedom

As if these obstacles were not enough, there was an addi-tional problem that Kant did not anticipate. The Christian world view was being gradually eclipsed by the scientific. Even if Kant had proposed to ground moral education on historical Christianity, he would have found that project swept away by subsequent cultural changes. The project could not have succeeded in the climate of opinion of the nineteenth and twentieth centuries, in which the scientific world view was enormously strengthened by the work of Darwin, Freud, Einstein, and their many brilliant collaborators. Concomitantly, and without any direct encouragement from Kant, Christianity was rationalized and demythologized. As it gained in sophistication, Christianity lost much of its appeal to the average person. The scientific world view was indifferent to the ultimate questions concerning the meaning of life, and left these to the realm of uncertainty. The civilization based on the Christian world view was dissolving into smaller and competing social elements. Each of these could claim to be validated by the scientific world view, whose presumption of value neutrality endorsed ethical relativism, and to some extent encouraged an intellectual climate of political and moral anarchy.

The pervasive influence of the scientific world view in the twentieth century — as the implications of value neutrality and ethical relativism were applied with extraordinary crassness to justify the opinions and beliefs of any and everyone — has contributed to the disintegration of the social and legal order. The respect of individuals for law and the discipline that moral persons impose on themselves in the fulfillment of freedom have been extensively undermined by social relativism and indifference.

Kant did not have the option of proposing the imposition of a religion contrived to achieve ethical orthodoxy, which could provide the motivational force of a mythic religion. Kant was, of course, aware of this possibility from his reading of Plato.

Plato had proposed in the fourth century B.C. a scheme of general education whereby a society might be transformed and an ideal state of ideal citizens brought into existence. In order to achieve this social objective, Plato proposed a new mythic religion whose tenets were consistent with the aims of the state. He proposed a great fable in which all citizens of his republic would be nurtured. They would be taught to believe that God had made human beings of three basic substances: gold, silver, or iron and bronze. They would come to believe on faith, as if it were a mundane truth, that their natures were thus differentiated at birth. Those of gold would become rulers; those of silver, auxiliaries; and those of bronze or iron, farmers or craft artisans.[45]

Plato's proposal to invent mythic roots as incentives to moral conduct was not, however, acceptable to Kant. It involved not merely the propagation of falsehoods and a mistaken concept of the good as homogeneous, but its success required also a totalitarian state that destroyed freedom and hence the possibility of morality.[46] Kant demonstrated the falseness of Plato's ethical position and that of the Stoics by proving the heterogeneity of the good. He showed that the plausibility of the Platonic and Stoic concept of good depended on the assumption of a homogeneous concept of the good in which virtue and happiness are confused.[47] Once the mistaken notion of a homogeneous good is corrected, Plato's theory of motivation is destroyed. Individuals no longer automatically desire to do the good as a means to both virtue and happiness; rather they find themselves torn between the appeals of happiness (the natural good) and the demands of moral obligation on which depend their virtue (the moral good) and their worthiness to be happy.

Although Kant exposed a fundamental confusion in Plato's concept of the good and demolished Plato's theory of motivation, which derived its plausibility from that confused notion, Kant did not and could not refute the efficacy of Plato's educational proposal. He understood that it was entirely possible to change human behavior by a totalitarian educational program.

Unfortunately, subsequent history has amply shown that Plato's theory of totalitarian education works effectively in practice. Marx, Lenin, Stalin, and Mao all proposed, and all save Marx established, educational programs with the scope and thoroughness of Plato's scheme, programs that put down the mythic roots of their secular religions. They project a new vision of society and of human beings within that society. That vision is indoctrinated into children as a mythic religion, and children come to consciousness in an ethos in which the state is watching and judging and will reward and punish them. The diabolical religion of National Socialism was inculcated in the same way—by terror and totalitarianism. It incorporated Norse sagas into a new state religion whose end remained Ragnarok.

However benign or malignant their objectives, these totalitarian states have inculcated contrived mythic religions that promise to "free the human race." But the freedom that is promised is not the freedom more precious than life itself, the freedom that makes possible "all that makes life worthwhile,"[48] the freedom on which human dignity and one's worthiness to be happy are grounded. Rather, it is only an *ersatz* freedom of mere conformity to party objectives, a legality devoid of autonomy.

It would appear that Kant stood between two worlds — one dying and the other powerless during his lifetime to be born. The civilization based on mythic Christianity was dissolving in the solvent of the scientific world view and the neo-religions of socialism were as yet scarcely emerging. Kant could not subvert the ethical by introducing the coercive motivations of mythic religion. But he was by no means indifferent to the need for moral incentive. He thus presented a theory of ethics of maximal rational purity, grounded in human freedom and the law of its expression, and revealing the human person as a being worthy beyond price. Those who understand and accept Kant's conception of humanity are immunized against the temptations of the secular heterodoxies, the totalitarian schemes for human betterment without freedom.

Kant's ethics has its mythic roots, but they lie rather in Christian pietism than in reason. And his fully developed ethical theory proscribes the use of any mythic religion that is not subject to the test of ethical orthodoxy. By eschewing mythic roots, Kant's theory only lost what it could never really have had. Having reached the limits of reason in providing moral incentive, Kant stopped. And perhaps he did enough: his ethical theory clearly provides the principles of criticism and procedural guidance for personal and political conduct. Although the force of moral feeling produced by reason may be weak, it continually gives rise to the conviction that freedom is the natural end of the human race and that each of us should subordinate life itself to those principles that make life worthwhile.

The limited incentive of moral feeling is perhaps best understood as a moral sea anchor that, although incapable of providing the motive power to move a ship to harbor, may yet prevent its foundering on the rocks.

NOTES

1. Immanuel Kant, *Was Ist Aufklärung?* KGS 8:35, p. 286. In this essay I have abbreviated the titles of the works cited as shown below. I have usually cited both the German text and an English translation.

KGS: *Kants Gesammelte Schriften* (Königlich Preussische Akademie der Wissenschaften).

Gr: *Grundlegund zur Metaphysik der Sitten* (KGS 4).

Paton: *The Moral Law: Kant's Groundwork of the Metaphysic of Morals,* trans. H. J. Paton (London: Hutchinson University Library, 1948).

KdrV: *Kritik der reinen Vernunft* (KGS 3).

Smith: *A Translation of Kant's Critique of Pure Reason,* trans. N. Kemp Smith (London: Macmillan, 1929).

KdpV: *Kritik der praktischen Vernunft* (KGS 5).

Beck: *Critique of Practical Reason and Other Writings in Moral Philosophy,* trans. Lewis White Beck (Chicago: University of Chicago Press, 1949).

Rel: *Die Religion innerhalb der Grenzen der blossen Vernunft* (KGS 6).

Greene: *Religion within the Limits of Reason Alone,* trans. Theodore M. Greene and Hoyt H. Hudson (La Salle, Ill.: Open Court Publ. Co., 1960).

Abbott: *Kant's Critique of Practical Reason and Other Works on the Theory of Ethics,* trans. Thomas Kingmill Abbott (London: Longmans, Green, 1948).

A: *Anthropologie in pragmatischer Hinsicht* (KGS 7).

Gregor: *Anthropology from a Pragmatic Point of View,* trans. Mary J. Gregor (The Hague: Martinus Nijhoff, 1974).

TuP: *Über den Gemeinspruch: Das mag in der Theorie richtig sein, taugt aber nicht für die Praxis* (KGS 8).

TaP: *On the Old Saw: That May Be Right in Theory But It Won't Work in Practice,* trans. E. B. Ashton (Philadelphia: University of Pennsylvania Press, 1974).

KdU: *Kritik der Urteilskraft* (KGS 5).

CoaJ *Kant's Critique of Aesthetic Judgment,* trans. James C. Meredith (Oxford: Clarendon Press, 1911).

CotJ: *Kant's Critique of Teleological Judgment*, trans. James C. Meredith (Oxford: Clarendon Press, 1928).

MdS: *Die Metaphysik der Sitten* (KGS 6).

MoM: *The Doctrine of Virtue, Part 2 of the Metaphysic of Morals*, trans. Mary J. Gregor (Philadelphia: University of Pennsylvania Press, 1971).

Päd: *Über die Pädagogik* (KGS 9).

Ed: *Education*, trans. Annette Churton (Ann Arbor, Mich.: University of Michigan Press, 1960).

2. Carl Becker, *The Heavenly City of the Eighteenth-Century Philosophers* (New Haven: Yale University Press, 1932), p. 19.

3. John Hill Burton, *Life and Correspondence of David Hume*, 2 vols. (New York: B. Franklin Press, 1967), 1:64; Becker, *Heavenly City* p. 38.

4. Becker, *Heavenly City*, p. 80. Note the expression of Diderot's view in Kant's famous statement, "It is impossible to conceive anything at all in the world, or even out of it, which can be taken as good without qualification, except a *good will*" (Gr, p. 393; Paton, p. 61). This point is elaborated below.

5. Denis Diderot, *Oeuvres Complètes*, 20 vols. (Paris: Garnier, 1875–77), 19:464; Becker, *Heavenly City*, p. 81.

6. Diderot, *Oeuvres Complètes*, 23:45; Becker, *Heavenly City*, p. 80.

7. KdrV, p. 130; Smith, p. 29.

8. Gr, p. 392; Paton, p. 60.

9. KdpV, p. 151; Beck, p. 249.

10. Becker, *Heavenly City*, pp. 126, 128.

11. Gr, p. 393; Paton, p. 61.

12. Rel, p. 44; Greene, p. 40. The responsibility for the origin of evil is thus transferred from God to human beings. It is a possibility that is introduced by freedom and, though not logically or causally necessary, appears to be an ineluctable consequence of human volition.

13. KdpV, p. 143; Beck, p. 245.

14. For a fuller explication of these views, see John R. Silber, "The Metaphysical Importance of the Highest Good as the Canon of Pure Reason in Kant's Philosophy," *The University of Texas Studies in Literature and Language* 1:2 (1959): 240–42; and John R. Silber, "The Importance of the Highest Good in Kant's Ethics," *Ethics* 73 (1963): 179–97.

15. KdpV, p. 192; Beck, p. 232.

16. A, p. 295; Gregor, p. 166. The English translation is my own,

though I here cite Gregor's translation. The words "honesty," "sincerity," and "integrity," singly and alone, inadequately translate *Wahrhaftigkeit*. In this context, its meaning encompasses not only "honesty," but also "sincerity" (*Aufrichtigkeit*), "conscientiousness" (*Gewissenhaftigkeit*), and "integrity" (an English word for which there is no single German equivalent). "Integrity," however, which presupposes a consistent and dependable moral character through time — as contrasted with "sincerity," an instant virtue — most adequately conveys the full meaning of *Wahrhaftigkeit* as used by Kant.

17. Sören Kierkegaard, *Fear and Trembling and Sickness unto Death*, trans. Walter Lowrie (Garden City, N.Y.: Doubleday, 1954), p. 29.

18. Gr, p. 389; Paton, p. 57.

19. "O Sincerity! Thou Astraea, that hast fled from earth to heaven, how mayest thou [the basis of conscience and hence of all inner religion] be drawn down thence to us again?" (Rel, p. 190; Greene, p. 178); and, "Duty! Thou sublime and mighty name that dost embrace nothing charming or insinuating but requirest submission and yet seekest not to move the will by threatening aught that would arouse natural aversion or terror but only holdest forth a law which of itself finds entrance into the mind and yet gains reluctant reverence (though not always obedience) — a law before which all inclinations are dumb even though they secretly work against it: what origin is there worthy of thee, and where is to be found the root of thy noble descent which proudly rejects all kinship with the inclinations and from which to be descended is the indispensable condition of the only worth which men can give themselves?" (KdpV, p. 86; Beck, p. 193).

20. Reinhold Niebuhr, *An Interpretation of Christian Ethics* (New York: Harper, 1935), p. 206.

21. Gr, p. 389; Paton, p. 57. I have dealt with the role of judgment in the application of the moral law at greater length in "Verfahrensformalismus in Kants Ethik," *Akten des 4. Internationalen Kant-Kongresses, Teil III* (Berlin, 1974): 149–85; "Procedural Formalism in Kant's Ethics," *Review of Metaphysics* 2 (1974): 197–236.

22. Gr, p. 460; Paton, p. 128.

23. KdU, pp. 245–46; CoaJ, pp. 91–92. See also Gr, p. 389; Paton, p. 57.

24. Gr, pp. 459–61; Paton, pp. 127–29.

25. KdpV, p. 32; Beck, p. 143.

26. Gr, p. 460; Paton, p. 128.

27. KdpV, p. 96; Beck, p. 202; Gr, pp. 461–63; Paton, pp. 129–31.

28. TuP, pp. 283–84; TaP, pp. 50–51; cf. KdpV, p. 76; Beck, p. 184. Since the issues raised by questions 1 and 2 are considered at length in

the section on 'Moral Feeling' in my essay "The Ethical Significance of Kant's *Religion*," Greene, lxxix–cxxxiv, I shall not elaborate these issues here.

29. KdU, p. 366; CotJ, p. 12.

30. MdS, p. 443; MoM, p. 109.

31. KdU, pp. 232–33, 298–99; CoaJ, pp. 75–76, 157; see secs. 41, 59, 60.

32. KdU, pp. 257–63; CoaJ, pp. 106–13.

33. KdPV, pp. 76–77; Beck, pp. 184–85.

34. KdpV, pp. 152–56; Beck, pp. 250–53; cf. MdS, pp. 428–40; MoM, pp. 92–106.

35. Päd, pp. 494–95; Ed, p. 112. Kant would agree with Kierkegaard that faith presupposes an objective uncertainty.

36. Päd, p. 481; Ed, p. 84.

37. KdpV, pp. 152, 159–60; Beck, pp. 250, 256–57.

38. A, pp. 325, 327; Gregor, pp. 186, 188.

39. Niebuhr, *Interpretation of Christian Ethics*, p. 206.

40. Päd, pp. 494–95; Ed, p. 112.

41. Päd, p. 493; Ed, p. 110.

42. Päd, p. 495; Ed, p. 112.

43. Päd, p. 494; Ed, p. 111.

44. Päd, p. 495; Ed, p. 113.

45. Plato, *The Republic*, Bk. 3, 414–15; trans. Francis Macdonald Cornford (Oxford: Clarendon Press, 1941), pp. 106–7.

46. In noting the totalitarian implications of the Platonic program, I wish to distance myself from the analysis by Karl R. Popper, who, in *The Open Society and Its Enemies* (Princeton: Princeton University Press, 1950), tried to credit Plato with ideas that lay behind Hitler's National Socialism. It was Plato's position that the state should serve the individual and guarantee the greatest personal fulfillment possible. It is highly anachronistic and irresponsible for a scholar to attribute to Plato an abuse of democratic freedoms and a support of totalitarian schemes of which he had no knowledge and about which he had no intentions.

47. John R. Silber, "The Copernican Revolution in Ethics: The Good Reexamined," *Kant-Studien* 51 (1959–60): 85–101.

48. Kdpv, p. 159; Beck, p. 256.

2

Reason, Tradition, Community: The Search for Ethical Foundations

CHARLES DAVIS

WHAT IS MEANT BY the search for ethical foundations?

A first approximation to its meaning may be given by saying that to search for ethical foundations is to seek the answer to the two questions Ronald Green uses as the framework for his recent study of religious reason,[1] namely: Why should there be morality? Why should I be moral? The questions as thus formulated do not, however, give any indication of what would count as an answer. Here Ronald Green himself points a direction by interpreting his two questions in a way that throws their meaning back upon that of reason. The first question becomes: What is the reason or rational justification for the institution of morality?[2] And the second question is now: Is it always rational for the individual to be moral? or, Is what is generally rational always rational for me? If we follow that direction, the search for ethical foundations is to be understood as the attempt to ground, not yet a particular morality, but morality as such, both as a social system and as a personal imperative, upon reason. But what do the terms *reason* and its derivatives, *rational* and *reasonable*,[3] mean in the moral realm?

The questions so far raised belong to metaethics. Metaethics is the level of ethical reflection that, presupposing the existence and functioning both of moralities and of theoretical ethical systems, considers the most general questions concerning the nature of the good and the right, what it means to make a moral judgment, the logic of moral statements, and so on. The preceding

37

level of reflection constitutes normative ethics.[4] The questions normative ethics asks are: What kind of action is good or right or obligatory? Is there a set of moral principles we can use in making particular moral judgments? Theoretical moral systems, such as utilitarianism, belong to normative ethics. Apart from the fact that any moral theory is the work of rational reflection, normative ethics inevitably raises the question of the relation between moral action and reason or rationality. Richard Brandt has recently suggested that the main traditional questions of moral philosophy can be rephrased as questions about what is rational. Thus, the questions: What is worth wanting or working for? What is the best thing for agents to do from their own point of view? What is morally right? What is morally just? may be reformulated as: What is it rational to want, for itself? What is it rational for agents to do, from their own point of view? Which kinds of action is it rational to approve morally? What kind of moral system for their society would it be rational for agents to support?[5] Clearly, agreement with the reformulation depends upon the concept of the rational presupposed here.

It is not my present purpose to discuss Brandt's own account of the rational. I simply wish to show that normative ethics is the application of reason to morality. To acknowledge that is not indeed to accept the pattern of rationality at present dominant in ethics. David Burrell and Stanley Hauerwas have attacked the standard account of moral rationality for its pursuit of an impersonal rationality and its consequent neglect of the indispensability of narrative for ethical reflection. No ethical system or normative moral theory can capture the substantive content of the many moral notions we inherit. These moral notions are embodied in the stories of our communities. What we need is not theory-building, but the development of the reflective capacity to analyze stories, so that we understand how they function.[6]

The transition from morality to normative ethics need not, then, be understood, as it generally is, as the articulation of a set of universal principles from which particular moral judgments can be derived. Rather than trying to mold the moral life into a system, ethics would offer an analysis of the functioning of stories and a set of criteria for discriminating among stories. But whether one is committed to the theoretical rationality of a moral system or to the practical rationality both exhibited and formed by narrative, the conscious reflection that shifts morality into an explicit ethic is rational reflection. We use reason to articulate and justify morality.

How far is morality itself an affair of reason? Morality, which I here distinguish from normative ethics and metaethics, is best understood as a cultural system of communally shared and transmitted authoritative models and norms for governing social and interpersonal behavior. A morality, consequently, is a tradition of models and norms, carried by a community and thus having legitimate force, that is, authority. The moral models and norms constituting morality not only exist in the form of moral statements, but are embodied in institutions and symbolic actions. Every person as a moral agent participates in a morality, which forms the context for ordinary moral judgments and decisions, even though he or she may not engage in the theoretical or self-conscious reflection of normative ethics or metaethics. A morality is a function of a tradition of the community that bears it. Is it also essentially a product of reason? In other words, does reason relate to moralities as a contentless, purely formal principle of order or is reason the originating source of the substantive content of the order of human existence, brought to expression in the norms and models of a morality?

There are, we find, two concepts of reason and two concepts of order as it relates to human existence. The first is the concept of substantive reason as the seat of a fundamental experience of reality, giving rise to morality, tradition, and community, when these are true or authentic. The order of human existence is in this conception grounded upon the structure of reality, to which human beings belong and must conform. The second concept is that of reason as tool or calculus. Its function is not to produce a content, but to order what is given in human existence. That given is not essentially rational, but a medley of ends and desires, which cannot themselves be judged or evaluated by reason. In establishing an order, reason acts as a purely formal principle. The order it establishes is not, therefore, a reflection of the structure of reality, but consists in the removal of conflict. Human beings are seen not as inhering in an order larger than themselves, but as self-defining subjects, producing their own orders from the material of their own interests and desires, which are not to be measured by other than human criteria.

The relation of each of these conceptions to tradition and community differs. Since in the second conception reason is purely formal, reason in its moral function is understood as independent of the content of particular traditions and of the sets of convictions governing the life of particular communities. The attempt is to produce a moral theory of universal validity in so far as moral judgments are derived from basic principles, themselves independent of any community or tradition. Moral principles and judgments are thus, it is thought, freed from involvement in mythical, cosmological, religious, or ideological world views, so as to constitute a cognitively independent ethics guided by universally valid principles and universally available procedures of rational will-formation and decision making. Ethical rationalization or the penetration of the moral field by reason is in this view the disengagement of moral insights, judgments, and principles from the ideals and beliefs proper to a particular community and distinctive of its tradition. Normative ethics thus replaces morality or conformity to tradition in those who are fully mature, moral adults.

Those who hold the first conception of reason as a substantive experience of the structure of reality and of the truth or true order of human existence must take account of the universality essential to any morality or ethics that claims cognitive force and rationality. How can this be done without falling into the dogmatism and ethnocentricity of claiming universal validity for the set of ideals and beliefs of a particular tradition? Universality can be saved in and through particularity by recognizing the overlapping and convergence of traditions and the equivalence of experiences and their symbolization.

This is not to deny the existence of real conflict among traditions and the need for a critical discrimination of the content of traditions. A community and its tradition may be and often is rendered inauthentic by failure or refusal to consider new data, by biased judgments and irresponsible actions. Nevertheless, conflict and inauthenticity in regard to meaning and value are not overcome by flight to a formal universality, but by a deepening and purification of the particular tradition, so as to release its dynamic convergence and equivalence with the other traditions that symbolize the truth of human existence. For this conception of reason, ethical systems or theories have a limited role as heuristic tools. They cannot replace the *phronesis* or practical wisdom of the *spoudaios* or mature person. Normative ethics or self-conscious ethical reflection is less the elaboration of a theoretical system than the analysis of the modes in which moral values are embodied and expressed, of the criteria for their discrimination, and of the processes for moral formation. The question of moral formation cannot be omitted, because the moral life does not consist in a set of choices between courses of action made by an unchanged agent, but is a process of moral becoming through deliberation, decision, and action.[7] Morality as lived rests upon the moral being of the community and of the individuals who participate in the life of that community.

I want to defend here the substantive conception of reason. For the basis of true or authentic morality is reason, and normative ethics and metaethics may be understood as the articulation and defense of that moral rationality. Reason here, however, is not a technical instrument for ordering the irrational components of human life into a conflict-free harmony, but a fundamental experience of reality, an experience that constitutes the source of order in human existence and thus the foundation of authentic human community and tradition. Such an experience is not distinct from religious faith, so that I am led to hold with Donald Evans[8] that authentic religious faith and genuine moral character share a common core, which consists of basic stances he refers to as attitude-virtues. They are religious attitudes as fundamental ways in which the self relates to the world as a whole; they are moral virtues, not so much ways of behaving as ways of being in the world. Whatever may rightly be said about the distinction of religious and moral statements and their logical relationship, both religious faith and moral convictions go back to a common concrete experience. That is why Ronald Green finds himself unable, in the last analysis, to answer the question, "Why should I be moral?" without appeal to religious reason.

The most forthright statement in recent thought of the substantive and religious character of human reason is given by Eric Voegelin. In his article "Reason: The Classic Experience,"[9] Voegelin describes the life of reason as it reached articulate self-consciousness in Plato and Aristotle and finds it very different from reason as cultivated in the modern West. The same account is given in his earlier article "The Gospel and Culture,"[10] but there he also argues that the noetic core is the same both in Greek philosophy and in the gospel movement. The gospel is not an alternative to philosophy, but the same noetic experience in a perfected state. What, then, is the noetic experience?

In resisting the disorder of their age, Socrates, Plato, and Aristotle experienced a force or source of order in the human *psyche*. To that force, and to the movements and the structure of the *psyche* it effected, they gave the name of *nous*. The reality experienced by the philosophers as specifically human is existence in a state of unrest. To be specifically human is to be a questioner, searching with a wondering question the ultimate ground and meaning of existence. The questioning is not merely a game to be played. The philosopher feels moved, drawn into the search by an unknown force. The questioning is a divine-human encounter:

> In the Platonic-Aristotelian experience, the questioning unrest carries assuaging answer within itself inasmuch as man is moved to his search of the ground by the divine ground of which he is in search. The ground is not a spatially distant thing but a divine presence that becomes manifest in the experience of unrest and the desire to know. The wondering and questioning is sensed as the beginning of a theophanic event that can become fully luminous to itself if it finds the proper response in the *psyche* of concrete human beings — as it does in the classic philosophers. Hence, philosophy in the classic sense is not a body of "ideas" or "opinions" about the divine ground dispensed by a person who calls himself a "philosopher," but a man's responsive pursuit of his questioning unrest to the divine source that has aroused it.[11]

Thus the reality expressed in the language of *nous* is the structure in the *psyche* of someone who is attuned to the divine order in the cosmos, not of someone who exists in revolt against it. Reason has a definite existential content of openness toward the ultimate ground. "If this context of the classic analysis is ignored and the symbols *nous* or *reason* are treated as if they referred to some human faculty independent from the tension toward the ground, the empirical basis from which the symbols derive their validity is lost; they become abstracts from nothing, and the vacuum of the pseudo-abstracts is ready to be filled with various nonrational contents."[12]

"The life of reason in the classic sense is existence in tension between life and death. . . . Man experiences himself as tending beyond his human imperfection toward the perfection of the divine ground that moves him."[13] It is life in what Voegelin, borrowing the concept from Plato in the *Symposium* and *Philebus*, calls "the metaxy" or "In-Between." The metaxy or In-Between is not an empty space between the poles of the tension. It is the realm of the spiritual, the reality of mutual participation of human in divine and divine in human, the movement somewhere between knowledge and ignorance of the spiritual person in quest of the ground, the experience of the noetic quest as a transition of *psyche* from mortality to immortality.

> Because of the divine presence that gives the unrest its direction, the unfolding of noetic consciousness is experienced as a process of immortalizing. With their discovery of man as the *zoon noun echon*, the classic philosophers have discovered man to be more than a *thnetos*, a mortal: he is an unfinished being, moving from the imperfection of death in this life to the perfection of life in death.[14]

Hence, if human beings exist in the metaxy, to conceive them as world-immanent beings will destroy the meaning of existence by depriving them of their specific humanity.

Existence in the metaxy or In-Between is a field of pulls (*helkein*) and counter-pulls (*anthelkein*). Human beings are free to engage in the action of "immortalizing" by following the pull of the divine *nous* or to choose death by following the counterpulls of the passions. Consequently, the human *psyche* is a battleground between the forces of life and of death. Life is not given, but offered, and requires human cooperation in order to be gained. But even if a person "mortalizes," he or she cannot escape from existence as a *zoon noun echon*. Rejection of reason will assume the form of reason, and the more radically one rejects reason, the more radically will one symbolize that rejection in some rational system. Hence the speculative systems of the Comtean, Hegelian, and Marxian type are not science, "but deformation of the life of reason through the magic practice of self-divination and self-salvation."[15]

The gospel, too, presents existence as a movement in which life can be death and death be life.[16] "For whoever would save his life will lose it, and whoever loses his life for my sake will find it" (Matt. 16:25). Human existence is likewise symbolized in the gospel as a field of pulls and counter-pulls. In the Gospel of John, Christ says, "And I when I am lifted up from the earth will draw (*helkein*) all men to myself" (John 12:32); and earlier in the same Gospel this drawing power of Christ is identified with the pull exerted by God: "No one can come to me unless the Father who sent me draws (*helkein*) him" (John 6:44). The gospel is not a message or doctrine, but the event of the divine Logos becoming present in the world through the representative life and death of a human person. The saving tale is the story of God's pull becoming effective in the world through Christ.

For Voegelin, then, the noetic core in the gospel is identified with that of classical philosophy. "There is the same field of pull and counter-pull, the same sense of gaining life through following the pull of the golden cord, the same consciousness of existence in an In-Between of human-divine participation, and the same experience of divine reality as the center of action in the movement from question to answer."[17] He rejects the distinction found in much Christian theology between "revelation" and "natural reason." The language symbols expressing existence in the metaxy are not invented by an observer who does not participate in the movement of that existence, but are engendered by participation, so that their ontological status is both human and divine.

This double status of the symbols which express the movement in the metaxy has been badly obscured in Western history by Christian theologians who have split the two components of symbolic truth, monopolizing, under the title of "revelation," for Christian symbols the divine component, while assigning, under the title of "natural reason," to philosophical symbols the human component. This theological doctrine is empirically untenable—Plato was just as conscious of the revelatory component in the truth of his *logos* as the prophets of Israel or the authors of the New Testament writings. The differences betwen prophecy, classic philosophy, and the gospel must be sought in the degrees of differentiation of existential truth.[18]

Further, although the greater differentiation leads prophecy, philosophy, and the gospel out from the more compact form of the cosmological myth, it does not lead from all myth. "Myth is not a primitive symbolic form, peculiar to early societies and progressively to be overcome by positive science, but the language in which the experiences of human-divine participation in the In-Between become articulate."[19] It should be added that cosmological cultures themselves, though undifferentiated in their experience of existence, "are not a domain of primitive 'idolatry', 'polytheism', or 'paganism', but highly sophisticated fields of mythical imagination, quite capable of finding the proper symbols for the concrete or typical cases of divine presence in a cosmos in which divine reality is omnipresent."[20]

The gospel and *nous* or reason, then, are not alternatives, but different degrees of differentiation of the same experience of specifically human existence. The noetic analysis of the Greek philosophers is in some respects superior to that of the gospel,[21] but the gospel surpasses Greek philosophy in its decisive differentiation of the Unknown God. "The strength of the gospel is its concentration on the one point that is all-important: that the truth of reality has its center not in the cosmos at large, not in nature or society or imperial rulership, but in the presence of the Unknown God in a man's existence to his death and life."[22]

The relevance to ethics of Voegelin's account of *nous* is put into relief by this passage from Aristotle's *Nicomachean Ethics,* referred to by Voegelin himself:

> If the intellect (*nous*) is divine compared with man, the life of the intellect must be divine compared with the life of a human creature. And we ought not to listen to those who counsel us, "O man, think as man should," and "O mortal, remember your mortality." Rather ought we, so far as in us lies, to put on immortality and to leave nothing unattempted in the effort to live in conformity with the highest thing within us. Small in bulk it may be, yet in power and preciousness it transcends all the rest.[23]

Only when experienced and conceived in this way, namely, as a participation in the divine and a movement toward the divine, can reason as the source of order found a morality by which we may live a truly human existence. In other articles, notably "Immortality: Experience and Symbol"[24] and "Equivalences of Experience and Symbolization in History",[25] Voegelin has elaborated the principles through which we may grasp reason in the noetic sense as a constituent of humanity at all times and in all places. The noetic experience, articulated as both philosophy and gospel, was the source of order for the Western *psyche* and for Western civilization. It is an experience of existence in the In-Between, which is an experience of existence in its specifically human, unfinished form. Our own mode of noetic experience should enable us to discern the noetic experience of other cultures and traditions, despite different degrees of differentiation and different sets of symbols.

I have contrasted the substantive conception of reason, according to which reason is a relationship with a normative order, with a formal conception, according to which reason is a calculating instrument for combining together and thereby removing conflict among the irrational elements of human nature. Utilitarian ethics is a clear representative of the formal conception. There is, however, a third, intermediate conception of the role of reason in morality. This begins with autonomous reason as the expression of the human person as a self-defining subject and, consequently, refuses the appeal to a larger rational order, not of human making. But instead of seeing reason as purely calculative, it attempts to find in autonomous reason as self-determinative or free the basic normative criteria for action.[26] This is the approach of Kant, for whom autonomous reason as rational will is the ground of obligation and the criterion of moral action. A more recent attempt to find an intermediate position between substantive reason in its classical sense and a purely formal conception of reason as a technical instrument is found in Jürgen Habermas.[27] Habermas belongs to the Marxist tradition and agrees with Marx in regarding autonomous, scientific reason as the ultimate source of knowledge of reality, to the exclusion of religious faith as a revelatory source of the truth of human existence. At the same time, Habermas shares a rejection of positivism with the older mem-

bers of the Frankfurt School and a consequent refusal to be satisfied with a purely technical or means-ends rationality. His aim
is to find in reason a normative basis for practical or moral — as
distinct from technical — human action, and for human society
as striving for emancipation. His analysis is well worth consideration as a remarkable attempt to overcome the humanly destructive
consequences of a positivistically conceived reason without a return to religious faith or an uncritical appeal to tradition.

Fundamental for Habermas is an irreducible distinction between two kinds of human action: purposive-rational (*zweck-
rational*) action and communicative action. Habermas draws upon
Weber in forming his concept of purposive-rational action, but
his concept and Weber's do not exactly correspond.[28] Purposive-
rational action is action directed to success in achieving some
concrete end by organized means. It may for Habermas be either
instrumental or strategic. Instrumental action is directed to achieving a successful physical intervention through technical means.
Strategic action follows rules of rational choice, as set forth in game
theory and decision theory, with the aim of achieving success in
influencing the decisions of others to fulfill one's own purposes.

Communicative action is directed, not to success in one's own
purposes, but to reaching an understanding among people trying
to come to an agreement. Such action is governed by consensual
norms, held in a communicatively achieved agreement or at least
intersubjectively presupposed. The context of communicative action is the life-world, understood as the total network of normatively regulated interpersonal relations. It is within the social
context of the life-world that there arises knowledge in the form
of interpretations, which is distinct in type from empirical knowledge in the form of information. The empirical sciences systematically pursue knowledge as information, whereas the hermeneutic and historical disciplines elaborate interpretations into the
systematic understanding of traditions.

Habermas therefore insists upon the distinctive rationality
of normatively regulated actions over against the rationality of
purposive-rational action. Normatively regulated actions incorporate a moral-practical knowledge, given in tradition and articulated in the hermeneutic and historical disciplines; purposive-
rational actions incorporate empirical knowledge, methodically

pursued in the empirical sciences. Habermas criticizes Weber's account of societal rationalization as concentrating too narrowly upon the institutionalization of purposive-rational action in the capitalist economy and the modern state, even though he admits that Weber's general concept of rationality was not limited to the means-ends relationship.[29] What Habermas attempts is a more comprehensive account of societal rationalization.

A first approach to that account may be made by noting that Habermas distinguishes the interpretation and application of tradition, a procedure systematized in the hermeneutic disciplines, from what he calls a critical appropriation of tradition. Critical appropriation releases the content of meaning in tradition, while refusing any claim that cannot be redeemed in rational discourse.[30] In other words, critical appropriation disengages the content of tradition from the authority of tradition. A normative agreement based on tradition is lower on the scale of rationality than one reached through rationally grounded procedures of will-formation.[31] Societal rationalization in the sphere of communicative action is thus a function of the opposition between normatively ascribed agreement and communicatively achieved agreement. The less cultural traditions and social structures predecide what has to be accepted and by whom, and the more a given consensus proceeds from interpretive processes of the participants themselves, the more rational is the social relationship.[32] However, that presupposes the possibility of a self-sufficient rational foundation for normative values, a foundation which is independent of any appeal to the authority of tradition. Habermas sets out to provide such a foundation. He considers that the type of reflection found in Kant in the form of a search for the transcendental subjective conditions of knowledge has now dropped the transcendental subject and become the rational reconstruction of generative rules and cognitive schemata, as for example in general linguistics. He argues that moral philosophy can achieve the same kind of status as a linguistic ethic (*Sprachethik*), by reflectively deriving universal ethical rules from the fundamental norms presupposed in every instance of rational speech.[33]

He disengages the fundamental norms implied in speech: every speech act carries four different types of validity claims with it, namely, truth, truthfulness, rightness, and comprehensibility. If any question arises about the truthfulness of the interlocutor or the comprehensibility of what is said, the only solution is to continue the communication until the doubt is resolved. The other two claims — namely, to the truth of the propositional content of the utterance and to the rightness of the norms presupposed or created by the interpersonal relationship of the speech act — if questioned, need to be redeemed in discourse (a specialized form of communication, disengaged from action and experience, in which we enter into argument). Claims are treated as hypothetical and through argument rationally grounded or rejected.

Habermas argues further that discourse itself implies a counterfactual supposition of what he calls the ideal speech situation. The ideal speech situation is presupposed and anticipated by discourse as a potentiality inherent in the present situation, though never completely actualized and in that sense counterfactual. Why does discourse presuppose the ideal speech situation? It does so because to take part in a discourse is to suppose that a genuine agreement is possible. Discourse would be rendered meaningless if a grounded consensus were not possible or could not be distinguished from a false consensus.

When is a consensus rationally grounded? Habermas maintains that a rational consensus can be characterized only formally. It is one achieved when discourse is unrestrained and universal, that is, where the only force is that of the better argument and where there is equal opportunity for participation. In other words, a consensus is rationally grounded only in so far as the discourse presupposes and anticipates the ideal speech situation.

Now if we follow up the requirements of the ideal speech situation, we find that they imply an ideal form of social life, that is, a form where the organization of society in its institutions and practices allows free, symmetrical, and unconstrained discourse. Consequently, ideal speech implies a society free from domination, organized on a principle of equality, and embodying the ideals of truth, freedom, and justice. To put it briefly: since every speech act has an essential relation to discourse, and discourse presupposes the ideal speech situation, and the ideal speech situation implies an emancipated society, every speech act necessarily implies the basic moral values of truth, freedom, equality, and justice.

Such, then, is the rational grounding in speech, taken as it-self rational, of an emancipatory ethic. How does this appeal to reason relate to tradition and to the normative orders the various traditions embody? As Habermas sees it, the traditional world views as represented by the religions have been dismantled beyond any prospect of restoration. A steady rationalization has brought area after area of life previously regulated by tradition under the con-trol of rational techniques. Habermas does not wish to deny or oppose the rationalization process. What he does do, however, is to insist that normatively regulated actions should be rationalized in a distinctive manner, namely, through the achievement of free and equal participation in rational will-formation.

The cultural life of societies, he goes on to argue, is not a random process. It follows a rationally reconstructible pattern of development. His argument runs as follows: The cultural life of society is constituted by socialization. Socialization is brought about through the medium of normative structures, in which human needs are interpreted and various actions permitted or declared obligatory. The normative claims thus made call for justification in discourse. But the discursive redemption of normative claims follows a rational sequence. Therefore, since socialization is depen-dent upon normative claims and their justification, it follows a rational pattern of development. In other words, the cultural life of society is directional and embodies an irreversible sequence. As long as the continuity of society is unbroken, socially attained stages of moral consciousness cannot be forgotten and any devia-tion is experienced as a regression.

What, then, is the rationally reconstructible pattern of de-velopment in the cultural life of social systems? There is an in-creasing demand for the discursive redemption of normative claims. That pressure leads from myth through religion to philosophy and critique. In the directional process the following irreversible trends are discernible: the expansion of the secular in relation to the sa-cred; the movement from heteronomy to autonomy; the emptying of the cognitive contents from world views, so that cosmology is replaced by a pure system of morality; the shift from tribal par-ticularism to universalistic and individualistic orientation; an in-creasing reflexivity of the mode of belief.[34] The directional move-ment is in effect the gradual freeing of normative validity claims from fusion with other claims. When that has occurred, the rightness of norms can be clearly recognized as a validity claim subject as such to discursive justification. We are then in the postconventional stage of moral and social development.

Döbert, a younger collaborator of Habermas, has taken up the theme of the increasing reflexivity of belief and interpreted the history of religious consciousness as the development of a process of reflection through which human beings gain clarity in regard to themselves and free themselves from the domination of normative systems that impose themselves with a nature-like compulsion.[35] The opposite of a nature-like compulsion of norms is a mutual agreement on norms, reached in a free reciprocal process of communication. Döbert therefore suggests that the development of religion may be conceived as the evolution of communicative competence. The end point in the development of religion, thus conceived as communicative competence, is this: persons as subjects will have become competent to test and render perspicuous for one another assertions and behavioral expectations through a linguistically mediated process of reciprocal reflexivity. In brief, the final stage or ideal, which marks the dissolution of religion into an autonomous and universalistic morality, is the reciprocal transparency of persons in a process of communication to decide upon norms for their relationships and actions.

In Habermas and Döbert, practical reason or moral rationality is disengaged from the stories and other symbolic contents of the religious traditions. Those traditional world views are regarded as devoid of any rationally defensible cognitive contents. Reason, therefore, stands on its own as autonomous. To be rational in the moral sphere is to be willing, when one's norms have been questioned, to enter into a discursive situation with others with a view to reaching a genuine agreement. Within practical discourse acceptance or rejection of norms will be rationally motivated according to the subject-matter to be regulated, the given contents, and the empirical consequences.[36] No prior commitment to any substantive order of human existence or to any unchanging moral principles or set of ideal norms is presupposed, except for the norms implied by the acceptance of discourse itself. But — and here Habermas departs from a purely formalistic conception of reason — practical discourse does presuppose the acceptance as normative of certain idealized preconditions of discourse, namely, freedom, justice, and equality. Those, therefore, become the fundamental norms of a communicative or linguistic ethic.

The serious oversight of this impressive theory, it seems to me, is the failure to consider the source of motivation in the moral agent. Bernstein has already remarked the lack in Habermas of "any illumination on the problem of human agency and motivation."[37] The crux is the question raised by Ronald Green as providing the dynamic for his analysis: Why should I be moral? Even granted that there is a rational justification for the institution of morality, why should I be moral when it is not in my personal interest to do so? Why should I submit normative claims that are in possession and that work to my advantage to modification by impartially organized discourse? What prevents me from dismissing communicative action (as opposed to strategic and instrumental action) as an empty ideal without any basis in the harsh reality of human existence and society? The distinctive moral rationality claimed for communicative action may be rejected as unrealistic and consequently irrational by those whose measure does not transcend the self.

The basic norms discerned by Habermas in the ideal speech situation and therefore as underlying discourse and communicative action are in effect a demand for self-transcendence on the part of human beings as moral agents. That demand is unsupported wishful thinking unless reason participates in a transcendent order. But if reason is such a participation and not merely a regulative procedure, the transcendent order of reality and human participation in it require expression in the stories and symbols of religion.

Reason cannot adequately ground morality if it is enclosed and totally self-defining, instead of being the openness of human beings to an order larger than themselves. When no longer linked to a self-transcendent source of motivation, reason becomes a tool of expediency. Hauerwas writes:

My basic difficulty with "rationality" as the "mark" of man, however, is that when reason is abstracted from the other goods that enhance our lives it becomes a technical instrument for man's attempt to secure survival. Reason thus often becomes wedded to self-interest as the tool to secure my existence against others.[38]

How true that is comes across with all the vividness of concrete experience in Langdon Gilkey's *Shantung Compound,* a reflective account of his experiences in a civilian internment camp in North China during the Second World War. The internees, though reduced to subsistence level in regard to the necessities of human living, were not subjected to any cruelty and were left completely free by the Japanese to organize their own life within the camp. The majority of those in the camp were the kind of educated people usually regarded as persons of principle. Here, then, was a situation that could be viewed as providing a test of the role of moral reason in organizing human affairs, and that is indeed how Gilkey treats it in his book. What he found was that under the kind of pressure experienced in the camp, the moral and rational powers become servants of self-concern. As he writes:

> In this situation, no amount of intelligence or of ideals and good intentions will change his behavior or free him from his selfishness so that he can be good. The more acute mind of the intelligent man may well fashion more plausible rationalizations than can the slower mind of his neighbor. In each of our crucial moral issues this pattern repeated itself: over and over the more educated and respectable people defended their self-concern with more elegant briefs. We came, indeed, to have a grudging respect for the open rascal. He, at least, was forthright in admitting his selfishness.[39]

Moral issues must be seen, therefore, as the expression in action of deeper issues. Gilkey goes on to say:

> A man's morality is his religion enacted in social existence. The rare power of selflessness, what we call true "morality" or "virtue," arises only when a life finds its ultimate devotion to lie beyond itself, thus allowing that person in times of crisis to forget his own concerns and to be free to love and help his neighbor.[40]

The source of deception in these matters is that when people's basic security is not threatened their moral and rational powers function with benevolence. That benevolence, which is the ground for the humanist's faith in human moral self-sufficiency, is in fact often a mere expansiveness due to easy circumstances. It disappears when the welfare of the self is fundamentally threatened. So, as I myself wrote in *Theology and Political Society*, with reference to the reliance of Habermas upon discourse for the validation of normative claims: "Detached discourse can only be carried on by those who are already leading a moderately contented existence. It has a limited context and function. It cannot bring salvation to the human race locked in institutionalized unreason and unfreedom."[41] The analysis Habermas gives of the distinctive rationality of moral action is logically elegant, but it remains remote from reality in its disregard of the concrete problems of moral motivation. But if like Habermas one excludes the religious dimension, how can one deal with sin as the choice of unreason when unreason suits the self-concern of the self-centered ego?

My conclusion is that reason as the autonomous power of a self-defining subject will not succeed in grounding morality. Moral action is self-transcendent action. That is what distinguishes it from strategic or instrumental — namely, from self-serving — action. If reason is to ground self-transcendent action, it must transcend the self. In other words, we come back to Voegelin's noetic experience as participation in the divine and only as such the ground and the source of order for human existence.

When reason is understood as that by which we experience the pull of the divine, the order it grounds is not just that of the individual, but of community. Reason is no longer an instrument by which the individual and group manipulate things and events for their own survival or welfare; it becomes a self-transcendent intentionality toward the goods that found authentic human community. As the source of human community, it is also the source of tradition, with its stories and symbols, its doctrines and precepts. Tradition should not be identified with the imposition and continuance of heteronomous authority. Tradition is the cumulative experience of successive generations; it is the memory of outstanding, originative experiences, to the heights of which subsequent generations must rise; it is the irreplaceable respository of experiences too rich for discursive reason adequately to objectify.[42] Its authority is therefore the authority of human cooperation across time and space.[43]

Morality is completely realized and expressed only in a community with its tradition. Underlying community and tradition when these are authentic is reason, not as a calculative instrument of self-interest, but as the movement of the human subject toward divine truth and goodness. That is whither our search for ethical foundations leads us and that is where it must end.

NOTES

1. Ronald M. Green, *Religious Reason: The Rational and Moral Basis of Religious Belief* (New York: Oxford University Press, 1978).
2. Ibid., p. 13.
3. For a distinction of meaning between the two terms *rational* and *reasonable,* see Chaim Perelman, "The Rational and the Reasonable," in *Rationality Today/La Rationalité Aujourd'hui,* ed. Theodore F. Geraets, Proceedings of the International Symposium on "Rationality Today" held at the University of Ottawa, October 27–30, 1977 (Ottawa: University of Ottawa Press, 1979), pp. 213–24.
4. Henry John McCloskey, *Meta-Ethics and Normative Ethics* (The Hague: Martinus Nijhoff, 1969).
5. Richard B. Brandt, *A Theory of the Good and the Right* (Oxford: Clarendon Press, 1979), pp. 1–2.
6. Stanley Hauerwas et al., *Truthfulness and Tragedy: Further Investigations in Christian Ethics* (Notre Dame, Ind.: University of Notre Dame Press, 1977).
7. Ibid.
8. Donald Evans, *Struggle and Fulfillment: The Inner Dynamics of Religion and Morality* (Cleveland, Ohio: Collins Press, 1979).
9. Eric Voegelin, *Anamnesis,* ed. and trans. Gerhardt Niemeyer (Notre Dame, Ind.: University of Notre Dame Press, 1978). See chapter on "Reason: The Classic Experience."
10. Eric Voegelin, "The Gospel and Culture," in *Jesus and Man's Hope,* ed. Donald G. Miller and D. Y. Hadidian, 2 vols. (Pittsburgh, Pa.: Pittsburgh Theological Seminary, 1971), 2:59–101.
11. Voegelin, *Anamnesis,* pp. 95–96.
12. Ibid., p. 97.
13. Ibid., p. 105.
14. Ibid., pp. 103–4.
15. Voegelin, "The Gospel and Culture," p. 76.
16. Ibid., p. 67.
17. Ibid., p. 80.
18. Ibid., p. 75.

19. Ibid., p. 76.

20. Ibid., p. 84.

21. Ibid., p. 97.

22. Ibid., p. 99.

23. Aristotle, *Nicomachean Ethics* 10.7.

24. Eric Voegelin, "Immortality: Experience and Symbol," *Harvard Theological Review* 60 (1967):236–79.

25. Eric Voegelin, "Equivalences of Experience and Symbolization in History," in *Eternità e Storia: I Valori Permanenti Nel Divenire Storico A Cura dell'Instituto Academico di Roma* (Firenze: Vallechi, 1976), pp. 215–34.

26. For a brief but very clear account of the different conceptions of reason, see Charles Taylor, *Hegel and Modern Society* (Cambridge: At the University Press, 1979), pp. 72–84.

27. Jürgen Habermas, "A Postscript to Knowledge and Human Interests," *Philosophy of the Social Sciences* 3 (1973): 157–89; Jürgen Habermas, *Legitimation Crisis*, trans. Thomas McCarthy (Boston: Beacon Press, 1975).

28. Thomas McCarthy, *The Critical Theory of Jürgen Habermas* (Cambridge, Mass.: M.I.T. Press, 1978), pp. 28–30.

29. Geraets, *Rationality Today.*

30. Habermas, *Legitimation Crisis*, p. 70.

31. Geraets, *Rationality Today*, p. 193.

32. Ibid., p. 202.

33. Habermas, "A Postscript," p. 183; Habermas, *Legitimation Crisis*, pp. 102–10.

34. Habermas, *Legitimation Crisis*, pp. 11–12.

35. Rainer Döbert, *Systemtheorie und die Entwicklung religiöser Deutunsystem: Zur Logic des sozialwissenschaftlichen Funktionalismus* (Frankfurt: Suhrkamp, 1973), p. 141.

36. Geraets, *Rationality Today*, p. 206.

37. Habermas, *Legitimation Crisis*, p. 224.

38. Hauerwas, *Truthfulness and Tragedy*, p. 63.

39. Langdon Gilkey, *Shantung Compound: The Story of Men and Women under Pressure* (New York: Harper & Row, 1966), p. 232.

40. Ibid., p. 233.

41. Charles Davis, *Theology and Political Society* (Cambridge: At the University Press, 1980), p. 102.

42. Ibid., pp. 96–103.

43. Bernard Lonergan, "Dialectic of Authority," in *Authority*, ed. Frederick J. Adelmann, Boston College Studies in Philosophy 3 (The Hague: Martinus Nijhoff, 1974), pp. 24–30.

3

"But We Do See Jesus": The Particularity of Incarnation and the Universality of Truth

JOHN HOWARD YODER

LET ME BEGIN WITH a landmark cliché, the words of Gotthold Ephraim Lessing which are so often taken as symbols of the threshold of modernity:

> Accidental truths of history can never become the proof of necessary truths of reason. . . . That . . . is the ugly, broad ditch which I cannot get across, however often and however earnestly I have tried to make the leap. If anyone can help me over it, let him do it, I beg him.[1]

It may be true for individuals that everything seems, only recently, to have come loose; but it is not true of the history of Christian thought. The new challenges which some take so seriously are not that new, except to them. It would be wrong to think that the issue of the credibility of particular claims is best represented only by some quite recent reformulation of historical skepticism, or religious pluralism, or the death-of-God language, or by the gap between contingent facts of history and the necessary truths of reason posited by Lessing, the dean of modern ditchdiggers. Each of those formulations is important. Yet none of them is at the bottom of our problem. None of them can find *beyond the ditch* a place to stand which would be less particular, more credible, less the product of one's own social location.

My task in this synthetic effort is not to respond to any one of those culture shifts alone in an adequate way, but rather to respond to the way in which they all address analogous challenges to a specifically Christian witness. Thereby several logically distinguishable critiques of particularity are telescoped. I shall not try to disentangle them:

1. There is the denunciation of the logical circularity of all claims to revelation.
2. There is the logical challenge of Lessing's dissatisfaction with particular proofs as not proving general truths.
3. There is the need for making sense to people of other backgrounds, who know ahead of time that our reasons are provincial.
4. Among the other backgrounds there is the special case of other faiths. Global cultural change no longer lets Christians assume the superiority of their belief system.
5. There is the need in public life (not only in politics) for a common denominator language in order to collaborate with relative strangers in running the world despite our abiding differences.
6. There is the need, in the interface of clashing or unrelated idea systems, for metalanguages to interpret why we misunderstand one another.
7. There is embarrassment about the provincialism of our predecessors, especially if they linked it with oppressive political and economic power.
8. There is doubt about the adequacy of the dichotomies between grace and nature, the ideal and the real, the natural and the supernatural, with which we have tried to classify our problems, and by means of which the more private traditions had been defending themselves.
9. There is the fear that what we used to believe can all be explained reductionistically by some causation language (Freudian, Marxian, Skinnerian) which the wider culture knows.

For present purposes I propose an obvious simplification, lumping these variations under the code label pluralism/relativism, without claiming to define rigorously even those terms.[2] What is pertinent for our purposes is the point at which this stance is forearmed to box in the claims of Christian witness in the ready-made pigeonhole of the old absolute which it had destroyed.

For many, the great variety of convictions held in different cultural settings makes any absolute position unsustainable. The self-evidence of this claim is most convincing if it is not examined too closely, and it is in that form that I shall respect it.

This excludes my being fully fair to any *one* explanation for the skepticism which any breakthrough to a wider culture teaches anyone to direct toward the belief system he or she came from. Any living community is always moving from smaller worlds into wider ones, always challenged by the psychic dominance of each next wider world. Let the phrase *wider world* substitute for *universality* in my title, and let *pluralism/relativism* stand in for the varied ways in which truth claims from the smaller world find their credibility challenged.

Six adaptive strategies

In the face of this challenge how many possible responses do we have among which to choose? Subject to the obvious limits of all reasoning with types, I suggest that there are at least six.

A first and obvious response is to stay by one's prior particular truth. But in the new context this fidelity will have a new meaning. What was before taken for granted as the way things are, simply "because my mother told me so," a natural identity, is now transformed by the threat into self-conscious narrow carefulness. Thereby the wider world has already exacted its tribute. Instead of being organic and natural as it had been "at home," the particularity will need to be defended against the wider spectrum of other particularities.

A second logical option is conversion. One grants that the wider world is not only larger and stronger but truer. Perhaps it is even thought to be truer just because it is larger and stronger.[3]

A third way will be that of the enlightened pedagogue. Since I was led — the convert says — from the smaller world to the larger one by an experience of rational growth and not by a simple irrational leap from one system to another, so I can with proper patience and intelligence lead along with me those who were born where I was and who should no less than I be helped by finding their way from there to here.

A fourth, more complex pattern is the apology. The *apologia* is a self-commendation or self-defense before a tribunal whose authority to judge one accepts. Yet instead of renouncing one's smaller identity, saying it had been wrong (the colloquial American meaning of *apology*), the apologete finds ways to commend his or her particular past by rephrasing it as another form of the mainstream value system, just as good as the other subforms.[4]

A fifth way, instead of looking for a common nature which is already there, would be to construct a new neutral meta-language, an artificial instrument to talk about talking, to construct by conscious artifice a pedestal beyond all parties to the past conversations, thus being ourselves creators of the still wider world.

A sixth standard type of response is to retain one's stated loyalty to one's particular identity, but to accentuate the humility with which one recognizes the wider context. One does not, like the apologete, try to prove the smaller system right by appealing to the criteria of meaningfulness which rule the larger, nor to prove the larger right by explaining it in terms that make sense in the smaller world. One simply stands them side-by-side and talks about the interface in terms that accept particular identity for oneself and yet relativize the notion of truth.

What these six patterns have in common, behind a host of variations in secondary characteristics, is the acceptance of one way of putting the problem in the first place: namely, the priority in truth and value of the meaning system of the world claiming to be wider. That priority is not the product of a careful, debatable demonstration. Its own definition of what constitutes a wider or more public proof is precisely what we should be interested in debating. But that wider world, in any one person's experience of pilgrimage or in any interface between two groups, is still a small place. It still speaks only one language at a time, and that is still insider language. One adolescent's breath of fresh air is another's ghetto. Any given wider world is still just one more place, even if what its slightly wider or slightly more prestigious circle of interpreters talk about is a better access to "universality." Thus the first mistake which tends to be made by the apologetic person emerging from the smaller world is thinking that that wider society is itself the universe, or that its ways of testing validity beyond the provincial have succeeded, by dint of a harder and more thorough hauling away at one's own definitional bootstraps, in transcending particularity. How can particular truths be proclaimed publicly?

I shall draw a pattern inductively from a series of testimonies of cultural transition found in the literature of the early Christian missionary culture.

An ancient paradigm

In a very coarse-grained way we can say that the New Testament is the document of a transition made by a message-bearing community from one world to another. Born in Aramaic-speaking Palestinian Jewry, praying and socializing and theologizing only in that small society and its tongue, with its Scriptures, the messianic movement in two generations had reached the capital of the world and had produced a core body of literature in the trade-and-culture language of the Gentile world. Admittedly, the hellenistic world was not one culture but a cosmopolitan melee; Jewry was already largely hellenized; and even Palestine had been infiltrated by hellenistic cities and hellenistic culture. Nonetheless, Jesus-believers with a relatively smaller, more homogeneous, poorer, less speculatively pretentious world view moved with their homegrown forms of faith into the encounter with peoples and meaning systems which have no place for their confident call to decision. The Jesus movement was utterly particular. The hellenistic Roman world was classically pluralistic.

I propose to look schematically at five New Testament texts, chosen not arbitrarily but because of parallelisms within their differences. In very different language forms, they have in common the evident fact that the particularity of the Jesus story, previously borne by predominantly Jewish communities into whose own world that story had first erupted, comes now, in the process of organic expansion into the hellenistic world, to encounter the call of believers (and perhaps also of doubters) for a higher level of generality. In what sense can the Jesus story be reported as true for non-Palestinians? For non-Jews? As answering questions never put to Jesus?

We can readily project that the six prototypical strategies of submission to the wider world just described could be spelled out in as many ways to link Jewishness and Gentileness. They are analogous to the choices faced by any young person who discovers the jargon world of the peers on the street or the intellectual world of the teacher at school to be wider than the world one's parents had led one into at home; or to the choices faced by any immigrant, or any minority youth going to university.

Which of these choices does the New Testament support? Conversion to Gentile pluralism? Apology? Or is there another? Having sharpened the question, I turn to the texts. In what sense do New Testament writers already speak to this question?

The Prologue to John (John 1:1–14) seems to be addressed to people holding to a proto-Gnostic cosmology, in which a long ladder of mediating entities stretches from God to earth. The ladder's function is as much to hold its ends apart as to connect them, and it symbolizes the pluralism of Mediterranean culture. The pure ineffable Divinity at the top wards off particularity and contingency, so to speak, by interposing the Logos, a kind of cosmic provost, as the principle of order and rationality. Such a cosmology would have a natural, honorable place for Jesus and thereby for Christian proclamation. The cosmology, however, was bigger than and prior to Jesus, as Greco-Roman culture was prior to the church.

But the seer of the Prologue won't let them put Jesus in that slot. Encouraged by the analogy of Proverbs 8, where Wisdom seems to be a facet of deity, he does not hesitate to accept the language which this cosmology offers. He affirms the Logos as light enlightening every person, and before that as creator of the visible world. Yet instead of tailoring Jesus to fit the slots prepared for him, John breaks the cosmology's rules. At the bottom of the ladder, the Logos is said to have become flesh, to have lived among us as in a tent, symbol of mortality, and to have suffered rejection by us creatures. At the top of the ladder, the Logos is claimed to be coeval with God, not merely the first of many emanations. But then there is no more ladder: the cosmology has been smashed, or melted down for recasting. Its language has been seized and used for a different message. No longer does the concept of Logos solve a problem of religion, reconciling the eternal with the temporal; it carries a proclamation of identification, incarnation, drawing all who believe into the power of becoming God's children.

The addressees of the Epistle to the Hebrews also had a settled cosmology. Angels at the top have access to the divine presence from which they bear the word of the divine will to earth. Priests at the bottom are raised from among their fellows to mediate by bringing to the altar, on their own behalf and for all, the gifts and sacrifices which can cover sin.

Instead of claiming for the Son of Adam his place just *beneath* the angels, however, Messiah is declared to be *above* them at the Lord's right hand, appointed Son, reflecting the stamp of the divine nature, upholding the universe. Yet this cosmic honor was no exemption from human limits. His perfection is not a timeless divine status but was *attained* through weakness with prayers and supplications, loud cries and tears. Fully assuming the priestly system, as both priest and victim, once for all he ends the claim of the sacrificial system to order the community of faith, putting in its place a new covenant, a new universalized priestly order, an unshakable kingdom.

Yet this cosmic sovereignty is not a simple possession. Our contribution to proving or bringing about this sovereignty is our faithfulness to Jesus.

As it is, we do not yet *see* everything in subjection to him. *But we do see Jesus,* who for a little while was made lower than the angels, [now] crowned with glory and honor because of the suffering of death. (Heb. 2:8–9)

The Christians at Colossae also had their cosmology ready, with a modest slot for the Jewish Jesus. The world is held together by a network of principalities and powers, visible and invisible. Religious behavior (fasting, festivals) helps one to find one's way through the tangle. Visions and angelolatry help to manipulate the powers.

Once again Jesus is proclaimed, by the Paul of Colossians, not as part of the cosmos but as its Lord. The powers are not illuminated, appeased, manipulated by him, but subdued and broken. The believer risen with Christ has died to them, and is no longer in their hold. That can be the case because the Son is the image of the invisible creator, holding all things together, reconciling all things, head of the body.

The first vision of the Apocalypse (Rev. 4:1–5:4) presents in classic visionary language the puzzle of history. No one is in sight able to break the seals on the scroll containing the meaning of it all. John weeps. There is no one worthy among the elders, the angels, or the seraphim. But then the Lamb appears, next to the throne, perfect in the sevenfoldness of his horns and eyes, able because he was slain to take history in his hands, unstick the seals, and unroll the world's judgment and salvation.

The fifth analogous text is one which we cannot locate in an initial communication context. It must have been in use in some churches as a hymn before Paul wove part of it into the letter to the Philippians (chapter 2). The imagery behind the hymn would seem to be that of a Prometheus/Adam/primeval king, who as representative of the human race grasped at equality with God, thereby representing the picture the poet projected of the human predicament. The contrast with that is not a more successful Prometheus or an unfallen Adam, but the willing self-emptying of the one who really had divine sonship in his grasp, to identify himself with humanity and in fact to die the death of a criminal. "Wherefore," the hymn goes on in a dramatic reversal of the *kenosis*, "he has been divinely exalted and given the name of Lord" (Phil. 2:9), which fact all of the cosmos shall one day acknowledge. The ground for this exaltation is the free willingness of his humiliation. The low point of the humiliation is not entering humanity but dying on the cross.

Five times, in utterly independent ways, an apostolic writer has responded to the challenge of a previously formed cosmic vision. Each time, in completely different vocabulary, and with no commonality of structure to indicate that one might have learned from one of the others, the writer makes the same moves. We could call it a syndrome or a deep structure. What are those moves? We have seen, each time:

1. That the writer becomes quite at home in the new linguistic world, using its language and facing its questions;
2. That instead of fitting the Jesus message into the slots the cosmic vision has ready for it, the writer places Jesus above the cosmos, in charge of it;
3. That there is in each case a powerful concentration upon being rejected and suffering in human form, beneath the

cosmic hierarchy, as that which accredits Christ for this lordship;

4. That instead of salvation constituting our integration into a salvation system which the cosmos holds ready for us to enter into through ritual or initiation, what we are called to enter into is the self-emptying and the death — and only by that path, and by grace, the resurrection — of the Son;

5. That behind the cosmic victory, enabling it, there is affirmed (without parallel in the Synoptic Gospels) what later confession called preexistence, co-essentiality with the Father, possession of the image of God, and the participation of the Son in creation and providence;

6. That the writer and the readers of these messages share by faith in all that that victory means.

> Brother and sister saints, who share in the heavenly call, contemplate Jesus, Apostle and High Priest of our confession. He was faithful in God's house. . . . Now Moses was faithful in all God's house as a servant, to testify to the things that were to be spoken later, but Christ was faithful over God's house as a Son. *We are his household,* as we hold fast our confidence and pride in our hope. (Heb. 3:1–2, 5–6)

To be fair to this event in the first century we must protect it against anachronistic tendencies which our twentieth-century agenda would impose upon it. One thing we cannot say about the impact of these texts upon their readers, or upon their readers' unbelieving neighbors, was that it was alien or meaningless. They addressed a profound challenge to the contemporary pagan mind, and they did it in terms familiar to that mind, from within its linguistic community.

The other thing we cannot say about this new communication move is that it leaves Judaism behind. That would be anachronism again; the writers of these texts and the singers of the hymn in Philippians were all Jews. They were proclaiming the pertinence and the priority of the meaning-frame of messianic Judaism, with all its concentration upon empirical community, particular history, synagogue worship, and particular lifestyle, over against the speculative and skeptical defenses of its cultured despisers. Instead of requesting free speech and room for one more stand in the Athenian marketplace of ideas for a new variant of already widely-respected diaspora Judaism, their claim was that now the Hebrew story had widened out to include everyone; that, with the inbreaking of the messianic era, the Jewish hope in process of fulfillment was wide enough to receive all the nations and their riches.

So we must step back a moment from our own concern with the usability of ancient language in our time, if we would follow how it was usable then. A handful of messianic Jews, moving beyond the defenses of their somewhat separate society to attack the intellectual bastions of majority culture, refused to contextualize their message by clothing it in the categories the world held ready. Instead, they seized the categories, hammered them into other shapes, and turned the cosmology on its head, with Jesus both at the bottom, crucified as a common criminal, and at the top, preexistent Son and creator, and the church his instrument in today's battle.

It is not the world, culture, civilization, which is the definitional category, which the church comes along to join up with, approve, and embellish with some correctives and complements. The Rule of God is the basic category. The rebellious but already (in principle) defeated cosmos is being brought to its knees by the Lamb. The development of a high Christology is the natural cultural ricochet of a missionary ecclesiology, when it collides as it must with whatever cosmology explains and governs the world it invades.

Particularity as good and as news

As I try to identify how the apostolic sample differs from the other ways of relating the wider and the smaller world with which I began, the best adjective I can find is *evangelical*.

I take the term in its root meaning. One is functionally evangelical if one confesses oneself to have been commissioned by the grace of God with a message which others who have not heard it should hear. It is *angellion* ("news") because they will not know it unless they are told it by a message-bearer. It is *good* news because hearing it will be for them not alienation or compulsion, oppression or brainwashing, but liberation. Because this news is only such when *received* as good, it can never be communicated coercively; nor can the message-bearer ever positively be assured that it will be received.

What distinguishes this view from the apologete and from the convert is the challenge it addresses to the truth claims or salvation claims of the wider world. This challenge does not prove that people at home in that other wider world view are bad. It simply brings them news.

Its reason for not remaining in the ghetto is not merely some kind of psychic drive, nor a sense of deprivation, or a lack of esteem projected upon ghetto dwellers by outsiders. The message cannot remain in the ghetto because the good news by its very nature is for and about the world. The good news is not information which will remain true even if people in a ghetto celebrate it only for themselves; it is about a community-building story for which the world beyond the ghetto is half of the reconciling event. It moves on from the verifiable fact that the world of the God of Abraham is higher and wider than the world of the mystery religions or the Athenian sophists. This is simply true of the story of the Abrahamic people, which has already run through its contacts with Babylonia, with Egypt, with Persia, as well as it is true of the Hebrew cosmology, which makes sense of the world as the meaningful product of the purposive activity of a single, coherent, invisible creator. Abrahamic particularity is not bad but good news, not embarrassing but worth sharing, not arcane but illuminating.

That the world of Abraham and Moses and Jeremiah was (and still is) larger than the world of the sophists and the gnostics is not an apologetic argument needing to be waged in the midst of ambivalent claims and counterclaims about what constitutes an argument for wider validity; it is a simple cultural experience. While messianic Jews in the first century are a sliver of a minority population, the story they tell has been around farther and longer than the Athenian story. That does not make it true. Age, like size, is not in itself verification. But the memory of centuries does support its credibility, and perhaps it explains why for those Jew-

ish witnesses their particularity was less embarrassing than ours
sometimes is for us.

How not to say it

It would have been the wrong question had the early Christians asked, "Shall messianic Jews enter the hellenistic world and
adjust to its concepts?" Should Paul use Greek? The question was
not whether to enter but how to *be* there: how in the transition
to render anew the genuine pertinence of the proclamation of
Christ's lordship, even in a context (*particularly* in a context) where
even the notion of such sovereignty is questionable.

Then must we not say the same for other times and places,
for here and now? Pluralism/relativism as a pervasive meaning
system is not, like Kantianism or Thomism, a total seamless unity;
it is more, like Greek or Fortran, a language. We are now called
to renew in the language world of pluralism/relativism an ana-
logue to what those first transcultural reconceptualizers did; not
to translate their results but to emulate their exercise.

The last thing we should ask, then, would be whether we
can translate into our time from theirs the notion of preexistence
or of the participation of the Son in creation. That would be to
contrast the rules of two language worlds instead of finding a message to express within both. That would be like asking whether
with the bases loaded you should try for a field goal or use a number three iron. What we need to find is the interworld transfor-
mational grammar to help us to discern what will need to happen
if the collision of the message of Jesus with our pluralist/relativist
world is to lead to a reconception of the shape of the world, instead of to rendering Jesus optional or innocuous. To ask, "Shall
we talk in pluralist/relativist terms?" would be as silly as to ask
in Greece, "Shall we talk Greek?" The question is what we shall
say. We shall say, "Jesus is Messiah and Lord"; but how do you
say that in pluralist/relativist language? If that language forbids
us to say that, do we respect the prohibition? Or do we find a
way to say it anyway?

We won't play with the utopia of getting out of our own
pluralist/relativist skins by going either backward or forward. It
is within these skins that we need to restate whatever our claims
are. Since for some even the phrase *truth claim* evokes echoes of

theocratic compulsion or of pretensions to infallibility, let us use the more biblical phrases *witness* and *proclamation* as naming forms of communication which do not coerce the hearer.

We shall not ask whether Christianity, or Jesus, or anything, is absolute or unique or universal in some way that could be supported, kept dry above the waves of relativity. A claim to absoluteness can be adjudicated meaningfully only in the frame in which it is pronounced, and then only if the way that that frame is self-understood provides some kind of fulcrum and a place to stand to make such a judgment.

What we need to try to do now may be further clarified by contrast with the six strategies of adaptation with which we began. Those strategies granted in different ways the priority, in the orders of both knowing and being, of the wider world. They then defended or diluted or translated the particular identity in subordination thereto. Now we are asking, in the same kind of intersystem encounter, what would be the shape of an evangelical alternative — one which would agree with the above strategies in the practical affirmation that the present world, the wider and the widest worlds of our day, is the arena within which it speaks; but one which would claim to have something more to say than to concede the sovereignty or the adequacy of the ideas currently dominating that wider arena.

What then can we do to transpose faithfully into a self-contained immanent frame the equivalence of the "Christ is Lord" claim, in some continuity with what it meant in the first-century context, where all parties to the conversation lived in cosmologies with the top open for transcendent validation?

There is no need to assume that that question can have only one answer. Maybe it has to have several, each fragmentary, but which might severally add up asymptotically to a functional equivalent of a proclamation of lordship. One partial answer might be that in an encounter between two different — not fully compatible but not fully alien — meaning frames, reference to Jesus might make it easier to converse about things which in both frames are important. Modern meaning systems being independent, might they still overlap? Might Jesus be located on common turf?

Jesus participates in localizable, datable history, as many religious hero figures do not. Jesus intervenes in the liberation from violence and he identifies with the poor as many savior figures do not. He contributes to the nuts-and-bolts reconstruction of forgiving community, as many people planning to change the world do not. His memories have created, despite much betrayal by his disciples, a nearly world-wide communion, as some of the great culture religions have not yet done. His message interpenetrates with the realms of politics and culture, as some forms of devotion do not. Let these specimens stand for the longer list of traits of *relative* fruitfulness of Jesus as mediator in culture clashes and changes.

But, you will say, these samples of transsystem meaningfulness are only relatively true; none is fully unique. Of course! It would have been contradictory to expect that Christian commitment — even less Christians' performance — should be at the top of every scale. What we are looking for, I repeat, is not a way to keep dry above the waves of relativity, but a way to stay within our bark, barely afloat and sometimes awash amidst those waves, yet neither dissolving into them nor being carried only where they want to push it.

Some meaning frames, such as the early modern natural science vision of the closed causative system, claim or assume no historical variability and therefore cannot handle historical particularity. They can neither verify nor falsify it. They cannot deny that Jesus is Lord because they have no definition of what affirming it would mean.

Sometimes the internal claim of a meaning system applies only criteria of inward consistency: wholeness, coherence, happiness, or self-fulfillment. Of course these will work as criteria only if we assume in a circular way that it is better to be whole or happy or coherent, however we measure those virtues, and that whatever meets those standards is true.

There are those whose skepticism is more thorough, and who will make a point of setting aside any hypothesis which they don't need. Yet that response does not remove them from the conversation, since the first-century witness never understood itself as a hypothesis needing to verify itself by someone else's standards. No communication in any meaning framework needs to accept being tested by people who have decided ahead of time not to listen. Then an evangelical vision will seek no validation and fear no falsification.

A second usable choice would be to look again for other extant meaning frames in which larger questions can still function. Is there some still wider world? There is, for instance, the wider world of past history which, although interpretations of it will keep changing *somewhat*, is not completely a wax nose. Historical memory of the Hebraic and Christian contributions to Western culture may then contribute to reordering any debates between later meaning systems, all of which claim to take account of the past.

A third line of advocacy would be to make more of the family of epistemological paradoxes which gather around the truth claim of relativism/pluralism itself, whose proponents constantly tend to disregard its own warnings and to claim the authority to accredit other value systems with more substance than their own. The pluralist/relativist view differs from (some) other value systems in that it is our own world, the air we breathe. It is also a second-order system, which lives from interpreting other views. It leaves much of morality and more of worship to other communities. It does not baptize babies (or adults). It does not fight just wars (or love its enemies). It does name heretics, but when it does so firmly it tends to refute itself.

Another path we noted could be projected to reach past the varieties of peoples to a knowledge of nature which is common to all, as we could know it either by finding it everywhere or by constructing it out of necessary truths of reason. Instead of being a renunciation of particular claims, can it be made usable as an evangelical instrument? Perhaps, but a fair test of that alternative would take us too far.

To glance back for a moment at our starting point: we shall no longer try to help Gotthold Ephraim Lessing to leap across his ditch, nor to build him a bridge. The solidity of the necessary truths of reason concerning fundamental ideas of the nature of the Godhead, which Lessing's doubt posited on the other side of the ditch, is not there, should not be, need not be. The solid ground beyond the ditch is not there. The less narrow truth over there is still also provincial. Reality always was pluralistic and relativistic, that is, historical. The idea that it could be otherwise was itself an illusion laid on us by Greek ontology language, Roman sovereignty language, and other borrowings from the Germans, the Moors, and the other rulers of Europe. Yet within this relativity and in the style of noncoerciveness, we can and must still proclaim a Lord and invite to repentance. We report an event that occurred in our listeners' own world, and ask them to respond to it. What could be more universal than that?

This debate about the context in which it again makes sense to talk of Jesus has been the bulk of my assignment. What then remains to be resaid cannot be new, but only the context for restating it.

This land is our land

To begin that restatement I would take my first cue from the early proclaimers' confidence that they were not on foreign ground when they laid claim to the hellenist cosmologies as one more place to make peace. They believed they were mopping up after an invasion in which their general had already established his lordship. Similarly pluralism/relativism is a confusing world but it is not an alien one. It is the child of the Hebrew and Christian intervention in cultural history. It is the spinoff from missionary mobility, from the love of the enemy, from the relativizing of political sovereignty, from a dialogical vision of the church, from a charismatic vision of the many members of the body, from the disavowal of empire and of theocracy. It lays before us the challenge of convincing interlocutors who are not our dependents, of affirming a particular witness to be good news without being interested in showing that other people are bad. Its corrosive critical power seems at first to be alien to the claim of the witness to bear good news, when that critical perspective is first encountered as a threat to the self-evidence of the smaller world in which one grew up. Yet it still is the case that pluralism/relativism is itself a part of the ripple effect of the gospel's impact upon Western culture.

What the challenges of relativism do threaten, and threaten profoundly, are two other kinds of epistemology. One of those, the epistemology of the establishment, was validated by placing the power of political authority and social consensus behind a particular belief system. In the primitive tribe, in an ancient Near-Eastern metropolis, or in Caesaro-Papism from Constantine to recent times, the vision of a local monocultural unity could remove all subjective choice from the belief question. This still is the normative vision in most of the world. Not until Vatican II did the Church of Rome reject it formally. But the knowledge of geography and the interpenetration of cultures make that option logically inaccessible for us even if we had found it psychologically attractive.

The other option to reject is one we have not finished dallying with, which we described at the outset as a subset of the apologetic approach: the search for some operation — be it linguistic, statistical, or logical — to define a kind of solid ground no longer subject to the reproach of others or to self-doubt as being vitiated by any kind of particularity. This is to renew the vain effort to find assurance beyond the flux of unendingly meeting new worlds, or to create a meta-language above the clash, in order to renew for tomorrow the trustworthiness and irresistibility of the answers of the past.

By confessing that Messiah has been placed by God above and not within the cosmology and culture of the world they invade, the messianic Jewish witnesses also affirmed that under his lordship that cosmos will find its true coherence and meaning. To use the example of Colossians, the powers are not merely defeated in their claim to sovereignty, and humbled; they are also reenlisted in the original creative purpose of the service of humanity and the praise of God. Or in John, the *logos/sophia* vision of the rationality of the universe and of history is not only dethroned but is also put to work illuminating everyone who comes into the world, and empowering sons and daughters. To know that the Lamb who was slain was worthy to receive power not only enables his disciples to face martyrdom when they must; it also encourages them to go about their daily crafts and trades, to do their duties as parents and neighbors, without being driven to despair by cosmic doubt. Even before the broken world can be made whole by the Second Coming, the witnesses to the first coming — through the very fact that they proclaim Christ above the powers, the Son above the angels — are enabled to go on proleptically in the redemption of creation. Only this evangelical Christology can found a truly transformationist approach to culture.

We still do not *see* that the world has been set straight. We still have no *proof* that right is right. We still have not found a bridge or a way to leap from historical uncertainty to some other more solid base, that would oblige people to believe, or make our own believing sure.

> As it is, we do not see everything in subjection to him. *But we do see Jesus*, revealing the grace of God by tasting death for everyone. (Heb. 2:8–9)

That should be enough for us to begin reconstructing God-language on this side of the ditch. We shall often be tactical allies of some apologetic thrust, when it rejects the results of a previous too-close identification of church and dominion. We may be tactical allies of the pluralist/relativist deconstruction of deceptive orthodox claims to logically coercive certainty, without making of relativism itself a new monism. We will share tactical use of liberation language to dismantle the alliance of church with privilege, without letting the promises made by some in the name of revolution become a new opiate. For the reconstruction we shall find other tactical allies. In the realm of ethics we shall not grant, with Tolstoy and Reinhold Niebuhr, that to renounce violence is to renounce power. We may then find tactical alliances with Gandhi, as did Boston University's most prominent black Baptist alumnus, or with the Enlightenment, as did Quakers and Baptists in the century after their expulsion from the Puritan colonies.

For our world it will be in his ordinariness as villager, as rabbi, as king on a donkey and as liberator on a cross that we shall be able to express the claims which the apostolic proclaimers to hellenism expressed in the language of preexistence and condescension. This is not to lower our sights or to retract our proclamation. It is to renew the description of Christ crucified as the wisdom and the power of God. This is the low road to general validity. It frees us from needing to be apologetic in either the popular or the technical sense. It thereby frees us to use any language, to enter any world in which people eat bread and pursue debtors, hope for power and execute subversives. The ordinariness of the humanness of Jesus is the warrant for the generalizability of his reconciliation. The nonterritorial particularity of his Jewishness defends us against selling out to *any* wider world's claim to be really wider, or to be self-validating.

Paul Ricoeur speaks of a second naïveté in which, after having taken all the critical distance we must, both from a text as literary product and from its ideas as artifacts of a not fully recoverable cultural matrix, we after all read a text as it stands. It is such a second level of ordinariness for which our tactical alliance with pluralism/relativism/historicism has freed us, by suspecting all the remaining claims of any wider worlds, however accredited, to have the authority to pass judgment on the Lord. The particularity of incarnation *is* the universality of the good. There is no road but the low road. The truth has come to our side of the ditch.

But then my assigned problem was not the real problem, but a screen. The real issue is not whether Jesus can make sense in a world far from Galilee, but whether — when he meets us in our world, as he does in fact — we want to follow him. We don't have to, as they didn't then. That we don't have to is the profoundest proof of his condescension, and thereby of his glory.

NOTES

1. Gotthold Ephraim Lessing, *Lessing's Theological Writings*, trans. Henry Chadwick [A Library of Modern Religious Thought] (Stanford: Stanford University Press, 1957), pp. 53, 55.

2. Relativism is a mood more than a position. As the fairest viewers tend to agree (Arthur Dyck, *On Human Care: An Introduction to Ethics* [Nashville: Abingdon Press, 1977], pp. 144ff.; and Bernard Arthur Owen Williams, *Morality: An Introduction to Ethics* [Cambridge: At the University Press, pp. 20ff.]), it can weaken the claims of others but can never rationally sustain its own nor solidly falsify another's.

3. A most dignified and careful exposition of the claim that to be wider is to be truer is the distinctive usage made of the adjective *public* by David Tracy, "Defending the Public Character of Theology," in *Christian Century* 98 (1 April 1981): 350ff. What is most striking in his exposition is the circularity of his assumption that we share his definition of what it means to prove "publicly" the truth of what one argues, without any accounting for the selection of the particular value biases of the several "publics" one seeks to communicate to.

4. This would seem to be a fair though coarse characterization of what Paul Van Buren was seeking to do in his *Secular Meaning of the Gospel* (New York: Macmillan, 1963), pp. 158ff.

4

Pilgrimage to
Communitarian Personalism

WALTER G. MUELDER

THERE ARE NO COMPLETELY original modes of ethics today, and all types of moral theory are to some degree consciously correcting some other tradition or school of thought. When Marx said that philosophers have only differently interpreted the world but the point is to change it, he was trying to correct the Hegelian dictum that the owl of Minerva only flies at night. But Marx stands nevertheless in the Hegelian tradition as well as in that of biblical prophecy and historical eschatology. When John Dewey pleaded for prospective pragmatism, he was in the tradition of both Bacon, who sought science in order to control nature, and Aristotle, who enumerated proximate and intrinsic ends. Ethics, like philosophy, is at the same time its history, criticism of that history, and current reconstruction. My pilgrimage to communitarian personalism reflects all three.

The traditions that inform ethics are not only philosophical but religious and theological as well. The biblical tradition has profoundly affected Western ethics because it has helped shape Western culture and civilization. Conceptions of law, faith, righteousness, love, persons, family, the economic order, and politics — as well as ideas of past, present, and future — bear the imprint of Judeo-Christian and Muslim personal and community life. Jesus Christ and institutional Christianity have stimulated modes of ethics that developed sectarian, mystical, and church-type heritages of meaning and value. The interaction of religion and culture has begotten a great perennial Tradition and many particularistic traditions. Ecumenical ethics in both the World Council of Churches and in the Second Vatican Council reflects the tensions of this pluralism. On the one hand, for example, stands the systematic synthesis of philosophy and theology as in Thomism. On the other hand, theologians and ethicists have asked, "What has Jerusalem to do with Athens?" Some Christian ethicists would reject philosophical ethics entirely; some like Paul Lehmann even reject the imperative for the indicative mode.

Ethics must consider the heritages not only of philosophy and theology but also of modern science. The scientific heritage profoundly affects ethics, either in partnership with philosophy or theology, or through conflict. Science is not value-free, but at times it has asserted complete autonomy. The claim to autonomy is, of course, a more-than-scientific claim. In any case the relations of science to philosophy and theology have helped shape contemporary religious ethics. Though not value-free, science has had a more descriptive function; the other two disciplines deal with ultimate issues. Science cannot be ignored in clarifying the facts of situations, helping trace the possible consequences of alternative choices, and devising programs that move from moral decision to policy implementation. The pilgrimage of this essay employs a dialogue between theology, philosophy, and science.

These three disciplines, together with technology, have increasingly shaped the ideological context of modern Christian ethics. At all levels of reflection and application this complex context must be considered. Within this context ethics has a degree of autonomy because it appeals to a nonreducible moral experience, but it is dependent on and points to more ultimate factors such as the moral subject (agent) and the nature of the moral order. All ethics is reflection on moral experience involving choice and decision in accordance with what is right or good. Christian ethics is inescapably influenced by its distinctively theological components, the contributions of empirical sciences and history, and the principles of philosophical ethics which help bridge the gaps between the traditions of Christian faith and modern science. The goal of the disciplined reflection on all the factors affecting choice is an emergent coherence, about which more will be said below.

The appeal to emergent coherence implies that Christian ethics as a discipline is still theoretically and practically incomplete.

The present state of the art is therefore eclectic. Aristotle argued that ethics is a branch of politics, personal morality being an aspect of social morality. Similarly Christian ethics is an aspect of Christian social ethics. Within theological ethics, the profound inward ethics of the Sermon on the Mount is part of the comprehensive Kingdom-of-God ethics of the messianic gospel tradition. This general thesis is especially relevant here because social ethics is not a problem of how to apply personal ethics in society. Rather the converse is the case, since the concrete whole is person-in-community. The inner and outer cannot be reduced to each other, nor disjoined.

My experience confirms the eclectic character of the present state of Christian social ethics. Its constituent elements cannot be reduced to each other, and efforts to do so have failed at both theoretical and practical levels. Theology makes philosophical assumptions; philosophy feeds on the religious substance of Western culture; and science has roots in both their value systems and assumptions. Their appropriate relationships are dialogical and their integrated goal is coherence as the criterion of truth. Eclecticism has its perils, but the risks are unavoidable. As a Christian social ethicist active in the ecumenical movement I am less eager to create an original theory than to support methods of reflection that will strengthen a global ethical witness by the churches. Here history has much to teach. Among the great contributions of the history of the social teachings of the churches, the permanent values stated by Ernst Troeltsch seem persuasive: (1) a conviction of personality and individuality, based on personal theism, which no naturalism or pessimism can disturb; (2) a socialism which, through its conception of God's love, embraces and unites all souls and transcends all natural connections; (3) a resolution of the problem of equality and inequality through mutual obligation which transmutes natural differences into the ethical values of caring; and (4) the virtue of active helpfulness based on the values of personality and love, as a fruit of the Christian spirit. (5) Beyond these the Christian ethic gives to all social life and aspiration a goal which transcends the relativities of earthly life.[1] Philip Wogamann has more recently summarized the dominant consensus of Christian ethical values in terms of positive and negative presumptions: (a) the goodness of created existence; (b) the value of individual human life; (c) the unity of the human family in God; (d) the equality of persons in God; (e) the fact of human finitude; and (f) the reality of human sinfulness.[2] The similarities of Wogamann's list to that of Troeltsch, both appealing to personal theism, are striking.

With the above as an introduction, this essay on a pilgrimage to communitarian personalism will be sketched as follows: (1) the moral experient as person-in-community; (2) the centrality of the person as subject and agent; (3) the dialogue between theology and philosophy; (4) autobiographical confessions and influences; (5) rejection of naturalism and neo-orthodoxy, and affirmation of personal idealism; (6) moral laws as regulative; (7) the sacredness of human life as a Christian contribution; (8) the role of science in ethics; (9) Jesus Christ and the distinctiveness of Christian ethics; and (10) the ecumenical movement in contemporary Christian social ethics.

I. THE EXPERIENT AS PERSON-IN-COMMUNITY

Farewell to the autonomous individual impartial spectator! Since ethics is reflection on moral experience, the inescapable starting point is the moral experient. Understanding the nature of the experient is theoretically and practically crucial. I am my experience and the experient. The experient is the moral subject, the moral agent. These are not two, but one. Moreover, the one who reflects and the one who acts are the same person. As a person I am both my history and my possible future existence, both my past choices and my present freedom in choosing, to the extent that I am truly free. My experience is complex. As a *unitas multiplex*, as a *socius* with a private center, I am experientially both a historically molded person and a self-conscious agent who chooses, decides, and acts with limited freedom. No final dualism exists between social self and creative ego, however puzzling it may be to verbalize precisely the relationships between formative social contexts and personal subject. The experient is logically and existentially prior to the abstractions called social environment and moral agent. The experient is a multidimensional unity of experiences, a person-in-community.

Behind this unity stands no substantial soul, no self-existent independent subject who *has* these experiences. Self-transcendence is an aspect of person-in-community experience. I *am* my social relations as part of my identity and I am my process of present moral activity and my reflections on that activity. Personal experience is a process and is itself at once social activity, private individuality, flow of consciousness, reflections on that consciousness, anticipator of the future, entertainer of value possibilities, and decider of moral behavior. To affirm, as one should, that the moral subject, the human individual, is more than an ensemble of social relations means an appeal not to a substantial transcendent entity "behind" or "under" experience taken as a whole, but to personal experience as an *ontic* unity, that is, as real in a philosophical sense.

II. THE PERSON AS CENTRAL

What is a person? A person is a consciousness, an experient, capable of reason, ideal values, and willing. A person is more than a self, for a self may be simply any consciousness taken as a whole, whereas a person is a self who thinks and chooses in terms of criticized values. What are values? Values are the conscious objects of any desire, interest, need, preference, concern, and the like. They may be intrinsic or instrumental or both. Criticized values or true values conform to a norm, ideal, or standard. Personhood requires experiences of self-transcendence, for persons are primary moral subjects, moral agents. If there are other moral agents — such as groups, associations, corporations, institutions — they are secondary or derivative. Their moral significance depends on their meaning for persons. Persons are persons-in-community, but the collectivity exists for the person as realized in the collectivity.

There are benefits in ethical theory in this conception of person and its centrality, particularly in issues involving race, sex, and class. First, person transcends the category of race. Human worth is not determined by the historical or cultural baggage of prior social conditions, such as slavery, nor by biological externalities. The principle of personhood exposes the presence or absence of racism in social structures and roles. In resolving racial and ethnic tensions it does not beg the question whether the good society will be assimilationist, diversified, or simply ethnically tol-

erant and nonassimilationist. It frees the ethical discussion of being a mere corrective of present discriminatory practices, thus
freeing the moral subject to express optimal autonomy.

In analogous ways person transcends the categories of sex
and sexism. The differentiation of males and females is much more
complex than race, and hence sexism may be harder in the long
run to overcome than racism. What the good society would be
like in terms of personhood freed of all sexist taint can probably
not be culturally formulated today. Yet person points to all sex-
role differentiation as freed from power concentrated in the hands
of males, institutions, and ideologies which conserve such present
power, and freed from practices that restrict and prevent women
from living the kinds of lives that persons ought to be able to choose
as moral subjects with optimal autonomy.

So, too, a person also transcends the categories of class whether
stated in terms of religious caste, natural abilities, economic factors, or social functions. Though persons are always specifically
persons-in-community, and are placed in various degrees of participation in a continuum from the realm of necessity to the realm
of real freedom — and hence are never classless — as moral agents
they have equal dignity and an obligation to help achieve a mutually responsible society, as we shall note more fully below.

The metaphysical, logical, and moral priorities of persons
in transcending race, sex, or class do not imply that increasing
their moral freedoms is always preferable to fewer liberties. The
principles are that optimal autonomy is a prerequisite to responsible reflection on these issues, and that the freedom of the person
as participating subject is ethically and logically prior to specific
liberties which are claimed in matters of race, sex, or class relationships. In short, the principle of personality is the presumption
of all serious reflection on matters of morals, for all values are
of, by, and for persons.

III. THE DIALOGUE BETWEEN THEOLOGY
AND PHILOSOPHY

We turn now from the person as experient to the dialogue
between theology and philosophy in Christian social ethics. Formally, their perspectives are conflictual. Theology logically be-

gins with a dialogue (covenant) initiated by God with finite persons and through this dialogue tends to draw all human morality into its scheme of creation and redemption. God initiates and human beings are called to respond. There are many Christian theologies, but all of them tend to demand that any philosophical ethics, viewed as part of the above response, be made coherent with the historical action in the covenant of salvation. Christian ethics, when it recognizes the dialogical character of moral decisions, insists that the horizontal person-to-person moral dialogue is not qualitatively comparable to the vertical covenant of salvation. This qualitative differentiation is not confined to Barthians. Jesus clearly distinguished the dimensions of the two great commandments. God initiates and sustains the covenant despite rebellion.

Philosophy, on the contrary, begins ethical reflection with situations involving a choice of values. It insists on the relative autonomy of ethics as one of the philosophical disciplines and seeks to formulate ethical principles (laws), to define the virtues, to identify norms or standards, and to consider ends (the good). It proceeds, finally, to what Brightman called the metaphysical law of ethics: all persons ought to consider the source and ground of the whole moral order. Thus, the order of reflection is different in theology and philosophy. Nevertheless, philosophical ethics must consider the claims made by theological ethics and by rival metaphysical proposals. In so doing the appeal to empirical rational coherence as the criterion of truth is not limited to a prior or privileged faith claim as in the biblical covenant. The autonomy of coherence is not the same as the coherence of philosophy within theology.

For this reason, the dialogue between theology and philosophy with respect to ethics can never be completed; but it can be conducted with mutual respect. The human experient is the subject of theology, philosophy, and science taken as a whole experience. I myself accept the Christian faith as a practical commitment, and philosophical coherence (including the dialogue with science) as the theoretical criterion of truth. Yet I hold that the realm of salvation and the realm of ethics should not be and logically cannot be conflated. They are resources for each other in dialogue. When theology makes exclusive claims by absorbing all mundane morality into salvation ethics, the autonomy of reason is compromised and patent common-ground experience is neglected. When, on the contrary, philosophy fails to listen to the call of Christ, it is in danger of reductionism by ignoring the distinctive and unique quality of the historical community of faith. Human experience is so constituted that faith and reason are dimensions lying within each other. Apart from dialogue, theology tends to impose a heteronomous view of moral imperatives. Antitheological philosophy tends toward closed autonomy in ethics. Since, as I shall show, the *proprium* of Christian ethics is the person of Jesus Christ, the highest principle is *agape*/love. But this norm is both divine and human, and thus belongs to both theology and philosophy. Love is the highest expression of the *humanum;* hence love is theonomous, having its source in God and its personal moral imperative as a self-imposed true value.

IV. AUTOBIOGRAPHICAL CONFESSIONS

I come from a Methodist clergy family, the second oldest of seven children. With a father and mother dedicated to ministry among German-speaking immigrants and their offspring, and family experience shaped by both pietistic devotion and social gospel imperatives, my religious and moral development had nurturance both in the interior life and in matters of social justice. As a model my father cultivated both critical biblical liberalism and philosophy, in which he had an earned doctorate. I emerged in the early 1920s from the uncritical conscience of childhood into the pluralistic mores of high school and the work world of night shifts in bakeries, summer day shifts in railroad repair shops, and the intellectual arena of debates on science and religion. Church and society conspired to demand a critical conscience on both evolution and labor strikes. The great post-World War I railroad strike deeply divided Burlington, Iowa, and the local church. A whetstone for sharpening my critical conscience was the high school national debate question: Resolved that the federal government should own and operate the coal mines and the railroads. Since the United States government did operate the railroads during World War I, this issue was emotionally charged with partisan politics and economic ideology. My favorite social science teacher was writing her dissertation at the time on Eugene V. Debs, who had been jailed during the Pullman Strike and was imprisoned in Atlanta for opposing World War I. I emerged from this situation with strong pro-labor and socialist opinions. These I took with me to Knox College and later to Boston University School of Theology.

At college I joined the mid-twenties revulsion to the lies and absurdities of World War I and the Versailles Treaty and helped lead a student protest against the R.O.T.C. My pacifism was reinforced by a number of the plentiful biographies of Jesus which portrayed him as a nonviolent leader of the early church in obedience to the Kingdom-of-God conception of love. I became aware that Jesus was the inspiration of leaders like Tolstoy, Gandhi, Schweitzer, and Kagawa. Student peace movements had an international appeal.

When I decided to enter the Christian ministry, I was already predisposed to a liberal critical historical interpretation of the Bible, to personal idealism in philosophy, as well as to socialism and pacifism. The first two were reinforced by studies under A. C. Knudson and E. S. Brightman. Subsequently, a year at the University of Frankfurt under Paul Tillich and Max Horkheimer reinforced religious socialism and a constructive critical approach to Marx. The thirties put the twenties into radical perspective under the impact of the Great Depression, economic and nationalistic crises in Germany, the spread of totalitarianism, and the Spanish Civil War. The churches moved to the left in politics and economics, but the tension between theological liberalism and neo-orthodoxy became divisive.

On the theoretical side my personalism became communitarian through the study of Hegel, Marx, and Troeltsch. Yet each of them fell short of an adequate theory of person-in-community. Hegel finally lost the individual in his devotion to the state and process of the Absolute; Marx's humanism was submerged in economic causality and class consciousness, the doctrine of alienation leaving the idea of the individual undeveloped; and Troeltsch's historicism and relativism sacrificed personality as a universally valid category when he reflected on Christian thought in relation to non-Christian cultures and civilizations. To this day I owe much to the following: Brightman (organic pluralism and moral law); Hegel (dialectical understanding of wholes as process); Marx (historical materialism, the dialectic of capitalism, the socialist vision); and Troeltsch (the nature of historical wholes as unities of meaning and value, the logic of the inner development of institutions). These perspectives have been validated in my critical studies of neo-orthodoxy, naturalism, logical empiricism, and ecumenism, and in the historical contexts of World War II, the Korean War, the McCarthy era, the dissolution of European colonialism, the Civil Rights struggle under King, the Indochina War, the developmental crises in Third World countries, and the current ecological dilemmas. These contexts are noted to emphasize that person-in-community has been an operational research method in developing Christian social ethics. I needed interactive models for interdisciplinary work in the midst of world revolution.

In subsequent sections, I will make philosophical, theological, and scientific aspects of communitarian personalism more explicit.

V. PERSONAL IDEALISM

My philosophical attitude toward realism and science entailed rejection of both neo-orthodoxy's attack on the pride of reason and naturalism's tendency toward scientism. Science represents not pride of reason but humility before empirical fact, constant correction of hypotheses, and openness to new evidence. Scientism was never a temptation for me since proximate control, prediction, and description are methodologically distinct from ultimate interpretation and unconditional concerns of people. Naturalism hardly tempted me because it seemed obviously seduced by science. There is an inherent bipolar ambiguity in naturalistic philosophies. On the one hand, they tend to anthropocentrism since everything, including religion, is viewed as revolving around finite persons and their interests. On the other hand, naturalism tends to reduce the human presence in nature to purely local significance. Here two idealistic principles of Hocking seem a good corrective: (1) meaning descends from the whole to the part, for if the whole has no meaning the part has no meaning; and (2) meaning rises inductively from the part to the whole; thus the part may be a key to reality. The human presence in nature has cosmic significance.

In theology neo-orthodoxy was disturbing because of its radical bifurcation of faith and reason as well as its assault on the pride of reason. As indicated above, reason in its critical role is a principle of humility, and in its courage to venture synoptic hypotheses it has analogues to faith. In the thirties and forties neo-orthodox militancy seemed paranoid in its human pessimism and its identification of philosophical liberalism with superficial optimism. I could not recognize myself in what was being said about philosophical idealism. Yet neo-orthodoxy had a useful corrective function in pushing the religious world to face the ubiquity of sin and the unreality of the dogma of progress. Particularly in Germany Barthianism assisted in resisting the cultural relativism which too easily accommodated to National Socialism. However, philosophy was sometimes used by Barthians to sweep the ideological floor clean so that theology could have the monopoly on floor space. The idea that faith is not as anthropocentric as reason, just because it gives a privileged status to the Bible, seemed to me to harbor a dangerous arrogance passing as humble faith. I recall a personal debate in Europe with a Danish theologian who argued that philosophy did not even belong in the forecourt of theology because there should be no philosophical dirt dragged into the temple of faith. My response then and now is that all theologies have philosophical presuppositions. All are very human — and very rational — constructions, the unity of the biblical revelation having many interpretations.

In the dialogue of theology with philosophy, idealistic perspectives have certain advantages. Personalism and the idealisms of Hocking and Whitehead all vigorously reject reductionism. Knudson combated all tendencies that reduced religion to an illusion; Brightman combated views that abstracted analytical aspects of value from synoptic experience; Hocking defended mind from "near-mind"; and Whitehead stressed the organic character of reality, the aliveness of nature, and the ubiquity of purpose. Personal idealism includes the testimony of faith, stresses the objectivity of value, is open to science, interprets the relation of the Supreme Person to finite persons as organic pluralism, and links the trustworthiness of reason to empirical coherence. The objectivity of the moral order in God does not restrict ethics to heteronomy or deontology; the autonomy of the moral person does not imply that a self-imposed ideal is a self-manufactured one. Purposes are more than local events. Hence the watershed issue between all naturalisms and personal theism is whether there is more-than-human purpose in the world. On this common ground theology and philosophy can have a fruitful dialogue.

VI. MORAL LAWS AS REGULATIVE

In the contingent world of history Christian social ethics must be dynamic, not static. No rule, no regulation, no code suffices for all occasions. But there is abiding relatedness that can be formulated philosophically in regulative moral laws. Though "natural" or "rational" law cannot express the universal moral imperatives of humanity in particular legal absolutes, a philosophical regulative moral law can mediate between theological insight and the scientifically described empirical order. What the moral law commands, the Christian's relation to Jesus Christ and the eternal moral order fulfill in intentionality and ideal form. Moral laws as here presented are not prescriptive in cultural terms, but they form a system that is universally relevant and in terms of which "middle axioms" and substantive commands may be formulated.

My indebtedness to Edgar S. Brightman in approaching certain moral laws is substantial, as also to L. Harold DeWolf for supplementing them. Their motifs have appeared in the work by Peter Bertocci and Richard Millard, *Personality and the Good;*[3] and DeWolf's latest version is found in *Responsible Freedom.*[4] The spirit of these moral laws is a hallmark of the ethics of Boston Personalism whose principal tradition was shaped by Borden Parker Bowne and developed by Francis J. McConnell, R. T. Flewelling, A. C. Knudson, and E. S. Brightman. To these moral principles I now turn.

The validity of regulatory moral laws lies in their systematic rationality and openness to the whole range of moral experience; in their constant appeal found in the history of ethics; in their coherent common sense; and in the fact that authors who reject philosophical ethics nevertheless assume or appeal to them. I have read no theological ethicist who could validly omit what they command. These laws refer to all persons. The system proceeds from the most formal or abstract aspects of ethical reflection to the most concrete (comprehensive relations) principles of person-in-community. The final law (metaphysical) commands exploration of the source and ground of the whole moral order. The principle of personality, as the key to reality, links the finite laws of ethics to the finite/infinite person of God. In personality we find the only true intrinsic value we know or conceive, all values being but forms of personal experience. When, then, we relate the theological idea of love to the philosophical idea of reason in these moral laws, we may say that the regulative moral laws taken as a whole are expressions of love in partnership with reason. Such an affirmation would illustrate an outcome of the metaphysical law noted above.

These moral laws, then, are a system of rational principles proceeding from the most abstract ethical imperatives and moving with ever richer appeal to empirical values toward fully relational laws of community. The formal laws are called the logical law and the law of autonomy. The first commands consistency and universality, ideas that are implicit in all valid moral judgments. If these are denied, impossible or contradictory consequences will follow. The second law states that self-imposed ideals are imperative. This is the great Kantian principle of the categorical imperative. Integrity and sincerity ought never to be compromised.

A second group of laws, the axiological, deal with value choices. The general axiological principle is that values should be coherent; the law of consequences holds that we should elaborate and approve the foreseeable consequences of choices; the law of the best possible recognizes compromise; the law of specification demands relevance; the law of the most inclusive end balances specification; and the law of ideal control requires the formulation of norms to guide the selection of values. In other words, within the realm of values there is a hierarchy of values which must be clarified, criticized, and chosen.

A third group of laws comprise the laws of personality, principles which relate formal and axiological choosing to the person as experient and agent. The law of individualism recognizes the worth of the moral agent; the law of altruism recognizes that all other persons are ends in themselves; and the law of the ideal of personality commands the formulation of a conception of what a person ought to become. For Christians such an ideal derives from the person of Jesus Christ in his fullness, not simply from one aspect of his life or teaching.

A fourth group of laws deal explicitly with persons-in-community. These laws, in harmony with all the other laws, place the free and responsible person in the context of the free and responsible society. In what social context ought we to choose? We should participate and do so cooperatively. We ought also to do so with devotion to the social good. Finally, "all persons ought to form and choose all of their ideals and values in loyalty to their ideals (in harmony with the other laws) of what the whole community ought to become; and to participate responsibly in groups to help them similarly choose and form all their ideals and choices."[5] Then, having regulated choice by these rational and empirical imperatives, all persons ought to obey the metaphysical law already explained.

VII. SACREDNESS OF PERSONALITY
AS A CHRISTIAN CONTRIBUTION

Though the inherent value of personality is presupposed in these moral laws, the sacredness of personality has a religious meaning which owes much to the history of Christianity. From this perspective God created and cares for persons. They reflect the "divine image." So stated the religious view is distinguishable from the philosophically ethical idea. The issue is, moreover, dialogical. To base the worth of human life exclusively on God's valuing it is extreme since it denies all inherent features of personality and regards human value as only extrinsic or relational. If all moral subjects (viewed apart from God) are only value ciphers, then relational attributes do not confer anything. There is intrinsic value in being a creature capable of making value choices. Kant's second version of the categorical imperative expresses the explicit ethical view in contrast to a wholly derivative type of religious view: "Act so that you treat humanity whether in your own person or

that of another always as an end and never as a means only."[6]
The capacity to be a moral agent (person) makes us worthy of
respect by all. Yet Kant was reared in the Christian West, and
historians of morals have pointed out the role of Christianity in
establishing the idea of the sacredness of personality. We have already noted from Troeltsch's historical summary how the sociality of all persons in God and in the love of Christ is linked to
individual human worth. A generation earlier, W. E. H. Lecky
in his *History of European Morals* argued that "nature does not
tell man that it is wrong to slay without provocation his fellow-
men." In Christ all this is different:

> Considered as immortal beings, destined for the extremes of
> happiness or of misery, and united to one another by a spe-
> cial community of redemption, the first and most manifest
> duty of a Christian man was to look upon his fellow-men
> as sacred beings, and from this notion grew up the eminently
> Christian idea of the sanctity of all human life. . . . (Indeed)
> it was one of the most important services of Christianity, that
> besides quickening greatly our benevolent affections, it defi-
> nitely and dogmatically asserted the sinfulness of all destruc-
> tion of human life as a matter of amusement, or of simple
> convenience, and thereby formed a new standard higher than
> any which then existed in the world. . . . This minute and
> scrupulous care for human life and human virtue in the hum-
> blest forms, in the slave, the gladiator, the savage, or the in-
> fant, was indeed wholly foreign to the genius of Paganism.
> It was produced by the Christian doctrine of the inestimable
> value of each immortal soul.[7]

Even when allowance is made for non-Christian roots of human
worth, it is well for philosophers to acknowledge the historical
origin of principles like personality which are later established
on more philosophically autonomous grounds.

VIII. THE ROLE OF SCIENCE IN ETHICS

Thus far we have not sufficiently noted the role of science
in the dialectic of theology, philosophy, and science in Christian

social ethics. Within a general ethical framework which seeks the resolution of social problems like racism, sexism, war, class conflict, ecological pollution, or abortion, three perspectives are important. First, there is the actual state of affairs in a culture, society, or nation; second, the ideal or norm in terms of which the situation and problem are evaluated and the approved state of affairs is affirmed; and third, the means or instrumentalities by which one proceeds to eradicate the difficulty or improve the situation under the mandate or guidance of the norm. Science is particularly relevant in formulating the first and third perspectives. Adequate description of both the state of affairs and its tendencies is essential for the first perspective. Projection of consequences with respect to alternative proposed solutions (both short-run and long-run, objective and subjective) is crucial in decision-making and in the third perspective. Science can help clarify the moral problem and the instrumentalities appropriate to ethical social policy.

One of the serious limitations of applied theological ethics is manifest when it appeals only to conventional or nonscientific definitions of a social problem. Even perceptive religious intuition does not suffice, for it is often informed by a factual error. And the refusal even to consider consequences out of loyalty to an ideal, however theologically sincere, is a refusal to be as intelligent as possible, and hence this attitude is in violation of the formal moral laws and the axiological law of consequences. On the other hand, theology can often illuminate the norms of evaluation required and shares common ground with philosophical ethics. Theology and philosophy are both indispensable in defining the importance of the problem which science clarifies descriptively and in evaluating eventual outcomes of decisions and policies. As a technical process science cannot ultimately evaluate itself and consequences do not evaluate themselves. Issues involving values are religious and moral before they become scientific problems and they continue to be so after science has completed its work.

Science is enriched when it includes a historical perspective. As I noted earlier, my pilgrimage to communitarian personalism was assisted by the interpretative historical methods of Marx and Troeltsch. To these I must now add acknowledgments for the holistic perspectives of Gunnar Myrdal and Rober MacIver, especially with respect to the role of valuation in social science. Myrdal contributed three theoretical concepts: (1) the principle of plural causation; (2) the idea of cumulative causation; and (3) the method according to which valuations in social science are best dealt with by making them explicit. Multiple and cumulative causation rule out single-cause solutions and stress the need for broad many-faceted planned social action. Furthermore, since causal factors can be placed in a rank order of importance, planned social change should have priorities. Such priorities must appeal (according to the system of moral laws) to the ethical principles of ideal control, the ideal of personality, and the ideal community. Myrdal is a democratic socialistic meliorist whose advocacy of social change is generally directed toward the institutional structures of a nation, with a strong bias toward equality.

MacIver, drawing on sociology and anthropology, contributed ideas about social cohesion, the ubiquity of government, and the nature of social coercion. Through these concepts he also influenced my conceptions of social change and power, supplementing those of Myrdal. Society, according to MacIver, exhibits a myth-structure and a technical structure. The former holds society together by self-enforcing values and beliefs. Society and government in particular do not rest primarily on force. This latter notion is one of these "half truths that beget total error." Moreover, since government is ubiquitous in social institutions, and since community must be distinguished from the political state, the intermediary structures between the person and the family, on one hand, and the state, on the other, have special significance. In this schema all government should be approached constructively and the state should be seen as much more than a negative or restraining element on personal freedom. All freedoms are historical combinations of liberty and restraint. Hence the real ethical question is: What combination of liberty and restraint in a given situation serves the chief end of person-in-community? As in Myrdal, so in MacIver, this question goes to the heart of the discipline of social ethics.

Applying Myrdal and MacIver to issues like racism, sexism, and classism the implication is that an *interactive* model is preferable to single-cause analysis that concentrates exclusively on factors of race, sex, or class. Such an interactive model is a genuine contribution of social science to ethics when linked to social philosophy. It is a model that would not generally emerge from traditional theological method alone or from philosophical ethics built exclusively on the ideal of the single autonomous impartial spectator. Biblical teachings, even the most prophetic ones, tend to go along single-issue pathways of reform like economic justice, peace, sexual ethics, or universal brotherhood and sisterhood. The inclusive category of the covenant does not of itself lead to an interactive analysis or strategy, evils being various modes of sin. Troeltsch was correct in observing that the New Testament knows nothing of the "social problem" in its modern systemic sense. It is to the merit of Francis Greenwood Peabody to have lifted up "the correlation of the social problems."[8] From such a principle an interactive model of a comprehensive sort fits well into the ecumenical norm of a responsible world society. Thus the contribution of social science to Christian ethics is constructive and substantial.

IX. THE PERSON OF CHRIST

We come once again to the question: Are there distinctive elements in Christian ethics? The response must finally be yes, but not primarily by seeking them in explicit teachings of Jesus. The distinctly Christian is Jesus Christ himself, who in his person illuminates the truly human and discloses the ultimate nature of God. Christian ethics does not stand apart from universal humanism in a disjunctive sense, nor by being a mere additive to philosophical ethics. Christians are related to all human persons through what is universally human, including rational moral reflection. Through their relation to Jesus Christ, his followers, both individually and communally, find their highest and holiest human fulfillment, that is, *agape*, the unlimited liability of sacrificial love. It is the intention of Christians to realize in their personal and collective existence the highest human manifestation of the good as seen and experienced in faithful discipleship. Beyond this, the believer and follower sees in Christ the self-disclosure of God. Hence the source and guarantor of the moral order is grasped as the God of Jesus Christ.

Though there are deontological and teleological aspects in

Christian social ethics, the ethic is relational in that it embodies (1) a universal rational humanity; (2) a special intention to be loyal to the person of Jesus Christ; and (3) an ultimate orientation to God. God calls all persons to respond to love in and through love. Forgiveness and redemption are relational, not only duties and goals. In this sense the particularity of Jesus as a historical person illumines the normative universality implicit in the whole human moral enterprise. Hence the relationship to non-Christians is not dichotomous but inclusively theonomous. God's holy otherness is immanent as the sustaining personal ground of all persons as they strive morally in the contingent historical world. For Christians the profoundest autonomy in moral decision making and the highest fulfillment of value are seen as expressing Christlike theonomy. Thus theonomy is distinguished both from heteronomy and from pantheism, for the relationship to God is an organic pluralism. The transcendent God loves the world of finite persons and manifests this love on the cross in Jesus Christ. The cross symbolizes the response of the transcendent/immanent God to the human predicament of alienation, sinfulness, and moral failure.

The person of Jesus Christ is a revelational given. He is God's gift of salvation to the world. Hence a person's relation to Christ is an indicative relation, since all are forgiven sinners and all moral choices are made in his eternal presence. Yet the relationship is also an imperative since the motivation, content, and goal of Christ's love is one of love. Love is the law of laws, the demand that defines intention, virtue, behavior, and realization. Love is the choice, decision, act, and personal fulfillment that is both autonomous and sacrificial service to the neighbor. The moral law is fulfilled in the law of love because it is autonomous (self-imposed); because it integrates all true value; because it respects both self and neighbor; because it creates reconciled community; and because it is a full response to the indicative/imperative moral order (Christ disclosing the governance of God). Love satisfies the demands of the regulative moral laws and the metaphysical law.

X. ECUMENISM AS COMMUNITARIAN PERSONALISM

The exaltation of Jesus Christ in ethics and theology manifests the faith of the Christian community and lays upon it the

obligation to serve the unity of the church and the unity of human-
kind. The Christian community serves the world both through
theoretical dialogue with it and through practical service. The
ecumenical movement embraces the microdialogues within and
among the churches on all matters that divide Christians from
one another and the macrodialogue of the Church with the cultural order as a whole. There have been many modes and method-
ologies of ethics within the Orthodox-Catholic-Protestant effort
to receive Christ's gift of reconciliation and to respond to this unity
as a task. During my whole adult life I have been nurtured by
participation both in microdialogues and in the great macrodialogue. This essay may be read as a modest reflection of them
on my pilgrimage to communitarian personalism.

Since there can be no serious or informed Christian ethics
today outside the ecumenical movement, a historical note about
its social ethics is relevant in conclusion. A landmark was the Oxford Conference of 1937. Its imperative was the slogan "Let the
Church be the Church!" The distinctive quality of Oxford was
expressed by William A. Visser't Hooft in *The Church and Its
Function in Society*, a preparatory volume for the conference. He
wrote: "Over against false conceptions of state and community,
the Church needs to affirm the existence of a God-given community which transcends all human divisions, and that as a reality
and not merely as an ideal; and that therefore the Conference
should not only speak about the Church, but manifest the living
actuality of the Church and its relevance to the world."[9] In terms
of the "message" of the Oxford Conference, which took place on
the eve of World War II, the words composed by Archbishop William Temple became the charter for the ecumenical movement
during that war and contain the nucleus of its theology in relation to ethics even at the present period of dialogue: "If war breaks
out, then pre-eminently the Church must manifestly be the Church,
still united as the one Body of Christ, though the nations wherein
it is planted fight each other, consciously offering the same prayer
that God's name may be hallowed, his kingdom come, and his
will be done in both, or all, of the warring nations."[10] On this
basis pacifists can escape sectarianism and work with nonpacifist
Christians, for although war is sin, individual Christians may see
their conscientious duties differently in the nations where the
Church is seeking to manifest the gospel. Similarly, Christian com-

munity ought to manifest itself across the strife of racism, sexism, and class conflict.

An ecumenical ethic must be more specific than the natural moral law in general, though it must embrace at least as much common ground among churches as it affirms in world society. For example, Marxist humanists and Christians have expressed a common responsibility for the future with respect to peace and social justice. Through the World Council of Churches the middle axioms of ecumenical consensus have taken the names of "the responsible society" and "a just, participatory, and sustainable world society." Experience shows that these middle axioms have stimulated profound moral dialogue among theologians, philosophers, and social scientists. Much common ground has been discovered. The material human situation is common to persons of all ideological persuasions; the moral demands are common; but the dialogue is essential because the motives and the ultimate context are not the same for the believer and the nonbeliever. Yet the believer needs the philosopher and the scientist, as these need the radical faith, hope, and love of the ecumenical disciple. Emerging coherence encourages the pilgrimage to communitarian personalism wherein the moral experient finds Christian love in partnership with reason.

NOTES

1. Ernst Troeltsch, *The Social Teachings of the Christian Churches*, 2 vols. (London: George Allen & Unwin, 1930), 2:1004–6.

2. J. Philip Wogamann, *A Christian Method of Moral Judgment* (Philadelphia: Westminster Press, 1976), chaps. 3, 4.

3. Peter Bertocci and Richard Millard, *Personality and the Good* (New York: David McKay, 1963).

4. L. Harold DeWolf, *Responsible Freedom* (New York: Harper & Row, 1971).

5. Walter G. Muelder, *Moral Laws in Christian Social Ethics* (Richmond, Va.: John Knox Press, 1966), p. 119.

6. Immanuel Kant, *Critique of Practical Reason*, trans. Lewis White Beck (Indianapolis, Ind.: Bobbs-Merrill Educational Publishing, 1977), p. 90.

7. William Edward Hartpole Lecky, *History of European Morals*, 2 vols. (New York: Appleton, 1870), 2:19, 21ff., 36.

8. Francis Greenwood Peabody, *Jesus Christ and the Social Question* (New York: Macmillan, 1925), chap. 7.

9. William Adolph Visser't Hooft, *Memoirs* (London: SCM Press, 1973), p. 71.

10. Ibid., p. 73.

PART II

Issues in Philosophical Ethics

5

Utilitarianism and the Goodness of Persons

LYNDA SHARP PAINE

DOES UTILITARIANISM SOMETIMES require an act which a morally good person would not do? If it does, is this a reason for rejecting utilitarianism? I will approach these questions through an inquiry into the relation between right conduct, as defined by utilitarianism, and the goodness of a person.

By *utilitarianism* I mean both act utilitarianism, which holds that an action is right if it has consequences equal to or better than the consequences of the alternative actions open to the agent, and rule utilitarianism, which holds that an action is right if it conforms to a general principle whose general acceptance has best consequences.

It should be noted that utilitarian theories are typically *maximizing* theories. Actions and principles are not evaluated by reference solely to their own consequences: right actions and principles must have consequences better than those of available alternatives. A right action is a maximizing action or one conforming to a maximizing principle. This comparative element distinguishes utilitarianism from other types of consequentialism.

Many utilitarians have either ignored the relation between right conduct and good persons, or have assumed that right conduct would naturally be performed by good people. G. E. Moore, for example, suggests that virtue can be understood in terms of dispositions to act in ways which generally produce the best possible results.[1] Similarly, Sidgwick holds that particular virtues are designations for the most important aspects of right conduct.[2]

101

J. J. C. Smart, an act utilitarian, believes that a person's moral goodness is a function of his or her success at performing maximizing actions.[3] For the typical utilitarian, motives and attitudes lack independent moral significance; their importance lies in their capacity to influence actions.[4]

It is implicit in these utilitarian views that the moral character of persons is in several senses secondary to the moral value of their actions.[5] First, identifying right actions does not require prior moral evaluation of the agent. Second, moral qualities we ascribe to persons are explicable in terms of the moral value of the acts they do. And finally, we should be interested in motives and attitudes mainly as a means of facilitating the performance of right actions.

I believe that attitudes, motives, emotions, and other qualities of agents must occupy a fundamental position in an acceptable moral theory, and that the moral values we attribute to persons and their characteristics cannot be adequately explained by reference to maximizing action. Thus, versions of utilitarianism which deny a fundamental theoretical position to such qualities of the agent should be rejected. Any acceptable form of utilitarianism will treat maximizing action as only one of several central concepts.

I

Many utilitarians insist on the importance of a distinction between the moral value of an action and the moral value of the agent.[6] This distinction does indeed have an appropriate place in our moral thinking, as when a good person acts wrongly in a particular instance, or when we do not praise someone who does the right thing for the wrong reason.

I do not deny that sometimes we ought to distinguish the moral value of the action from the moral value of the agent. I argue, however, that this distinction is not a basic one. The moral value of an action, even upon an act-utilitarian standard, cannot be assessed independently of characteristics of the agent. At the fundamental level of both act and rule utilitarianism — the level at which we determine which actions are right — the moral character of the actor is relevant. In order to maximize welfare a utilitarian must take into account the personal qualities of the agent. Only in this way can he or she accurately determine the level of preference satisfaction which will be achieved by the actions in question. This is one sense in which the agent must be a primary focus, and not merely a secondary one.

It is clear that the attitudes, intentions, and motives accompanying independently describable and deliberately chosen actions affect the consequences of those actions. As Oliver Wendell Holmes, Jr., noted, even a dog knows the difference between being kicked and being stepped on.[7] It also appears that merely holding certain values may affect the interests of others. Values which affect others in very important ways are manifested through habitual actions, looks, gestures, offhand comments, and tones of voice, and not only through deliberate action. These considerations cast doubt on the proposition that our interest in character is secondary to our interest in conduct. Even on a utilitarian analysis, characteristics of the agent are morally significant since they directly affect the welfare of others. In addition, as features of complex behavior they in part determine its effects on others.

Is it possible for a utilitarian to acknowledge the importance of character and the intricate relation between the agent's characteristics and the moral value of his or her actions? The answer depends on the nature and complexity of the utilitarian theory under consideration. I want to examine several versions of utilitarianism with this question in mind. I will begin with act utilitarianism and then turn to rule utilitarianism.

The situations in which moral evaluations typically occur may be divided into two broad categories: (1) situations in which the evaluation is prelude to or part of action; and (2) situations in which the evaluation is made from a detached critical perspective. Different pressures and standards govern in the two types of situations.[8] The available information and the perceived alternatives may be quite different when deciding what to do in the context of action and when deciding from a critical perspective what ought to be done in a given situation.

The context of action creates the most readily identifiable difficulties for the act utilitarian who would include qualities of the agent in action evaluations. A one-level act-utilitarian theory advises that the right action is the one with best consequences. Presumably, this standard applies in the context of action as well as in the context of critical evaluation. Thus, in deciding what we ought to do in the context of action, we should evaluate the likely consequences of the available alternatives and do what we expect will maximize the satisfaction of affected interests. It is in this context, however, that the effects of the intentions of the agent cannot be taken into account. The reasons for this are in part psychological and in part theoretical.

In deciding which of the available actions ought to be done, the contemplated actions have a life of their own. The actions and their consequences, not the person acting, are the focus of thought. It is easy for the agent to overlook the effects of his or her own personal characteristics on the persons whose interests are in question. But even if the agent were sufficiently self-reflective to realize the importance of attitudes in such a context, he or she could not be fully objective about their effects.

Moreover, and this raises the theoretical point, it is difficult to see how manner, attitudes, and intentions could be systematically included in utilitarian calculations. Application of the act-utilitarian principle requires that the agent consider the probable consequences of all the available alternatives. But what are the available alternative manners or attitudes or intentions that one could adopt? And when considering alternative courses, must one consider all the available manners in which each available action could be done? The problem of individuating alternatives — what is *one* manner or attitude? — is obvious.

In the characteristic act-utilitarian problem, mutually exclusive actions must be evaluated. Unlike actions, however, attitudes are not typically mutually exclusive. One does not, for instance, have to choose to be respectful rather than kind, or sincere rather than generous. We do not sharply differentiate these attitudes. They often can coexist quite harmoniously. The fact that attitudes cannot be individuated and ranked creates major difficulties for the act utilitarian who would include them in calculation.

In addition to the problems of identifying and individuating attitudes and intentions, there is also the problem of changing them if required by utilitarian analysis. Of course, to some extent one can adapt one's manner to suit the situation; however, one's most fundamental attitudes and purposes are not so malleable.[9] This is a crucial point. Insofar as act utilitarianism requires that we make each choice in light of the immediate situation, without the influence of our own previously held attitudes, beliefs, and commitments, it is unrealistic.[10] Moreover, it is questionable whether we should even want to become good act utilitarians if such flexibility were necessary.

Even if I realize that the beneficiaries of my charity find my pity for them offensive, for example, I cannot simply replace my actual feelings with more felicitous ones. I cannot simply *choose* to have a new attitude. Admittedly, it is possible through sustained effort to control one's feelings, but the process involved is vastly different from the act-utilitarian approach. We do not survey the alternative possible feelings (what would they be?) and adopt one on the spot to satisfy the relevant interests. Indeed, it appears that widespread cultivation of such a chameleon-like personality would undermine the whole act-utilitarian enterprise. If people's interests were flexible at will, it would be infinitely more difficult, if not impossible, to choose particular maximizing actions.

But the shortcomings of a simple act-utilitarian theory are not limited to the context of action. From the critical perspective the logical problems in applying the maximizing schema are significant. The concept of maximizing is appropriate only in the context of choice from a delimited class of alternatives and within the framework of a standard of comparison. But traits of the agent, such as attitudes, cannot be assessed in this way. Moreover, in reflecting on what would have been right in an actual situation, the act utilitarian who tries to take into account characteristics of the agent faces both the logical problems of individuating attitudes and intentions and the psychological problems inherent in determining what alternative attitudes and intentions were open to the agent.[11]

In addition to its inability to accommodate characteristics of the agent in action evaluations, act utilitarianism suffers from another serious inadequacy. Often we attribute moral value directly to characteristics of agents without regard to the relation between these characteristics and particular maximizing actions. Act utilitarianism lacks concepts to explain why this practice is justifiable, and fails to show why it is incorrect.

This investigation into the application of act utilitarianism suggests that major moral decisions must be made at a level more general than that addressed by act utilitarianism. Act utilitarianism is tailored to deal with very specific choices among actions, but not with the more fundamental and more general moral assessments of basic attitudes, dispositions, commitments, and purposes. These general orientations are fundamental in that they provide the backdrop for the specific choices which arise. They in part determine what specific choices present themselves to us as such. And further, they serve as standards for assessing which particular decisions would be maximizing.

These general orientations are also fundamental in another sense. Often they are not deliberately chosen. Children, for instance, seem to assimilate without conscious awareness many of the facial expressions, tones of voice, and attitudes of their parents. Adoption of manners or attitudes seems to result merely from exposure to others. When these fundamental general orientations are deliberately chosen, they can be implemented only with great difficulty. It requires great effort and an unusual degree of self-awareness for adults to recognize their own most fundamental traits and attitudes, and an even greater effort of will to change them.

Unfortunately, this is not the place to ask how such awareness and change might be accomplished. I wish simply to point out the great importance of this range of moral issues — issues which are not addressed and cannot be addressed by a simple act-utilitarian theory.

II

If at this point we had exhausted the investigation of utilitarianism, the question asked at the beginning of this essay would appear to be well taken. Act utilitarianism lacks concepts to explain ideals of character. Thus, it cannot explain the apparent inconsistency between what is required by utilitarianism and what is required by certain ideals of character. In countering a critic, the act utilitarian could simply deny the importance of character ideals as we know them and argue that we abandon them, but this reply is not philosophically satisfying. Besides, our consideration of act utilitarianism does not exhaust the field, and there are forms of utilitarianism more hospitable to concepts related to character.

Indeed, some forms of utilitarianism explicitly acknowledge the need for general principles concerning attitudes, dispositions, purposes, and actions. The two-level utilitarian theory proposed by R. M. Hare, for instance, allots a place to such principles. Professor Hare proposes a utilitarian theory with two levels of moral reasoning: an intuitive level and a critical level. Moral thinking at the intuitive level occurs in the context of action and consists in the application of *prima facie* principles. These *prima facie* principles are justified through moral reasoning at the second, or critical, level. Besides Hare's two-level theory, certain pure rule-utilitarian theories also allot a central place to general rules or principles.

Among those rule-utilitarian theories endorsing general principles, we should distinguish two types: those in which general principles are justified by reference to maximizing actions and those in which the principles are justified directly. By *direct justification* I mean a justification which rests on the consequences of adherence to the principle, but which does not depend upon maximizing the performance of right actions. Rule-utilitarian theories in the first category assume that principles are generalizations about maximizing actions. The others treat general principles as themselves basic and not derived from conclusions about particular maximizing actions.

Let me illustrate the difference. Moore's definition of virtue as a "habitual disposition to perform certain actions, which generally produce the best possible results" illustrates the view that the good character of the agent is based on his or her tendency to do good actions. According to this approach, which I call the "generalization approach" and which is related to what John Rawls has called the "summary" view of rules, a principle is justified by the fact that conformity to it produces, for the most part, right actions.[12] What counts as a right action is determined by the independent application of the act-utilitarian standard to particular cases falling under the principle.

Philippa Foot's theory of the virtues illustrates the direct justification view. Virtues are values for her because they correct human shortcomings.[13] Similarly, Professor Hare justifies altruism as a corrective to our tendency to overrate our own interests.[14]

Despite their differences, both types of justification are consequentialist. Moreover, it is my belief that a moral theory which rests on the view that the ultimate purpose of morality is to advance the welfare of society must rely on both types of justification. I have not, however, worked out a persuasive account of the proper place of each type of justification. The difference between these types of justification to which I wish to draw attention is the extent to which it is supposed that moral principles concerning persons and their qualities are reducible to principles concerning right actions. In the first part of this essay, I noted the utilitarian view that our interest in motives and qualities of the agent is secondary to our interest in right conduct. I believe that this view is wrong.

I agree, of course, that telling the truth, for example, is in most cases a maximizing action, even when done with the worst of motives, and on this basis I would argue for adherence to a principle of truth-telling. But it is by no means clear that even all action principles are justifiable in this way. Principles calling for general performance of actions necessary to produce certain public goods would seem to be justifiable only by reference to the strength of preferences for the goods to be secured. Moreover, when following such principles involves significant costs to the individual, it is not necessarily true that most conforming actions are maximizing actions according to the act-utilitarian standard.[15]

We may question the strategy of justifying general principles by reference to act-utilitarian calculations. However, my purpose here is more limited: to examine the use of this strategy for selecting principles concerning traits of persons. In my view, these principles must be justified directly, by reference to the desirable consequences of holding certain attitudes, motivations, and dispositions, and from the desirable consequences of general adherence to principles governing these matters. The generalization approach supposes that the act-utilitarian method of decision is in principle always applicable. But this, I argued above, is not the case: the act-utilitarian method is in principle inapplicable to decisions about traits of the agent.

Moreover, morally valuable traits such as kindness, respect, hopefulness, fidelity, and conscientiousness cannot be equated with conformity to general rules of action. These virtues cannot be reduced to general rules or sets of rules requiring particular types of actions. Their vagueness in this respect is perhaps what led Bentham to characterize the virtues as dangerous or at least useless to the practical moralist.[16] Unlike truthfulness, which is manifested by telling the truth, kindness and charity may be shown in a great variety of ways. Such traits involve beliefs, spontaneous actions, gestures, and expressions, as well as deliberate actions. All of these facts support my claim that we cannot justify principles governing these traits by reference to the likelihood of performing right actions.

The generalization approach can justify the generality of some broad principles. It can explain why we should follow a general principle concerning certain classes of cases rather than apply the act-utilitarian method directly. It does not, however, tell us how to select general moral principles governing matters to which the act-utilitarian method is in principle inapplicable.

There is an additional reason for rejecting the notion that general moral principles are no more than generalizations about right action. The reasoning is circular, as in a typical generalization justification for the principle of loyalty to one's own children.

The argument is often made that loyalty or preferential treatment for one's own children is desirable since more right actions will result from following this rather than some other principle. Normally, one knows one's own children better, has stronger affections for them, and so on. Thus, one is more likely in particular cases to maximize the satisfaction of interests all around by helping them rather than others. The aim is to ground the principle of parental loyalty on the greater likelihood of actually performing maximizing action by following this principle than by following a principle of impartiality or principles based on some other configuration of loyalties.

It is not surprising that such reasoning supports the conclusion that preferring one's children is in most instances right. In particular situations where the loyalty principle is invoked, the very preferences and expectations whose satisfaction is at stake reflect the fact that the principle is already generally adhered to.

It is only *because* a principle of parental loyalty and responsibility is common currency that most parents can in fact do more to benefit their own children. It is easy to imagine a society, not necessarily a desirable one, in which this were not the case.

My point, of course, is not that favoring one's own children is unjustifiable, but that the justification cannot proceed by generalizing over particular instances. It is only because general principles are what they are that questions arise concerning the correctness of favoring one's own children in particular cases. These particular cases involve the consideration of preferences which exist only because parents normally do favor their own children. For instance, the question of whether to add a foster child to one's family inevitably raises issues of the primacy of obligations to one's own children. The particular judgments relevant for justifying a general principle of parental loyalty presuppose that general principle: the general principle determines whom we identify as affected parties, and determines to some extent the nature and strength of their interests. Thus, we cannot without circularity justify the general principle by showing that following it would be right in most cases.

The generalization approach tells us that, practically speaking, in our society it is rational to follow a general principle of loyalty to our children rather than to adopt a case-by-case approach. But it does not tell us whether loyalty to one's children is preferable to some other configuration of loyalties. A justification which shows that adherence to the principle will in most actual cases lead to actions which maximize preference satisfaction all around does not explain why we should acknowledge preferences based on the principle, or why we should attribute moral value to those preferences. This form of justification will not distinguish among generally accepted principles which ought to be accepted and those which ought not to be.

To avoid circularity and to answer the latter questions, the principle must be justified directly — by the desirable consequences which would result from its general acceptance. A direct justification might begin by showing that people are generally better off when particular loyalties, rather than total impartiality, prevail. The proof that familial loyalties are preferable to some other configurations of loyalties would be more difficult. Such comparisons require empirical data which, as in this case, are largely unavailable. As with so many basic choices — such as whether to produce children — the utilitarian standard of maximizing preference satisfaction is difficult to apply. The decision itself may introduce unexpected preferences and change the priorities assigned to existing preferences. Faced with such difficulties in applying the utilitarian standard of maximizing preference satisfaction, we may be forced to resort to less precise standards such as advancing happiness. A rough comparative consequentialist justification may be the best justification that can be provided.

In any case, these are distinct claims: (1) good consequences will result from general acceptance of a principle; and (2) preference satisfaction will be maximized by following the principle. The first claim addresses the issue of justifying preferences, and this is the issue typically at stake when we ask for justification of a general principle. The second claim leaves the underlying preferences unexamined: given a configuration of affected parties and their preferences (which may be partially a result of general acceptance of the principle in question), action conforming to that principle will satisfy those preferences to a degree higher than action in accordance with some other principle.

In summary, the notion that evaluations of general principles can rest upon generalizations about right actions in particular cases is incorrect in two sorts of cases. It is incorrect in the case of general principles which are not associated with or manifested in any particular class of maximizing actions. It is also incorrect when the evaluation is circular because the preferences underlying the particular action assessments depend for their validity on the general principle in question. It appears that many general moral principles may themselves be basic and prior, in the epistemological sense, to specific moral judgments.

III

I began this essay by proposing that we inquire into the relation between good persons and right conduct as defined by utilitarianism. Having examined different forms of utilitarianism, we have found that some can accommodate a theory of virtues or principles governing traits of character, attitudes, and so on. Nevertheless, I have argued that the relation between the goodness of persons, as determined by their adherence to these principles, and right conduct is somewhat different from that often supposed by utilitarians. In particular, the principles concerning traits of the person are not secondary in either a practical or epistemological sense to determinations of right conduct. These principles are not simply heads for the various types of right conduct, as Sidgwick suggested, nor is our interest in the motives and purposes of agents important simply as a means of encouraging the performance of maximizing actions.

My view is that a theory of good persons, or of virtue, must be accorded primacy in a utilitarian moral theory. It cannot be regarded simply as a derivative of the theory of right conduct. Consequentialist reasoning is applicable to the range of questions concerning the moral worth of agents and certain of their traits, but it does not take the form used in determinations of right conduct in an act-utilitarian theory.

Finally, I want to return to the claim with which I began — the claim that utilitarianism sometimes requires an act which a decent person would not do or could not do easily. It should be obvious from the preceding discussion that utilitarians will respond to this claim in various ways. An act utilitarian might say that this situation is impossible since a decent person will always do what utilitarianism requires. Most rule utilitarians and a proponent of Hare's two-level theory would, I think, acknowledge such situations of conflict. But they would differ in their recommendations of what ought to be done.

In my view, the possibility of conflicts between the requirements of particular situations and general principles governing character traits does nothing to undermine versions of utilitarianism which can accommodate principles governing characteristics of the person. These versions of utilitarianism implicitly acknowledge the possibility of such conflicts. Admittedly, the resolution of the conflict is a problem, but it is not a problem peculiar to utilitarianism. Unless one's moral evaluations of particular actions are simply reflections of what one shrinks from doing, it is possible that situations will arise in which a good person would be disinclined to do what, according to other principles, he or she thinks ought to be done.

Before closing, I want to point out that the version of utilitarianism which accommodates general principles concerning the traits of persons departs from the rigorous version of act utilitarianism with which we began. In fact some might claim that this less rigorous version is not utilitarian at all since the notion of maximizing action is not the only basic concept in the theory. Not only is the maximizing strategy forsaken as a general strategy of moral choice and justification, but the principles which have taken its place are not justified by reference to maximizing actions. Undoubtedly, such a theory is consequentialist, and is thus distinct from nonteleological theories. I shall not decide whether such a theory is appropriately called "utilitarian," but shall simply acknowledge the points of difference from other versions of utilitarianism. I shall leave for another day the issue of defining more specifically the place of utilitarian thinking, understood as the application of the maximizing strategy, within a complex utilitarian theory.[17]

NOTES

1. G. E. Moore, *Principia Ethica* (1903; reprint ed., Cambridge: At the University Press, 1968), pp. 172–82.

2. Henry Sidgwick, *The Methods of Ethics* (1907; reprint ed., New York: Dover, 1966), p. 219, n. 1; p. 493.

3. John Jamieson Carswell Smart, "An Outline of a System of Utilitarian Ethics," in John Jamieson Carswell Smart and Bernard Williams, *Utilitarianism For and Against* (Cambridge: At the University Press, 1973), p. 48.

4. See Peter Singer, *Practical Ethics* (Cambridge: At the University Press, 1979), pp. 209–11.

5. See D. H. Hodgson, *Consequences of Utilitarianism* (Oxford: Clarendon Press, 1967), pp. 12–14; David Lyons, *The Forms and Limits of Utilitarianism* (Oxford: Clarendon Press, 1965), pp. 26–27.

6. The insistence on the distinction is not peculiar to utilitarians. See David Ross, *The Right and the Good* (1930; reprint ed., Oxford: Clarendon Press, 1973), p. 156.

7. I have heard this comment attributed to Justice Holmes, but I do not know its source.

8. See R.M. Hare, "Principles," *Proceedings of the Aristotelian Society* 73 (1972–1973): 17–18.

9. See Geoffrey James Warnock, "On Choosing Values," in *Mid-*

west Studies in Philosophy 3, Studies in Ethical Theory, ed. Peter A. French, Theodore E. Uehling, Jr., Howard Wettstein (Morris, Minn.: University of Minnesota Press, 1978), p. 28.

10. See Iris Murdoch, *The Sovereignty of Good* (Cambridge: At the University Press, 1967).

11. The view that an agent's motives have utilitarian significance which cannot be captured by act utilitarianism is also found in Robert M. Adams, "Motive Utilitarianism," *Journal of Philosophy* 73 (1976): 467.

12. John Rawls, "Two Concepts of Rules," *Philosophical Review* 64 (1955): 3.

13. Philippa Foot, "Virtues and Vices," in *Virtues and Vices and Other Essays in Moral Philosophy* (Berkeley and Los Angeles: University of California Press, 1978), p. 1.

14. R. M. Hare, *Moral Thinking* (Oxford: Clarendon Press, 1981), p. 129.

15. See Frank Miller and Rolf Sartorius, "Population Policy and Public Goods," *Philosophy and Public Affairs* 8 (1979): 148.

16. Jeremy Bentham, *Deontology: The Science of Morality* (London, 1834), 1:196. I owe this reference to Arthur Flemming's review "Reviving the Virtues," *Ethics* 90 (1980): 587.

17. I want to express my appreciation to Professor R. M. Hare for his helpful criticism of an earlier version of this paper. His comments convinced me that certain forms of utilitarianism can accommodate principles governing character traits. I also want to thank Joel Kupperman and the other participants in the philosophy colloquium held April 9, 1981, at the University of Connecticut at Storrs for their comments on a draft of this paper.

6

Rights, Privacy, and Tainted Ideals

EDWARD W. JAMES

THE GENERAL ARGUMENT FOR rights seeks to present them in some way as a means to or as constitutive of one's personhood. Rawls sees rights as a means to protect our own basic interests against the demands of others; Gewirth takes rights to follow from one's necessary commitment to freedom and well-being; Dworkin views rights as derived from human dignity and equality. As such, rights appear as desired possessions, positive in spirit; Rawls speaks of a *fair* bargain, Gewirth of *human* action, and Dworkin of political *trumps*—what we all want to make, do, or be dealt. Rights are what we seek, for they are fundamental to our projects or interests.[1]

The argument for privacy, which is usually defined as the right to control information concerning ourselves, has pretty much followed suit. Granted, the argument traditionally has begun with an appeal to liberty: we want privacy and all else is equal, so we should not be prevented from having it. But it has turned out that not all else is equal. Some charge privacy with creating false needs, such as that of isolating ourselves in those small-minded havens we label "family" and "close friends." And others accuse it of indirectly underwriting forces of evil by hindering the conviction of even the middle management of organized crime, forcing us instead to be satisfied with the kitchen help.[2] Consequently, some thinkers, like Fried and Reiman, have tried to connect privacy to a fundamental value, such as friendship or autonomy. Only through controlling information about ourselves may we reveal ourselves discriminately to our intimates and thereby show them how special they are to us (Fried), or achieve a sense of ourselves as our own persons (Reiman).[3] I hope to show, however, that such a strategy is inescapably invalid; for the ideals aimed at are so encompassing that they offer myriad ways to them, so that they may be attained not just by the means of privacy. Surely in the case of friendship, for instance, we show others that they are special to us not so much by dropping them personal tidbits as by standing fast by them in times of trouble, rejoicing with them in their successes, and the like. The upshot is to call for an all-encompassing new view of rights. Instead of seeing rights as positive, as a means to or a component of our dearest desires, we should see them as negative — as measures taken to compensate for the various failures of our cherished views, our philosophical systems themselves. Rights on this count are more akin to roadblocks or other compensatory make-do devices; they are not wanted but nonetheless are needed to protect our moral and political systems from their own shortcomings.

I

To begin, let us grant that privacy is culturally connected to such fundamental values as friendship or autonomy, in that it represents a significant way our culture has adopted to advance these values. Reiman stresses this idea in speaking of privacy as a "social ritual by means of which an individual's moral title to his existence is conferred."[4] The difficulty with such a defense of privacy, however, is that rituals are of course conventional and consequently may be replaced by other rites to achieve the same effect. Why not achieve moral title to our existence through other measures than that of privacy, say by those procedures stressing commitments and choices? For instance, Reiman argues that we gain a sense of our selves as our own through a moral ownership of our bodies, which entails two "essential conditions": "the right to do with my body what I wish, and the right to control when and by whom my body is experienced."[5] But surely the first condition is the more fundamental, for by making choices concerning what we do through our bodies we develop a sense of owning ourselves and our bodies. Why, in other words, do we need privacy, the other "essential" condition?

Reiman himself appears to be somewhat aware of this difficulty in his ambiguous representation of privacy. For in the end he switches from his specific initial definition, where privacy is seen as the traditional right to control information concerning one's self, to a much more general notion, where privacy is presented as "the right to the existence of a social practice which makes it possible for me to think of this existence as *mine*."[6] But many social practices other than privacy as traditionally understood may establish one's existence as one's own. Indeed, as we shall see, institutions eradicating traditional privacy may achieve such a result. Consequently, while Reiman would like to have shown the necessity of privacy in the traditional sense, all that he can claim to have shown is that privacy in the extended or Pickwickian sense — as an institution, any social practice whatever that guarantees a sense of self — is necessary. Privacy in the traditional sense ends up as a mere convention.

The lesson behind this failure of the effort to link privacy (and by extension any right) to a fundamental value like friendship or autonomy is the dilemma of the tight tie: make the value fundamental and its very richness rules out any necessary connection to privacy; yet make the tie tight and the value is so narrowed in meaning that it is no longer fundamental. Either the value is fundamental and the connection loose, or the connection remains fast but the value no longer fundamental. One source of this dilemma lies in the way our values become fundamental, namely, by being so extensive that they permeate our lives in myriad ways. With such a profound breadth to our fundamental values, no specific means to their attainment can be necessary. For example, autonomy, the key value behind Reiman's thinking, embraces such ideas as "being one's own person," freedom, rationality, choice, moral growth, self-criticism, and so on. To say that privacy is essential to reach this complexus of values is to ignore what it most obviously is, a complexus, which consequently may be approached by many routes. Moreover, another source of the dilemma lies in the notion that not one of the components of the complexus is itself indispensable to the fundamental value. They only more or less go together, as in a family resemblance. Hence we may achieve autonomy or some other fundamental value without attaining some of its usual characteristics — say, choice in just this area or criticality in that — precisely where privacy may be a necessary means.

II

To understand the argument for privacy in particular and for rights in general, we must discuss why a culture would wish to eradicate any one of them. A culture that effectively eliminates a right like privacy must be more than merely willing to do so. It must be, in an extended sense of the word, able — either through technological intervention, as in some extension of electronic eyes as directed by a central control; or through some enhanced mode of awareness, like telepathy, arising possibly through a transformation of the community. In either case we are facing a staggering venture which stands in opposition to the ideals traditionally connected with privacy: ideals that pursue a libertarian or individualist model of society by warning of the evils of governmental constraints, advocating extensive liberties achieved through a minimally regulated society, and seeking the creativity and promise of a Walden.

Why then would any culture wish to deny privacy totally? As we have already glimpsed in our initial criticisms against the need for privacy as well as in the ways of effectively eradicating it, the reply can assume two forms. One, the centralist model, has stressed the threat of a Walden lapsing into chaos, disparaged the ideal of responsible monads or a preestablished harmony of self-interested desires, and insisted on the consequent necessity to promote order through a central control, with a Platonic Republic, for example, as its goal. The other, the communal model, has excoriated the various forms of alienation arising within a Walden, derided the idea of a spontaneous and self-interested order, and extolled the joys of participatory love found in the promise of a beloved or organic society of a Paul or a Marx. Each of these forms, like the ideals commonly yoked to privacy, represents an ideal-cluster, a set of mutually strengthening or interconnected ideals. Clearly, then, given the vast commitment of energy required to eradicate privacy as well as the power of the ideals within which it traditionally nests, any reason to reject privacy totally must emerge as a focal point of much larger issues. It is no mere matter of considering whether a practice like privacy is tied to a value like friendship.

Accordingly, I am for the nonce considering a worst-case situation, where the denial of privacy is thorough; namely, where it is both extensive and effective. While we should and shall further scrutinize this worst-case strategy — for it does have important limitations — let us for the moment note that it is not peculiar to this analysis. Such a spectre has been raised, albeit more discreetly, by the other major defenses of privacy. Fried, for instance, starts us out and ends with his "immodest proposal" of "electronic monitoring," all to stage dramatically the conclusion that "without privacy" love and friendship "are simply inconceivable."[7] Similarly, at the heart of Reiman's considerations lies the concept of the "total institution," one that seeks "mortification of the self" — with the total denial of privacy taken to be "an essential ingredient in the regimen."[8] From such thorough denials of privacy as these, Fried and Reiman proceed to argue that disastrous results follow. However, as we shall see, even these worst-case appeals fail to establish the need for privacy, for by themselves they deny neither friendship nor autonomy. Yet, ironically, it is just here, in the initial failure of the appeal to the worst case as a defense of privacy, that we find the beginning of a new defense of it and of rights in general.

III

With the general discussion behind us, let us now consider a specific ideal-cluster, the "City of God" as found in Augustine, one that dimly but necessarily shines in the mundane through God's grace. As Augustine observes, "If a man confess to you, he does not reveal his inmost thoughts to you as though you did not know them, for the heart may shut itself away, but it cannot hide from your sight."[9] God knows all; there is no escaping; yet the Saint did not feel violated — for the obvious reason that God did not stress power to Augustine but rather love. So we hear of "the wicked," how they "do not know that you are everywhere. . . . Let them then turn back and look for you. They will find that you have not deserted your creatures as they have deserted their Creator. . . . Gently you wipe away their tears."[10] Here God is no spy, no infinitely able central control or organic order, aiming to record our transgressions so that we will suffer later. Instead God is ever present in case we call. The eradication of privacy by such an omniscient and omnipotent Being is secondary, or, to borrow a notion from jesuitical casuistry, an "indirect consequence" of the constant and guaranteed Presence that overcomes all reason for loneliness and fear. Consequently, more is required for the thorough denial of privacy to be a violation. For within Augustine's City, or at least in this borough, God of necessity denies privacy and yet allows the Saint and us the possibility of our personhood, autonomy, and the like. Hence if the aim is not directly to deny privacy in order to impose a set of predetermined values; if privacy is denied, as it were, accidentally, as a kind of second effect of some legitimate aim (such as divine love), then it seems that privacy denied is not personhood — or any other fundamental value — rendered impossible.

However, as we shall now see, there lies a Greek tragedy within this medieval play. For in making our ideals work, in giving them force and application, we soon see them falling from a heaven to a hell. Indeed we need not wait long before the loving caress of Augustine's beloved Companion metamorphoses into the cruel and cutting sword of the wrathful Judge. For what happens to those sinners who in the end do not sense the presence of God? Are they, too, embraced? The answer lies within Augustine, but particularly in one who made it the central point of the human condition, Jonathan Edwards. More than a millennium after the saint, this Puritan divine viewed us all as sinners in the hands of an angry God, threatened by an "exquisite horrible misery . . . a boundless duration . . . punishment [which] will indeed be infinite."[11] Edwards's God, unlike the many-sided God of Augustine, condemnably eradicates our privacy. With Edwards we do right primarily to avoid the wrath of the inescapable Avenger. We no longer choose because of love for the values themselves; we no longer bring those values to bear in our own way within our persons. Now the all-seeing Eye tells us what the values are and how they are to be lived and what exquisitely horrible consequences follow if they are not.

Consequently, in dealing with the wicked, with those who do not confess — a task that marks our world for both Augustine and Edwards — we find that the ideal inexorably slides from eternal Presence to eternal punishment. But what we find in the specific instance of the City of God is the general and necessary failure of all our ideal-clusters. For these ideals must be more than bedecked intellectual offerings to the sky. They must function or work, develop specific programs, and so face the evils and limitations of our world. Yet in meeting these limitations and evils our ideals must compromise, as Augustine's loving Father becomes the unmovable Judge. The denial of privacy is not a side effect but is instead a major means of imposing ideals on and thereby controlling the subjects. Our ideals, in sum, have within them an alluring ambiguity, that in one hand carries peace and prosperity and in the other war and famine — in the latter a war hammer or a cross, in the former a harvest sickle or a risen Lord. We find such irreconcilable tensions not just within the City of God, presided over by the Loving-Judge, but within all of our ideals, from Plato's Republic to Marx's communism.

This ambiguity is found in Plato's representative of a god on earth, the philosopher-king, who is at once reflective and active, philosophical and managerial, and thus capable of establishing and maintaining the Republic. Here once again privacy (or freedom of the press or assembly or worship) is denied by accident. The aim is to ensure that the citizens are fitted to their tasks. This aim demands a thorough knowledge of the citizens, a knowledge that we would gladly grant for the guarantee that we are in the best possible station. Yet such a leader in our world is forced to stress reflection or activity — one cannot by the logic of the matter stress both — and then degenerates, as Plato himself fears, into either an incompetent bungler or an all-too-competent tyrant. As Plato tells the story (with his many appeals to the Muses warning us that the exact mechanism is mere speculation), the defective guardians "first as guardians begin to neglect us, paying too little heed to music and then to gymnastics, so that our young men . . . deteriorate in their culture."[12] That is, the guardians first fail as managers or as activists, dwelling instead on their own cultural interests or visions. But when this neglect leads to strife, which in turn calls for order, those who respond do so by "enslaving and subjecting . . . their former friends and supporters."[13] The guardians turn to their managerial side at the expense of their theoretical, and impose their will and power on their fellow citizens.

This internal tension among our ideal-clusters is found again in the organic community, that perfect Society of Love where each person is defined in terms of the community and the community in terms of each person. Through a complete unity of minds (and with it, by the way, an utter loss of our traditional rights like privacy, or even the institution of promise-keeping), conflict and confusion give way to organic and spontaneous participation. Yet the traditional problem of such idealisms remains. For how the individual and the community can be defined in terms of each other without one of them being basic not only remains a mystery but also places the two in vicious competition — precisely what the ideal means to overcome! Bradley, for instance, speaks of the system as "real in the details of its functions. . . . The organs are always at work for the whole, the whole is at work in the organs. And I am one of the organs."[14] So far so good. But then in the next sentence Bradley tells us what this means: "The universal then which I am to realize is the system which penetrates and subordinates to itself the particulars of all lives."[15] Here the system or whole is dominant, subordinating all the particulars within it. But soon after, Bradley insists that "there must also be a soul. . . . The point here is that you can not have the moral world unless it is willed; that to be willed it must be willed by a person. . . ."[16] Now the individual looms large — but not for long. For "these persons . . . have the moral world as the content of their wills."[17] And so it goes, back and forth. To tell us in the end that we need both, as Bradley does, where "moral institutions are carcasses without personal morality, and personal morality apart from moral institutions is an unreality, a soul without a body"[18] is to tell us little. For it is to substitute impassioned rhetoric for the cold analysis needed to show what individual and community are and how they can mutually exist. Hence such a society, in a striking irony, dialectically finds itself of necessity in conflict, concluding with the forced choice between the anarchic chaos of rampaging individualism or a tyrannic dictatorship of the community or resident power.

Marxism-Leninism tried to solve this dilemma by that peculiar entity both social and political — the Party. The Party is social in its doctrines of the vanishing of the State immediately after the Revolution (or at least within a generation) and of the primacy of spontaneity in the individual, where for Marx one may "hunt in the morning, fish in the afternoon, rear cattle in the evening, criticize after dinner, just as I have a mind, without ever becoming fisherman, shepherd, or critic."[19] Here individual choice and autonomy are kept sacred through the knowledge and direction of the Party (which indirectly eradicates the standard non-interference rights like privacy). Yet, even after the Revolution, the Party remains political; for when faced with the problem of how this community is ever going to come about, the Party arrogates to itself the sole source of moral truth, subordinates the spontaneity of the individual to the conformity of the worker, and relegates the socialist society either to ignorance (where we hear Lenin say, "What socialism will look like when it takes its final form we do not know and cannot say")[20] or to the mystical (where he says, "The bricks are not yet made with which socialism will be built").[21] Hence Marxism-Leninism in the name of community creates the dictatorship of the Party, which is yet another rendition of the resident power or central control.

In sum, an acceptable eradication of privacy (or of any standard right) helps to allow an end that is fundamentally an end in our interest: the peace of God, the satisfaction of doing one's best in and for society, the joy of participatory unity in the organic society. Hence the denial is not negative, a mere means to an end from which it is divorced, but rather occurs in a more positive way, as an expression of the end itself. As such it is an affirmation of some great good. In the City of God the good being affirmed is God's divine love. Yet this includes God's divine knowledge, which eradicates privacy and the right to a trial before one's peers. The good affirmed in Plato's Republic is the philosopher-ruler's correct judgments concerning each citizen's contribution to the Republic. The philosopher-ruler's knowledge, however, eradicates privacy and the freedom of assembly. What we find here is the irrelevance of privacy and other standard non-interference rights in the light of what is affirmed and attained. No crucial interests, as determined by our ideal-clusters themselves, are denied. In contrast, an unacceptable eradication of privacy occurs in the expression of the power of the one—of God, the philosopher-ruler, the society, the Party—over persons. Privacy is eradicated as a means to express and maintain the powers that be and so to control completely the would-be persons under them.

Moreover, the point to underline here is that any seemingly acceptable eradication of privacy necessarily becomes unacceptable. For, as we have seen, our ideal-clusters in general and thus those denying privacy in particular are two-edged, presenting a salvation that slips and slides into a damnation—from a Republic that degenerates into a 1984, whether it be that of Big Brother or the Party, to an organic society that declines into a draconian dynasty or a mindless hive. The tragedy of the utopia is that, to function, it must confront the hardness of this world, and in so doing inexorably lose its grip on the gentility of the ideal. Nor does it lose its grip, as so far portrayed, in just one way. For the tensions embedded within our ideals are legion: in the City of God not just the Loving-Judge but also the Eternal-Act and the Unitary-Infinite; in Marx not just the social-political but also the unorganized organization of the communist society, the unalienated but directed worker, the society without any productive forms to define it as a society.[22] All of these ideals become tainted when faced with the world, our world.

Yet after saying this we must still leave the utopian door open, through which we may not travel but will definitely peer. For these ideals are so compelling in their insights and commanding in their vision that attempts to develop them into a coherent and even practiced notion will, with justification, persist. But we must keep clear that these ideal-clusters eradicating privacy are not ordinary values, like courage or self-criticism, but are—self-admittedly—radical. They call for a dramatic transformation of person and society. They offer us the hope of integrating love with justice, reflection with activity, the community with the individual, the political with the social. Hence these theories of the ideal ultimately demand a distinct break with the past, cry for a new world with new laws and ways, propose an annihilation of the evils and limitations necessitating our many compromises, and thus allow for the eradication of rights like privacy without the subsequent eradication of our personhood. So it is that Augustine pleads for

God's transforming grace or Marx prophesies that the chosen "will have to pass through long struggles, through a series of historic processes, transforming circumstances and men."[23] Such appeals necessarily fail to materialize in our imperfect world; but it would be foolish indeed for us to insist that this world must always be, that such hopes are for all times impossible, and that such lures are not even to be cast.

IV

What we have so far shown is still limited. Granted that a complete and effective violation of privacy leads to widespread encroachments on our personhood, all that this worst-case argument indicates is that we must prevent such a disaster. To be sure, this problem confronts all the major defenses of privacy that seek to link it to a fundamental value; as we have seen, both Fried and Reiman in the end depend upon a worst-case assumption by stressing the resulting horrors when privacy is eradicated. When Fried raises the spectre of the loss of friendship and Reiman speaks of the loss of a sense of self, they do so against a backdrop of an eradication of privacy and hence at best show that such a complete and effective denial of privacy should be prevented.

Our problem is akin to that faced by the traditional appeal, "What if everybody did that?" If everybody acted unethically, disaster would ensue. But to prevent the disaster all we need do is ensure that most people do not act so. Some may act unethically without a resulting disaster. Similarly, if privacy is eradicated disaster follows. But to prevent such a misfortune all we need do is obviate any *thorough* denial of privacy, seemingly allowing some to encroach somewhat on the privacy of others. Our society need not enforce privacy as a right and thereby may allow occasional, or even frequent, transgressions of it. How then can we translate what we have found regarding the worst case to our world?

To begin, we have learned from our excursus into the ideal that our various ideal-clusters, from the Republic to Walden, are all defective. Indeed we implicitly see this when the upholders of these various ideal-clusters criticize and dismiss each other for logically analagous reasons. Each charges the others with contradictions of the same sort, where the contradictions all originate from the failure of the ideal to meet fully the demands of the real.[24] Our ideals all turn out to be weak. Like light, they serve as a beacon but not as a road. While they provide us with pointers, organizational motifs for our lives, they do not give us much direction in our day-to-day living—in particular, as we have examined in this essay, when we face the difficulties of moral aberration. How do we deal with the recalcitrant, with our own failures and weaknesses, with those who follow different ideals? Here in the application of our ideal-clusters the tensions infecting them become manifest. Our position then is similar to those who return to Plato's Cave. They and we have become unchained by seeing the problems and issues, have journeyed into the realm of ideas and ideals, but now on returning we stumble. For the light of our ideals shines so sharply that it deforms what it illuminates.

It is just here, in the failure of our ideals, that we can see the need for rights in general and for privacy in particular. Although such rights do not light the way to the promised land, as do our revolutionary ideal-clusters, they serve as a beacon to help keep us, for all practical purposes, steady and off the rocks. While our ideals point us to the future and offer us a hope in a great good, whether through divine or historical grace, rights like privacy, ungainly as they may be, remain in the present and offer us a working warning. They are indispensable not because they link up, of practical and logical necessity, with some fundamental value, but because they prevent our value-clusters from becoming overweening. Like Jeffersonian government, rights like privacy endure, not as a necessary means to some fundamental value but as a safeguard against the dominance of any one end or value-cluster. They do so by checking the inroads of such ideal-clusters as individualism, centralism, and communalism. We devise compensatory adjustments and rights just where our ideal-clusters fail.

Let us return then to the analogy with the "What if everybody did that?" argument. An answer to the response, "But not everybody does do that!" is an appeal to fairness; all out of fairness should share the burden to avoid a possible disaster. When discussing rights, we argue, similarly, that even the moderate denials of privacy, as found in neglect or disdain, are, other things being equal, unjustified. For our ideal-clusters clash with each other. They do not by themselves suffice but require compensatory devices. Such devices, our rights, ensure that no one cluster becomes dominant by locating just where each is inadequate and needs the adjustment of rights.

V

To summarize, individual rights emerge from the essential limitations of our various ideal-clusters. This is a formal result in that it speaks of the logical limitations of a system — that a system cannot do or emphasize everything. Yet it is also an empirical result in so far as it respects what experimentalists, whether in science or in morality, have never tired of saying to theoreticians; namely, that their analyses may be wrong. In fact the philosopher-ruler is not to be found; in fact our ideals become sullied when lived. Moreover, the result is empirical because it tells us that to determine what the rights are we must look to the specific logical-empirical limitations of a given theory — especially regarding its applications. Hence the argument is nonmetaphysical in proclaiming rights to be independent of any individual theory. Yet it is profoundly metaphysical in speaking of rights as generated by the necessary limitations of any theory. Further, instead of starting with the individual as the possessor of rights, the argument begins with the theories that seem successfully to deny rights and works from the necessary failure of such theories to the demand for compensatory devices. To be sure, the argument does claim that there are fundamental interests of persons, as found in the important role autonomy plays throughout this discussion. But these interests are seen as granted by the theories themselves; Augustine's City of God and Plato's Republic and Bradley's social whole and Marx's communism all affirm the flowering of the individual.

Given, then, that rights arise out of the failures of our ideal-clusters to meet the demands of the world, let us make clear that there are two major forms of failure. The one we have already focused on in this discussion occurs when the system is excessive and overwhelms individual interests — thus generating the standard non-interference rights. The other takes place when the system is deficient and does not go far enough in allowing people to advance their own interests. The first type of failure calls for "roadblock" rights, as we have seen privacy function here. The second, though, calls for "springboard" rights, which instead of stopping the system's encroachments push the system to do more. Traditionally the first sort of right has been stressed by the democracies, while the second has been the subject of the socialist regimes, under the rubric of human rights. Both of these sorts of rights, however, appeal to the same fundamental justification: the failure of systems. What the springboard rights claim is that the individualist or libertarian organization of society fails — and for the same sort of reason that the totalitarian-communist systems fail. An organizational system, as justified by an ideal-cluster, cannot emphasize everything. For in the libertarian warnings of governmental interference we find implicit an inadequate address to human needs — to health, food, education, and the like.

To be sure it could be, and has been, argued that the libertarian system in its cooperative endeavor has human dignity at its heart, that human rights occupy a focal point of the position — as seen in the "trickle-down" doctrine of libertarianism. The libertarian denies that a special device like an *ad hoc* right is necessary when the entire system is designed to ensure the meeting of human needs. But what such an argument fails to see is that the same sort of reply is and has been given by communist societies and other ideal-clusters when the subject of non-interference rights has been introduced. For what is replied, as is by now notorious, is that such rights are just not important given the great goods arising out of socialist society. The counter, of course, is that the system, any system, fails. But to bring this claim home — which would still not be as powerful as a walk through a ghetto in a democracy or a visit to a dissident group in a communist society — we must show why a system, any system, fails. We must show that it doesn't fail merely by chance. It could not be touched up here and there or serve as the prototype to a new model; it fails ignominiously. There are basic limitations to a system. This is a matter of logic and a matter of the human condition. Put the two together and the result is the argument for rights.

Consequently, we can see how liberalism, the general and

insistent demand for rights, must be distinguished from any particular form of social organization or ideal-cluster. A libertarian need not be a liberal and a communist can be. For liberalism is an unwavering testimony to the need for all systems and is based on the claim that no system by itself suffices. As such it is not itself an ideal or ideal-cluster, but rather, after the manner of speaking in logic, a "meta-ideal-cluster" that provides an arena for the competition of the ideal-clusters so that no essential part of their various visions will be lost in guiding our daily lives. In doing so liberalism unifies the newer "positive" rights of socialism — the demand for health, education, a job — with the older "negative" rights of libertarianism — the prohibition against governmental infringement upon the freedoms of assembly, worship, speech, and, yes, information concerning oneself. In short, we need privacy and other rights to help meet the essential inadequacy of our various ideal-clusters and to help guarantee that no one ideal-cluster becomes dominant. Hence a threat to privacy or any right becomes a matter of grave concern — not just to the ideal-cluster traditionally connected with the threatened right, but also to all other ideal-clusters, and perhaps especially to the one that is threatening the right in question. For what satisfaction is there in winning when the victory results in unmitigated disaster?

Further, rights are of necessity somewhat *ad hoc* within a given political situation. For they point to the specific failures of the political organization, where the general attempt for a unified vision has failed. In making clear the aberrations and anomalies, where specific accommodations must be made, our rights thus make up a list rather than an organized theory. But this in turn is also why discussions concerning rights are always vital and always occupy the forefront of political issues. For they address the areas where our laws and ideal-clusters break down. Hence the observation in a recent survey on rights, that we "are for the most part unable to give full and precise specifications of the scope and weight of particular legal or moral rights,"[25] should come as no surprise; rights — the what, the weight, and the width — must be repeatedly scrutinized. As the society shifts and changes, giving dominance to one ideal-cluster over another, in this area rather than that, the need for the emphasis on certain rights diminishes or increases. We are faced here with the demand for constant vigilance and awareness of just where the conceptual pressure points in society are to be found. Consequently, the determination of rights is no eternal matter but is continually in flux and at the center of social-political controversy and promise, a matter of negotiation on the part of interested peoples and parties as well as a matter of understanding the conceptual underpinnings of the controversy.

In conclusion, rights are not part of any specific theory, in the sense that they arise out of the theory itself, but are instead awkward but necessary safeguards on the theory. It is in part for this reason that the issue of rights gives us philosophers as systematizers or theoreticians so much embarrassment. For we do not quite know what to do with them. As Judith Jarvis Thomson concludes in her essay on rights, "We are still in such deep dark in respect of rights."[26] Like rabbits pulled out of a hat, they amaze and delight —"Where did that one come from!"— but in the end, rights in Thomson seem to appear from nowhere. We have argued for a new model of rights, where rights are not integral to a system or ideal-cluster, arising out of its theses, but rather are *ad hoc* adjustments aimed at preventing a system from gaining too much power or specious success by making amends for its essential limitations. It is to be hoped that we have seen where the rights do come from, that magic is not the secret after all, and so have shed some light on the deep dark.[27]

NOTES

1. See, for instance, John Rawls, *A Theory of Justice* (Cambridge, Mass.: Belknap Press at Harvard University Press, 1971); Alan Gewirth, *Reason and Morality* (Chicago: University of Chicago Press, 1978); and Ronald Dworkin, *Taking Rights Seriously* (Cambridge, Mass.: Harvard University Press, 1978), pp. 266–78. For two fine general discussions on the problem of rights see Stanley I. Benn, "Rights," in *The Encyclopedia of Philosophy*, ed. Paul Edwards (New York: Macmillan, 1967); Rex Martin and James W. Nickel, "Recent Work on the Concept of Rights," *American Philosophical Quarterly* 17 (1980): 165–80. In these two essays the positive images in the representation of rights are continued — with rights portrayed as devices for parceling out legal advantage (Hohfield), legitimate claims (Feinberg), entitlements (McCloskey), possession of legal priority (Wellman).

2. For a fine review of these criticisms see Stanley I. Benn, "Privacy, Freedom, and Respect for Persons," in *Today's Moral Problems*, ed. Richard A. Wasserstrom (New York: Macmillan, 1975), pp. 1–21.

3. Charles Fried, "Privacy: A Rational Context," in Wasserstrom, *Today's Moral Problems*, pp. 21–33; Jeffrey H. Reiman, "Privacy, Intimacy, and Personhood," *Philosophy and Public Affairs* 6, no. 1 (1976): 26–44.

4. Reiman, "Privacy, Intimacy, and Personhood," p. 39.

5. Ibid., p. 42.

6. Ibid., p. 43. (The emphasis is Reiman's.)

7. Fried, "Privacy: A Rational Context," p. 23.

8. Reiman, "Privacy: Intimacy, and Personhood," p. 40.

9. Augustine, *Confessions*, trans. R. S. Pine-Coffin (Baltimore: Penguin Books, 1961), p. 90.

10. Ibid., p. 92.

11. Jonathan Edwards, "Sinners in the Hands of an Angry God," in *The American Tradition in Literature*, ed. Edward Sculley Bradley et al., 2 vols. (New York: W. W. Norton & Co., 1956), 1:119.

12. Plato, *Republic*, trans. Paul Shorey (London: W. Heinemann, 1930), 546d.

13. Ibid., 747b–c.

14. Francis Herbert Bradley, *Ethical Studies* (Oxford: Oxford University Press, 1927), p. 176.

15. Ibid., pp. 176–77.

16. Ibid., p. 177.

17. Ibid.

18. Ibid., p. 178.

19. Karl Marx and Friedrich Engels, *The German Ideology*, trans. C. J. Arthur (New York: International Publishers, 1970), p. 53.

20. Attributed to Lenin by Martin Buber in his classic study, *Paths in Utopia*, trans. R. F. C. Hull (Boston: Beacon Press, 1958), p. 115. For a study of current Soviet views on ethics see Richard T. DeGeorge, *Soviet Ethics and Morality* (Ann Arbor: University of Michigan Press, 1969), where the Party emerges as the "conscience of the people" (p. 80).

21. Attributed to Lenin in Buber, *Paths in Utopia*, p. 115.

22. For instance, see George G. Brenkert, "Freedom and Private Property in Marx," *Philosophy and Public Affairs* 8, no. 2 (1979): 122–47; Craig A. Conly, "Alienation, Sociality, and the Division of Labor: Contradiction in Marx's Ideal of 'Social Man,'" *Ethics* 89, no. 1 (1978): 82–94.

23. Karl Marx, "The Civil War in France," key excerpts found in *Marx and Engels: Basic Writings on Politics and Philosophy*, ed. Lewis Samuel Feuer (Garden City, N.Y.: Anchor Books, 1959), p. 370.

24. For further development of these ideas see my articles on ethi-

cal choice and ethical incoherence: "Working in and Working to Principles," *Ethics* 83, no. 1 (1972): 51–57; "A Reasoned Ethical Incoherence?" *Ethics* 89, no. 3 (1979): 240–53; and "Butler, Fanaticism, and Conscience," *Philosophy* 56 (1981): 517–32.

25. Martin and Nickel, "Recent Work on Rights," p. 173.

26. Judith Jarvis Thomson, "The Right to Privacy," *Philosophy and Public Affairs* 4 (1975): 314.

27. I wish to thank Professor David Cheney, who leveled many withering but constructive criticisms against earlier drafts of this essay, as well as Charlene Entwistle, who aided considerably in the writing of the essay. Neither, of course, is responsible for the essay's deficiencies.

7

Confession and Moral Choice

SISSELA BOK

PRACTICES OF CONFESSION — be they political, legal, religious, or therapeutic — link the concepts of the right and the good as experienced in individual lives. The claim made for such practices is that a life cannot be good until it has been set right — until what is not right about it has been accounted for, squared away, forgiven, healed, or punished. Unless such an account can be rendered, and rendered to someone fully empowered to respond, a person's life cannot be a good one to live, or to have lived.

In this paper, I shall inquire into this linking of the right and the good through practices of confession. I shall ask what moral considerations confront those who take part in such practices — those who receive or extract confessions, as well as those who offer or submit to them. Within each of these perspectives, I shall be tracing two clusters of moral distinctions: those, first of all, that have to do with openness and concealment in communication (and thus also with degrees of completeness, accuracy, and candor); second, those related to degrees of freedom or subjugation for the participants in such exchanges. Few practices illustrate the intricacies with which these distinctions interweave and affect one another as vividly as do the many forms of confessions.

Consider, as an example of the first set of distinctions, Rousseau's *Confessions*: an extraordinary blend of laying bare, disguise, concealment, and invention, of flaunting the self in public while yet nourishing a sense of mystery, and claiming the intention to "show myself to my fellow man in all the truth of nature."[1] Or take Clamence, the "judge-penitent" in Camus's *The Fall* — a past master at every nuance of confession, every shading of candor and

133

subterfuge. He tells how he has come to the point of liking to read only confessions, but that he has found that the authors of confessions write above all in order not to confess, so as to say nothing of what they know, and warns, "When they pretend to begin their avowals, be on your guard, it is time to put make-up on the corpse."[2]

For an example of the second set of distinctions, having to do with the degree of coercion or freedom accompanying the disclosures made in confessions, let us take the report of a group of Jesuits traveling among the Algonquin Indians in 1653, in the territory they called Nouvelle France.[3] They recount how the Indians tell of a land where the cold is so intense that all that is spoken freezes to ice. When the spring comes, the spoken words melt, and all that has been said during the winter can be heard "as if in a single moment." However that may be, wrote the Jesuits, the fact is that when spring comes, the Indians gather for a joint confession on the banks of a river, and all the evil that has been done in the great woods during the winter is disclosed. The Jesuits felt it necessary to add that these confessions took place "without torture or exaction." Their very disclaimer serves to remind readers of the role that torture has played, and still plays in large parts of the world, in extracting personal revelations.

Confessions provide extraordinary scope, then, for moral choice with respect to both sets of distinctions: openness and concealment, freedom and subjugation in all their modulations. These practices have offered a setting for the most intimate and highly charged confrontations. They have exhibited intricate strategies for pointing toward and away from the self. Used in every system of orthodoxy and domination, they have also served to heal and reconcile and transform. In studying the ethical issues of confession, therefore, we have an opportunity to see at close hand the ingenuity, the range, and the pitfalls of what human beings have thought to do for and to one another as well as themselves.

To confess something to someone is to avow what one has not previously disclosed to that person about oneself — often something one regrets or wishes one could regret. To confess is therefore different from the confiding among friends, relatives, and sometimes strangers without which human beings could not retain their links to one another nor to sanity itself.[4] Confession is an institutionalized, often ritualized practice. It promises more expert help than other forms of confiding, and at times access to the sacred; but it carries greater dangers as well.

In the Christian tradition, what is avowed in confession is a sin — what Aquinas defined as "a word, act, or desire that is against the eternal law."[5] Religious confessions as well as therapeutic self-revelations also probe the individual's past for what has been called the "pathogenic secret." In *The Discovery of the Unconscious*, H. F. Ellenberger traces the concept of the "pathogenic secret" back to the primitive healers, and the magnetists and hypnotists who worked at drawing intolerable and painful secrets into the open.[6] Origen, in the third century A.D., described the goal of confession in such terms: there were evil thoughts in people, he said, which, unless they were brought into the open, could not be "destroyed, slain, and . . . utterly done to death."[7]

Most confessions, religious as well as secular, are meant to reveal more than a trivial assortment of peripheral personal facts: something intimate and central to one's life — religious or political deviation, perhaps, or a dissolute or obsession-ridden life. They reveal a lack of harmony with accepted standards, and an effort to restore that harmony, often by making restitution, accepting a penance, or submitting to a ritual of purification.

People confess only to matters over which it is (or has been) possible, at least in principle, to exert some control, or for which they feel partial responsibility. Thus they may confess to incest or child abuse, but not to having unwittingly transmitted polio; confess to religious backsliding, but not to poverty. But they also seek support against forces they may regard as too strong for them to combat alone — addiction, perhaps, or weakness of will, or supernatural powers of evil. By confessing, they seek to align themselves with communal or sacred forces that will help in this battle. The change they seek may be from deviance to normalcy, from wrong to right, from ignorance about the self to insight. Their effort may be great enough to change their entire way of life, perhaps also to bring forgiveness and hope of salvation. Many have described the sense of purification and rebirth felt after such a change as similar to that felt after baptism. Bishop Cyprian of Carthage described it as follows, in *The New Life in the Spirit: A Personal Confession:*

> I was myself so entangled and constrained by the very many errors of my former life that I could not believe it possible for me to escape from them, so much was I subservient to the faults which clung to me; and in despair of improvement I cherished these evils of mine as if they had been my dearest possessions. But when the stain of my earlier life had been washed away by the help of the water of birth, and light from above had poured down on my heart, now cleansed and purified . . . then straightaway in a marvelous manner doubts began to be resolved, closed doors to open, dark places to grow light; what before had seemed difficult was now easy, what I had thought impossible now capable of accomplishment.[8]

The confession to crimes before civil authorities serves a different function. While it, too, may give a sense of unburdening and even of rebirth, its primary function is to realign with community norms and to give evidence in order to convict. Its scope and reliability have long been in dispute. The evidence that confessions provide has been acknowledged to be ambiguous. False self-accusations are common, commoner still when extracted by means of deceit or force. For this reason avowals in court are coming to be surrounded, in many societies, with increasing precautions. Discourse with those accused is carefully supervised to guard against undue pressure; the privilege against self-incrimination is upheld. In societies where political or religious orthodoxy is enforced by law, on the other hand, confession plays an entirely different role. Bringing the accused to see their error is what matters. The assumption is, at least in principle, that the accused will be grateful to have been brought in line. Proponents of coercive methods of thought reform may therefore take these methods to be in the best interests, not only of the state, but even of the individuals thus brought back to orthodoxy. And the confession is the crucial proof that this process has succeeded.

In all societies, the pressures for self-incrimination are strongest before the accused ever reach the court room. Police interrogation presents opportunities for every form of manipulation. Some have argued, as a result, that the evidence gained from confession ought to play as small a role as possible in assessing culpability; that the reliance on confession should gradually give way to other ways of obtaining evidence, just as has the ancient practice of subjecting individuals to ordeals to determine their innocence or guilt.

Religious debates, likewise, have considered the dangers and the benefits of confession, the degree to which it should be a required practice, and its role in keeping track of what individuals do and think. Innumerable spiritual traditions have employed practices of confession, from Buddhism to African rites, from Oriental mystery religions to Judaism and Hinduism. But it is the Christian tradition that has been more torn by disputes over its role than any other. Should confession be allowed only once after baptism, as Tertullian and Ambrose insisted, or more often? Should it concern only serious sins or every possible kind of lapse? Should revelations be public, before the entire community, or offered in private? If in private, should they be directed solely to God, or must they be made to a priest? Are repentance and confession sufficient, or must the sinner also do penance? And what are the links between penitence, penance, expiation, and guilt?

In the thirteenth century, Lateran IV decreed that "all the faithful, of both sexes, when they have arrived at the age of discretion, are to confess all their sins at least once a year to their own priest."[9] This stress on *all* sins was a departure from the earlier practice of including, in one's confession, a statement asking forgiveness also for possible forgotten sins. Confession was by then firmly established as part of the Holy Sacrament of Penance. And anxiety among believers about what to include was rising. Depictions of the suffering awaiting sinners after death were growing ever more literal. Many lived in terror of omitting some sins that were hard to pin down. Thus "consenting to pleasure" in one's thoughts (*consensus in delectationem*) was a sin which, unless confessed, could lead one to lose one's soul for eternity, according to Aquinas.[10] But just what is an instance of such a sin? Taking pleasure in sunsets or in food or in sexual intimacy? And even if the sin could be specified in all its variations, how could one make sure to avoid it, or even to remember it each time?

It was no wonder that individuals, faced with the threat of eternal damnation for sins so elusive and so hard to forestall, turned increasingly to their confessors in their concern not to offend God — the more so as they believed that God already knew each and every one of their sins, so that there could be no refuge in a false or too casual or incomplete confession. Nor was it a wonder that confessors took it upon themselves to probe ever more minutely into transgressions and into thoughts related to them. Probing and revelation of the most intimate recesses of the soul fed one another. Confessors' manuals came to treat in ever greater detail ways of overcoming the resistance and the reticence of confessants, and to suggest ways to assuage the resultant "scrupulosity" that tormented so many.

One who was beset with such scrupulosity to the point of exasperating his confessors was the young Martin Luther in the Augustinian monastery at Erfurt. His breach with the Roman Church over the issue of the nature of confession and penance split the Christian world. Luther fought the system of indulgences whereby penance in monetary form was required for the forgiveness of sins. He wrote that he was proud to have delivered believers from "the great eternal torture" of the obligation to confess one's sins to priests, and from "the terrible domination of the clergy over the laity." Christ, he argued, "manifestly gave the power of pronouncing forgiveness to anyone who had faith in him."[11] Yet the burden of sinfulness was not thereby lifted. For Luther held that all is sin that is not done in faith; and to determine the boundaries of such sin proved no easier than to delimit the sins that Aquinas and others had specified. Inherent human sinfulness could be wiped away by God alone, Luther held, not through confession or penance in themselves.

Contemporary practices of psychotherapy, and above all of psychoanalysis, echo the torment regarding guilt and confession in the Reformation and the Counter-Reformation, and the ever more precise and exhaustive soul-searching they inspired. As in those religious practices, current secular ones focus intensive and detailed probing on the individual's experience and past, and especially on sexuality in all its stages and manifestations. Both seek thereby to alleviate guilt, and to bring about a personal transformation. Just as religious confessors have urged those in their charge not to leave out of account a single sin or even a sinful thought, so analysts have pointed to the central rule of analysis: that not a single secret, no matter how seemingly irrelevant, be held back. Without such complete openness, both traditions have held that it might not be possible to help revealers overcome their suffering. Without it, the desired freedom and personal transformation would be out of reach.

Michel Foucault has pointed, in the *History of Sexuality* and in *Power/Knowledge,* to the roots of psychoanalysis in the earlier traditions of institutionalized confessions, and in the "medicalization" of sexuality — the view of it as an "area of particular pathological fragility"[12] — both of which he regards as peculiarly characteristic of the West. The links he discerns are striking; yet all evidence goes to show that the practice of confession, as well as the view of sexuality as thus problematic, have more ancient and extensive analogues in world cultures.

The institution of confession is so widespread because it is an unequaled method for bringing solace as well as for imposing orthodoxy of every kind. Robert Jay Lifton has shown its central role in practices of thought reform in his book *Thought Reform and the Psychology of Totalism.*[13] Studying Chinese practices in the 1950s, he shows how the writing and rewriting of confessions, sometimes for years on end, was the main task of political prisoners. It ceased only when they had produced a confession that was both satisfactory to their guards and in correspondence with their own changed views about their past guilt and their conversion.

Lifton, too, saw a parallel with psychoanalysis and with all efforts at profound human change. While psychoanalysis is, in principle, opposed to all that stands for control and thought reform, he argued, and while it aims for a freeing rather than a subjugation of the spirit, it runs great risks in practice. Unless care is taken in the training of analysts and in the treatment of patients, the process of self-revelation can be guided so as to ensure conformity and a doctrinal stance.

Theodor Reik, in *The Compulsion to Confess,* studied the links between practices of confession and psychoanalysis from a different point of view. He saw a near-universal compulsion to confess among individuals; it had been satisfied in the past through art, social custom, and religion. For the first time, he claimed, this compulsion could be dealt with rigorously and systematically.[14] Psychoanalysis would be the explicit and scientific method for eliciting repressed material. Its main concern ought therefore to be to assist and channel the compulsion to confess, and to find outlets for the need for penance.

Even Reik might be surprised, a half-century later, at the sheer number of professionals who now see it as their task to facilitate the compulsion to confess. Through analytic procedures of diverse kinds, through group therapies, and by means of encounter groups, hypnosis, and drug therapy, revelation is aided and interpreted. It is no longer so easy to be optimistic about the scientific nature of all these methods, nor about their therapeutic value. Recommendations of caution in the choice of the persons best qualified to listen to personal revelations are pressed with increasing urgency.

The caution is well founded. Studies of the psychology of self-revelation, while showing its importance in creating intimacy between individuals and in groups, and in channeling help to those most in need, have found it to flow in a direction opposite to that of authority, and thus to increase the vulnerability of those who expose themselves.[15] In ordinary practices of confiding, the flow is reciprocal, as the revelations of one person call forth those of the other; but in institutionalized practices, there is no such reciprocity. On the contrary, professionals who receive personal confidences are often taught to restrain the natural impulse to respond in kind.

While personal information does flow opposite to the flow of authority in many practices of confession, confessants may use the revelation to gain a measure of control in return. They may seek control through choosing what to reveal, what to hide, and how to shape the image others have of them. If damaging information is bound to come out about them, before legal authorities, for example, what they choose to say may influence the way in which it is interpreted. Confession may also mystify and tantalize. And confessants, in establishing an identity in the minds of listeners, come to matter to them in a new way. They no longer feel blurred and anonymous in the eyes of their confessors; the lives of the confessants have taken on a meaning for the listeners.

Confession may bring, as well, a gain in control over oneself. It may serve as a means for achieving a transformation of one's life. It may bring new self-understanding, and thus a chance to recreate oneself. For those who are not certain that they will be able to keep the errors and temptations of their past lives subdued, confession may be a call for help. Naming the temptations and the hostile forces may give the strength to resist them. This cannot easily be achieved through introspection alone. To seek out a confessor is then to look for someone who can share one's burdens, interpret one's revelations, confer forgiveness.

For such achievements, a loss in control over information about oneself may seem a small price to pay. The greater vulnerability of those who have thus exposed themselves may weigh little in the balance against intolerable guilt and suffering. And the burden they hope to alleviate may in itself be so heavy as to render them powerless, immobilized. Ironically, this burden has often been imposed from without in the first place, at times by the very authorities who then proffer assistance for soul-searching. Such was the case as the catalogues of sins multiplied in the Middle Ages, as sin weighed ever more heavily in the Calvinist and Puritan communities, and was hunted down by the Inquisition. Few documents express more poignantly the internalization of guilt imposed from without than do the confessions of the many women accused of witchcraft.

Given, then, that confessional practices can be exploited to upset the delicate balance protecting the self, to waylay the gullible and to insure unquestioning allegiance, but that they have also allowed human beings to seek intimacy and understanding and help, what factors might constitute danger signals in such practices? I shall but begin to suggest some answers to this question. In so doing, I shall leave to one side all the many harmless or beneficial aspects of confessions, and concentrate instead on the problematic ones; and among these, I shall try to point to some aspects of the two clusters of moral distinctions mentioned at the beginning of this paper: that of openness and concealment, and that of freedom and subjugation. I shall discuss them first from the point of view of the person listening to the confession, and then from that of the confessant.

A confessant confronts the listener with the conflicts shared by all who are faced with revelations from others. To what extent should they try to come closer, and probe in greater detail or depth? And if they do, what means do they feel justified in using? In addition, beyond the obligations they may ordinarily acknowledge toward others, do their roles in the institutions they serve offer special justifications for invasive probing, for exerting pressure in questioning and in interpreting, and for deceit or other manipulation?

In every institution encouraging confession, those who play the role of listeners tend to fall in with what is expected of them. Few look skeptically at the interpretations they have been taught to place on what is confessed. When they draw false or unprovable conclusions, the confessant is left with greater guilt and confusion, rather than with the hoped-for growth in self-knowledge. In this way, for instance, generations of women who have disclosed to clergy or to therapists their drive toward self-expression and growth have been told that they were acting out of a lack of feminine modesty or from sexual envy of men; they have been encouraged to fulfill themselves instead according to the prevailing stereotype of femininity. Whatever the current dogma, countless innocents have been similarly persuaded that their efforts to think for themselves revealed the sin of pride or the error of deviation or some grievous failure of solidarity.

For those listening to a confession, then, it is important to consider, first of all, not only their relationship with the confessant, but their role in the institution they represent, and the legitimacy of what it seeks to achieve. Equally important is a questioning stance with respect to the institutional justification for probing as deeply and as intimately as possible. Surely there are times when it is important to get to the bottom of certain questions of guilt. Thus the patient who discloses guilt feelings and pathological symptoms to a psychiatrist, but who does not see their connection to his or her having left the scene of an automobile accident in which he or she had caused the death of a child, clearly needs help in probing these links, and in considering, belatedly, what to do about them. But probing can be as invasive as surgery; and, when undertaken without clear need, it is as hard to justify as unnecessary surgery.

Even when probing is judged to be necessary, as in a great many criminal proceedings, it is important to question the reasons for using morally problematic means such as manipulation, deceit, and forcible coercion. Are there certain categories of persons

— those suspected of crimes, perhaps — toward whom it is right to use methods from which one would ordinarily refrain? Such questions have been at the center of debates among jurists, psychiatrists, and theologians.

In criminal law, to begin with, even in societies where force in extracting confessions is frowned upon, many regard other forms of pressure and deceit as entirely legitimate. They would not think it right to treat innocent persons with the combination of threats, invasions of privacy, and emotional manipulation that they advocate in criminal interrogation. The techniques are well known — alternating an abusive, contemptuous questioner with a gentler one, for instance, or falsely claiming that an associate has already confessed, or initiating bodily contacts felt to be degrading. The argument that persons who have broken the law ought not to be granted the same respect as others neglects the fact that the great majority of those thus interrogated are later found to have been innocent. Even if it were the case that guilty persons deserve less respectful treatment, therefore, the determination of who is and who is not guilty is precisely what is not ascertainable before the investigation.

A second argument for the use of otherwise troubling methods in seeking evidence and establishing guilt holds that society cannot afford to do without them. The current debate over the Abscam investigations raises precisely these questions. Most are uneasy about the methods used, yet worried about how else congressional corruption is to be combated. All would agree that there are infinite gradations in the degree of manipulativeness and invasiveness, and that criminal investigation and questioning will never, any more than other human efforts, be entirely without them. But the debate has to do with the lines to be drawn, even apart from the overt brutality and clear-cut entrapment that most would, at least in principle, reject. How far are we, in our society, prepared to go in bringing individuals to incriminate themselves? In seeking answers to this question, it is important not to neglect the undoubted injuries to the system and the risks of corruption of law enforcement agents that accompany the adoption of methods known to be problematic in their own right.

In therapeutic and religious traditions, a parallel choice arises. Some argue that reasons having to do with the best interest of the *revealer* justify inroads on the ordinary respect for persons, just as many argue, when it comes to criminal confessions, that reasons of social benefits provide such legitimacy. What if deceitful or forcible means might cure someone, or save someone? Would one not resort to force in order to save drowning persons, even against their will? Might one not lie to them as well? And would one not expect them to be grateful to have been thus rescued?

In psychotherapy, schools differ greatly in answering these questions. Freud, on the one hand, regarded coercion or deception of patients as serious infractions, and unlikely to benefit patients. "Since we demand strict truthfulness from our patients," he argued, "we jeopardize our whole authority if we let ourselves be caught by them in a departure from the truth."[16] Other schools are more manipulative. Some rely on the use of false statements to shock patients off their guard, and to force out their hidden thoughts. A therapist may, for instance, accuse a patient of a violent fantasy regarding a family member, and then watch the patient's reaction for clues to the underlying family pathology. And physical coercion, ranging from mild forms of pressure to near-complete subjugation, has been exercised to further self-revelation. Here, as in criminal interrogation, there has not yet been sufficient examination of the helpfulness claimed for such procedures. To manipulate and lie to the sick for their own good (as I have argued at greater length in my book *Lying*), injures everyone involved and distorts the therapeutic process.[17]

A related question is whether helpfulness either to society or to those engaged in self-revelation justifies inducing them to act in ways they would ordinarily reject toward intimates. Persons engaged in probing their own lives may be encouraged to believe, for instance, that it is all right to abandon all discretion in revealing, not only their own intimate problems, but those of others in their lives. Such assurances can be corrupting, the more so the younger or more inexperienced the persons thus encouraged to forgo all concern for reticence.

This leads us to ask about the choices facing the person doing the revealing. (I shall not discuss, in this context, the question of whether one can ever know or tell "the truth" about oneself, or of whether one can know more about oneself than another can. Rather, I shall consider just a few of the revealers' choices regarding what they take to be full or partial, correct or erroneous, truthful or deceptive information.)

Depending on the amount of coercion and manipulation they confront, on their need to confess, and on their belief that it should be done according to a particular form, their choices may be greatly reduced. The more critical the predicament, and the more oppressive the questioner, the more legitimate may be the revealers' own resorts to subterfuge in sheer self-defense. In a great many situations, however, there is scope for choice. Two problematic paths for someone engaged in self-revelation to take have to do with the implication of third parties, and with attempts at seduction of the listener.

Accusation of self is common in confession; accusation of others, implicitly or explicitly, hardly less so. Revelation, whether about self or others, offers opportunities for choice with respect to how complete or incomplete the revelations will be, and how accurate or inaccurate. As Camus said, a confession often signals the moment for applying make-up to the corpse; and part of the falsification may turn on implicating others in one's guilt, or placing it on their shoulders altogether. The question of accuracy is especially important in criminal confessions, because of what can befall those implicated; less so in therapeutic or religious confessions, from the point of view of the consequences for those drawn in, so long as the bond of confidentiality holds.

But accuracy is not all that is at issue; nor do those implicated regard the matter as insignificant so long as the revelations regarding them are held in confidence; nor, finally, do they have reason to trust that professional confidentiality will always be maintained. The questions of what ought to be revealed regarding third parties arise just as much when the revealer has the facts right. Even if what one has to say about others is not so much accusatory as exploring what one takes to be their weaknesses or obsessions or political excesses, it is important to ask whether one should drag them into one's revelations. What amount of discretion does one owe family members, for instance, or friends, as one undergoes psychotherapy? They may not be injured by any outward effects of the revelations; but to the extent that they find their personal affairs talked about, they may still feel intruded upon. Moreover, much depends on the nature of what is taken to be deviant or guilty. In some societies, for instance, children are pressed to report on any political or religious dissent in the home. Even if such reports are offered to a school psychologist with obligations of confidentiality, family members have reason for profound concern.

Apart from accusation or implication of those not present to give their side of the story the confessant may seek to manipulate the listener in many ways. Knowing that confessions among friends often bring revelations in return, some feign to confess in order to secure from the listener some response — confidences in return, or a bond that can be exploited.

Seduction offers the most striking examples of such manipulative confessions. In *Les Liaisons dangereuses*, by Choderlos de Laclos, the Vicomte de Valmont works on his most recalcitrant and unsuspecting victims alike by seeming to pour forth his heart in the tone most likely to gain access to them, and to elicit from them in return confidences and intimacy. In this way, he learns things about them that he can then use to apply pressure to them. And his partner in scheming to seduce and corrupt, the Marquise de Merteuil, confides to him that she regards it as a fundamental precaution to learn the secrets of those she uses for her purposes, saying of one young girl whose "disastrous amour" she had learned about:

> She knows, then, that her fate is in my keeping; and if the impossible happens and she defies these considerations, is it not obvious that her past, when it is revealed, not to speak of the punishment she must suffer, will deprive whatever she says of all credibility?[18]

Another form of manipulation in confessing is to choose as listener someone who cannot and should not be asked to carry the burden of the knowledge disclosed. This happens whenever people unburden themselves to the psychologically vulnerable, as in the case of parents who draw their children into confidences about intimate marital problems.

With respect to both accusation and manipulation, it is important to see the blurred boundaries of the pathological uses of confession. Masochists confess in order to draw others into their self-punishment; and sadists use confession to implicate others and to hurt them. For a view of both, consider again the "judge-penitent" in *The Fall* by Camus. His self-imposed penance is to confess his failures over and over to strangers, implicating them in his torment of self, taunting them, fanning their own guilt, in order to master them in the end:

> Since one cannot condemn others without thereby judging oneself, it was necessary to oppress oneself in order to have the right to judge others. Since every judge ends some day as penitent, I had to take that road in the opposite direction and take up the trade of penitent in order to finish as a judge.[19]

I have touched on some of the moral problems raised by practices of confessions. What is needed, I would like to suggest, is an interdisciplinary study of the casuistry of speaking and of listening in self-revelation. There is a wealth of cases and arguments to draw on in confessional handbooks, in the psychoanalytic literature, and in criminal law, to mention but the more prominent traditions in which debates have been carried on regarding the aims and the methods of confession. In the casuistry that I propose, it will be important to compare cases and arguments used in the different approaches, for all too often the debates have been carried on within a single tradition. They have not, as a result, questioned the fundamental premises concerning guilt, penance, social need, help to individuals, and the legitimacy of otherwise problematic methods. A cross-disciplinary inquiry is therefore essential.

At the beginning of this essay, I set forth the claim underlying many practices of confession: that a life cannot be good until it has been accounted for and set right. In ending, I would like to turn that claim back upon the practices themselves: to the extent that the conduct of practices of confession transgress — either in aims or in means used — the basic norms for what is right, to that extent they will not be good, either for those who take part in them or, in the long run, for the institutions sponsoring them.

NOTES

1. Jean-Jacques Rousseau, *Les Confessions* (Paris: Editions Garnier Frères, 1964), pp. 3–4.

2. Albert Camus, *La Chute* in *Théâtre, Récits, Nouvelles* (Paris: Bibliothèque de la Pléïade, 1962), pp. 1537–38.

3. See Raffaele Pettazoni, *La confessione dei peccati* (Bologna Forni Editore, 1968), 1:25–26.

4. *Confess* derives from the Latin *confidere*, and in turn from the Indo-European root **bheidh-; confide* derives from a different Latin term, *confiteri*, and in turn from the Indo-European root **bha-*.

5. Thomas Aquinas, *Summa Theologiae*, 1–2.71.6.

6. Henri F. Ellenberger, *The Discovery of the Unconscious* (New York Basic Books, 1970).

7. Henry Bettenson, ed. and trans., *The Early Christian Fathers* (Oxford: Oxford University Press, 1956), p. 253.

8. Ibid., p. 272.

9. Cited in James F. McCue, "*Simul iustus et peccator* in Augustine, Aquinas, and Luther: Toward Putting the Debate in Context," *Journal of the American Academy of Religion* 48:1, p. 88.

10. Aquinas, *Summa Theologiae*, 1–2.74.8.

11. Martin Luther, "Letter to a follower in Frankfurt," and "The Pagan Servitude of the Church," in *Martin Luther: Selections from his Writings*, ed. John Dillenberger (New York: Doubleday, 1961), pp. 345, 321.

12. Michel Foucault, *The History of Sexuality* (New York: Pantheon Books, 1978), pt. 3; Michel Foucault, *Power/Knowledge* (New York: Pantheon Books, 1980), pp. 199–200, 215.

13. Robert Jay Lifton, *Thought Reform and the Psychology of Totalism* (New York: W. W. Norton, 1961).

14. Theodore Reik, *The Compulsion to Confess* (New York: Farrar, Strauss, & Cudahy, 1959).

15. Nancy M. Henley, "Power, Sex, and Nonverbal Communication" in *Doing unto Others*, ed. Zick Rubin (Englewood Cliffs, N.J.: Prentice-Hall, 1974). See also Valerian J. Derlega and Alan L. Chaikin, "Privacy and Self-Disclosure in Social Relationships," *Journal of Social Issues* 33 (1977): 102–15; and Paul Cozby, "Self-Disclosure: A Literature Review," *Psychological Bulletin* 79:73–91.

16. Sigmund Freud, *Collected Papers*, ed. James Strachey (London: Hogarth Press, 1950), 2:383.

17. Sissela Bok, *Lying: Moral Choice in Public and Private Life* (New York: Pantheon Books, 1978).

18. Choderlos de Laclos, *Les Liaisons dangereuses* (Paris, 1782); trans. P. W. K. Stone (New York: Penguin Books, 1961), p. 187.

19. Camus, *La Chute*, p. 1546.

8

Supererogation: Artistry in Conduct

DANIEL R. DeNICOLA

THE LITERATURE OF MORAL philosophy contains several stock characters: there are, for example, the person who refuses to acknowledge moral obligations, the person who acknowledges moral obligations but fails to fulfill them, and the person who recognizes and fulfills moral obligations conscientiously. These characters usually merit our contempt, blame, and praise, respectively. With these roles, we are all too familiar. I wish, however, to spotlight a forgotten character who has disappeared from the repertory of the modern philosopher as the classical hero has vanished from contemporary drama. I am referring to the person who not only does his duty or fulfills her obligation, but who acts above and beyond that duty or obligation—the person who performs acts of supererogation.

Perhaps it is hyperbolic to say that supererogation has disappeared from ethical literature, but it is straightforwardly accurate to assert that supererogatory acts are treated as minor anomalies by most of today's prominent moral theorists.[1] This is both odd and interesting, because some acts of supererogation have, throughout history, been regarded as exemplars of the highest reaches of morality; such are the acts that make heroes and saints worthy of admiration and emulation.

The question I wish to put is: How are we to understand such a character and such acts, and what are the implications of this understanding for our ethical theories? The first part of this essay is a rehearsal of the conceptual history of supererogation, ending with a bewildering heap of ideas from recent discussions. The second is an attempt to dispel some of the confusion through a combination of critical points and constructive proposals of my own. The final part examines the implications of this account of supererogation for the foundations of ethics. In that section I will develop a heuristic simile suggested by supererogation: morality as an art form.

I

It seems helpful, though pedantic, to begin with etymology. The Latin verb *erogare* means "to expend, to take from the treasury with the consent of the people"; thus, *supererogare* means "to overexpend." This word appears in the Vulgate version of the Good Samaritan parable at Luke 10:35, which is rendered in one translation as: "He tooke forth two pence, and gave to the host, and said, 'Have care of him, and whatsoever thou shalt supererogate [spend beyond this], I at my returne will repay thee.'"

The Scholastics developed a technical, theological meaning for *supererogation*. They claimed that the merits of Christ were in sum greater than that required for the salvation of the human race; that the saints had also earned merits in excess of what God requires; that all these extra merits were deposited in a spiritual treasury; and that the Church may dispense these merits, through indulgences, to other souls who are deficient.[2] Those saintly works that provided the superabundant merits were called supererogatory. From this doctrinal usage, the term has come to mean "performance of more than duty or circumstances require."[3] We should mark in passing that supererogation is rooted in the financial context of debits and credits. Its meaning subtly shifts from "overexpending" to "overdepositing," yet it retains the notion of excess or superfluity. Its moral connotation is acquired only with Scholasticism, when the moral worth of actions is interpreted quantitatively.

With the resecularization of ethics that began in the Renaissance, the concept of supererogation was generally set aside. Much later, when Kant argued that the moral worth of actions derived from their adherence to duty, acts above and beyond duty were ignored. At best, supererogatory acts were reduced to a kind of moral one-upmanship; at worst, they were discarded from discussion as morally irrelevant. As moral philosophers focused their attention on universal ethical principles that could undergird legislation, it was easy to lose sight of the special acts of special people and to develop ethical theories that had no account of them.

Recent discussion of supererogation began with J. O. Urmson's classic article, "Saints and Heroes,"[4] though he never uses that term in the article. Urmson argues that the traditional tripartite division of actions into the obligatory, the permissible, and the forbidden, is deficient, as shown by a study of actions above and beyond duty. The estimable actions of saints and heroes in particular are often neither obligatory nor permissible and morally neutral. As Urmson says:

> . . . We may . . . call a person a saint . . . if he does actions that are far beyond the limits of his duty, whether by control of contrary inclination and interest or without effort; parallel to this we may call a person a hero . . . if he does actions that are far beyond the bounds of his duty, whether by control of natural fear or without effort. . . . Heroic and saintly actions are not the sole, but merely conspicuous, cases of actions that exceed the basic demands of duty.[5]

He cautions that such extraordinary actions, however inspirational they may be, cannot be made the expected standard of conduct in any moral code that would serve human needs; to make supererogation a standard is beyond reasonable hope and entitlement.

Building on Urmson's work, Joel Feinberg published an article entitled "Supererogation and Rules."[6] Feinberg asserts: "There are some actions which it would be desirable for a person to do, and which, indeed, he *ought* to do, even though they are actions he is under no *obligation* and has no *duty* to do."[7] Doing a favor is a rather humble example of such an action, for example, giving a match to a stranger. But there are some "favors" that go beyond duty in the amount of sacrifice they require, for example, a doctor's abandoning his or her remunerative private practice to join the medical forces in a plague-ridden city. These are supererogatory acts, says Feinberg, not duties, and they clearly have moral worth as actions and are thought to reflect moral virtue in the agents. However, because these actions are not required, their moral worth cannot derive from their requiredness; neither can one account for it by some complex of institutional concepts and rules for assigning moral debits and credits. The notion that laws and institutional house rules can serve "as models for the understanding of all counsels of wisdom and all forms of human worth" is a profound mistake, according to Feinberg.[8]

A somewhat different tack is taken by Roderick Chisholm in "Supererogation and Offence: A Conceptual Scheme for Ethics."[9] He makes the point that either the performance or the nonperformance of an act may be good or bad or neutral. He then defines a supererogatory act broadly and simply as "something which it would be good to do and neither good nor bad not to do."[10] If we compare the performance of a trifling favor with the performance of a demanding duty, we see, says Chisholm, that the difference between supererogation and moral obligation is not that the former is automatically more praiseworthy, more meritorious, or more beneficial than the latter. Unlike Urmson and Feinberg, who dwell on extraordinary feats as examples of supererogation, Chisholm considers very commonplace actions — ordinary politeness, for instance — to be supererogatory.

Still another approach is taken by David A. J. Richards in his book, A Theory of Reasons for Actions.[11] Richards operates within a Rawlsian social contract view, deriving moral principles from the hypothetical choices of rational beings in an initial position of fairness. He contends that in such a situation the contractors would agree to certain principles of supererogation over and above regular moral principles of justice, efficiency, and individual duty. He derives several, including principles of civility, mutual respect, mutual love, beneficence, kindness, and gratitude. These principles are called supererogatory because persons have the moral right or liberty to act in accordance with them or not, as they wish, since coercion and the threat of coercion are not justified in enforcing them.[12] Although coercion has been ruled out by the contractors as inefficient or violative of more basic principles, blame may be invoked. Richards writes: "The contractors would agree that forms of informal criticism, rebuke, and blame are justifiable in enforcing the principle's requirements."[13] In his unusual interpretation, supererogatory works are required of us all, yet we have a "moral right" not to do them; society is not justified in coercing us into doing them. Here supererogation has been identified with unenforceable moral requirements—yet blame and rebuke are used for motivating compliance.

By piling up these brief synopses of Urmson, Feinberg, Chisholm, and Richards—my "bewildering heap of ideas"—it becomes obvious that contemporary discussion of supererogation is hampered by definitional confusion and crossed purposes. Rather than add more synopses of later discussions to the pile, I want to begin to clear some philosophical ground; I hope to sort out some important issues while avoiding semantic quibbles, to articulate the features of supererogatory action clearly and distinctly.

II

I propose that we distinguish the moral sphere (or point of view) from the sphere of politeness or etiquette and from the sphere of custom.[14] Within each sphere, action is evaluated along a continuum: behavior in the etiquette sphere ranges from the rude to the polite; in the sphere of custom behavior ranges from the iconoclastic to the customary. But the spheres are distinct: to be rude is not to be immoral; to play the national anthem before athletic contests is customary, not polite or moral. While acts of politeness are outside of moral duties and obligations, they are not beyond them. They are not supererogatory moral acts because they are not moral acts at all. Actually, I suspect it may be possible to exceed the norms in each sphere, producing distinct varieties of supererogation. There may, for example, be supererogatory acts of politeness, acts beyond the requirements of good manners —perhaps one can even be heroically polite. But such acts are supererogatory in the sphere of etiquette; they are not morally supererogatory.

The failure to distinguish these spheres is part of the problem with Chisholm's accounts. For the sake of enriching the conceptual scheme of ethics, Chisholm creates an amorphous category of supererogatory acts that lumps together such trifling actions as being civil or polite and doing a favor with such extraordinarily risky and self-sacrificial actions as those of saints and heroes. It is a mistake to assume that all duties and obligations are moral duties and obligations. There are some acts which it is good to do that are not moral acts at all. Though acts of politeness and custom are undoubtedly relative to culture, there is age-old dispute over the cultural relativity of morality. Certainly these spheres are not sharply demarcated, but there is little to be gained by deliberately confounding them.[15] From this point on, I shall limit the discussion to moral actions.

What does it mean to say that an act is above and beyond one's moral duties? Feinberg has identified two kinds of cases. One may exceed one's duty in a quantitative sense, going beyond the dutiful level by a certain number of additive units, as for example when Sam promises to work four hours but actually works five, or when Mary gives ten dollars per month more than her fair share to the United Fund. Such acts are quantitative oversubscriptions. On the other hand, one may go beyond duty by performing a morally worthy act that is incommensurable with one's duties, as for example when the physician goes to the plague-infested city. In the latter case, we cannot say by how much the doctor exceeded his or her duty. Such acts are meritorious nonduties. Feinberg's distinction seems valid to me.[16]

However, classic cases of heroism and saintliness include additional varieties. Consider the case of permitting someone to fall short of his or her duty. There are morally worthy acts of forgiveness, grace, clemency, and mercy — acts which one is neither obliged nor duty-bound to perform — which may reasonably be termed supererogatory. These cases of permitting a deficiency have different moral constraints from cases of giving an excess. It is not always good to permit others to escape their obligations; there are circumstances in which one has no right to grant such permission. Moreover, before granting forgiveness, one should weigh the potential damage to the moral institution (social justice, for example) that may be induced by acting mercifully. There are, however, no comparable constraints on performance above and beyond one's own duty; in this case one need not consider possible damage to any moral institution, and one always has the right to exceed one's duty (assuming all other relevant duties are met).

These two distinctions define four types of supererogatory acts. Quantitative oversubscriptions and meritorious nonduties are both ways of acting above and beyond duty. Permitting others to fail to do their duty may also be assessed in quantitative terms in some cases (as when Julie forgives $500 of Bill's $1,000 debt to her) but not in others (as when Julie forgives Bill for lying to her).

I have one minor disagreement with Feinberg concerning the quantitative forms. He says that for these forms we can say by how much persons exceed their duty. Suppose I pay back a debt of $100 and give an extra $25 as well. It seems incorrect — even silly — to say that I exceeded my duty by $25 or by one-quarter. Just because our duties may involve quantitative transactions, we cannot therefore apply the quantitative relations to the duties themselves.

It is a cardinal principle of Kantian ethics that to have moral worth an action must be done from duty.[17] Supererogation flies in the face of that principle. As all of the contemporary philosophers mentioned above would agree, supererogatory acts have moral value (often very high moral value) yet by definition are not done from duty.[18] Since it cannot be conformity with duty or the requiredness of such acts that suffuses them with a halo of morality, on what basis do we affirm their moral worth?

Clearly, we must have a conception of duty before we can conceive of action that is above and beyond duty; in this way supererogatory is parasitic on a theory of obligation or duty. Supererogation is, as one recent writer has put it, "context-bound" to theories of obligation.[19] However, this fact does not establish the source of the moral worth of supererogatory acts; this source must lie outside obligation and duty. I believe that supererogatory acts derive their moral worth from the conformity of the act to the set of values we hold, and from the virtues they reveal in the agent. In this way, supererogation is tied to one's theories of values and virtues; it contributes to the attainment, realization, or expression of something thought to be worthwhile.

It might be thought that I am rejecting deontological theories in favor of teleological theories as providing the best account of supererogation. Teleologists do reduce rightness to the maximization of goodness; perhaps supererogation is simply an unusually conscientious adherence to the prescription to maximize goodness. The moral worth of supererogatory acts would then derive from the goodness they bring about and from the extraordinary conscientiousness of the agent. (Urmson may believe something like this, for he says that utilitarianism can best account for supererogation, though his reasons are unclear to me.)[20] This is in fact not my position. I believe the inference is incorrect, and when righted it will ironically supply a criticism of the teleological approach to ethics. First, teleologists are caught in an inconsistency. One basic duty is promulgated—"Maximize goodness"—and then supererogation is interpreted as unusually strict adherence to that duty. But supererogatory acts are those above and beyond duty; they transcend duty. Teleologists have not really accounted for supererogation; they have denied its existence and substituted instead the dogged maximization of the good. Second, we have laid bare a fundamental flaw in consequentialist theories, especially utilitarianism: they would require all moral agents to perform saintly and heroic actions—in fact, the most saintly, most heroic actions possible at any given moment—to comply with the basic prescription or duty to optimize the good. Far from the meanness with which utilitarianism is often charged, it is too exalted and idealistic a theory: it requires of us all what is impossible for most. It was Urmson himself who cautioned that we cannot make supererogatory actions the standard of a moral code; to do so is beyond reasonable hope and entitlement.

There is another interesting move that is designed to salvage the Kantian position that only when an action is done from duty does it have moral worth: this is to say that the saint or hero is in fact acting from duty, but from a moral duty not acknowledged or accepted by the average moral agent. Going beyond duty in a supererogatory act is really going beyond the duty recognized by the moral public. It is the peculiar and admirable trait of saints and heroes, on this view, that they accept and faithfully act from moral duties that the rest of us ignore.

A first line of response is that if the saint's duty is a genuine moral duty it is universalizable, and it therefore applies to all of us, and we (and the saint) should be blamed when we fail to act upon it. What is needed is moral education of the public and therapy for akrasia ("intemperance"). This response is not fully convincing, I think, because there are plausible counterexamples. Take the case of a vegetarian: suppose a woman follows a vegetarian diet on moral grounds—she feels obliged to avoid eating meat.

Though the moral public is not uniformly vegetarian, she might or might not want to blame those who aren't. She might be unsure whether her position is morally right, yet decide a vegetarian diet is more morally comfortable for her since she prefers not to risk wrongful action. Others live by their own lights, however, and the moral convictions vary. Though the vegetarian believes she is duty-bound, she is reluctant to universalize the duty and apply blame. A second sort of counterexample, stronger than the first, is the following: suppose Saint Francis of Assisi felt obliged to preach to the birds and believed this to be his obligation alone. Urmson discusses this example and allows that a saint or hero may "regard himself as being obliged to act as he does," but, "though he might say to himself that so to act was a duty, he could not say so beforehand to anyone else, and no one else could ever say it."[21] Urmson elaborates his point by picturing Saint Francis troubled by self-reproach for having hitherto failed to fulfill what he has just come to believe to be his obligation of preaching to the birds. Saint Francis might have urged others to preach to them, but even he would not have blamed anyone for not doing so, Urmson says. And no one could reproach Saint Francis for not doing so either, since "he alone can call such an action of his a duty."[22]

While Urmson's discussion of this example is helpful, it has a serious flaw: he blurs the distinction between a person who acts in a supererogatory manner and a person who conscientiously acts in accord with a duty he or she does not have. Consider a man who thought (wrongly) that it was his duty to convince people to repent of their sins before the imminent end of the world. Though he has no such duty, he runs about diligently acting from his nonduty. Though these characters are seldom treated in moral philosophy, they surely abound. Their actions may not be immoral; they may do no harm. They are irrational or mistaken or just bothersome. But whatever we say of such characters, they are not to be identified with persons who go beyond the duty they do have. The distinction is bolstered by the additional possibility of misguided souls who go above and beyond their nonduty, exceeding a duty they do not have. How are we to distinguish Saint Francis from the person who acts on a nonduty? Does Saint Francis really have the duty to preach to the birds or doesn't he? To reply that he does if he thinks he does makes him indistinguishable from the prophet of doom; and what sort of a duty is it if he can't be held accountable for it?

A way of strengthening the Saint Francis example is suggested by G. R. Grice in his book, *The Grounds of Moral Judgment.*[23] He introduces the term *ultra obligation* to refer to those genuine moral obligations that are beyond our basic obligations and apply only to special persons. Whereas Urmson would say that Saint Francis had no obligation to preach to the birds though he believed he did, Grice would say that Saint Francis had no basic obligation to preach to the birds, but he may have had an ultra obligation to do so. The difference is more than terminological for Grice, for he goes on to demonstrate that basic and ultra obligations have different grounds. Ultra obligations arise for those persons whose fulfillment requires devoting part of their lives to others. Different people find personal fulfillment in different modes of life, and the adoption of a mode of life reflects our nature and imposes obligations. As Grice says, "When a man's fulfillment consists in the devotion of his own capacities to the interests of others, the judgment that he ought to adopt this life is one of ultra obligation."[24] Saint Francis, therefore, being the sort of person he was and choosing the mode of life he did, had an ultra obligation to preach to the birds. Supererogation thus becomes action from ultra obligation, and the Kantian principle is saved: supererogatory acts do have moral worth only because they spring from duty. By redescribing supererogation as action above and beyond basic duty and in accord with ultra duty, Grice has accounted for the sense of being obliged that saints and heroes sometimes report and has shown the source of the moral worth of their actions.

Although I find Grice's position attractive in many respects, I have doubts about whether it does justice to the psychological facts in at least some supererogatory actions. I think there are many cases of supererogation in which the agent does not feel obliged in any way—whether by basic or ultra obligations. The act is freely done; it is gratuitous; and that is a distinctive part of its moral character. Sending a bouquet of flowers to a friend is a giving of gifts; knowing that the sender was not obliged to do this is part of the joy of receiving them. If the recipient learns that the sender felt duty-bound, the quality of the act is spoiled. Similarly with some significant moral actions: to say that the saint acts in a saintly manner out of a sense of nonuniversalizable, ultra duty, serves to rob the saint of his or her peculiar saintliness. The fact that a sacrifice is freely given, done out of affection or respect or whim that reveals personality, is part of the distinctive character of supererogation — at least in some classic cases. The gratuitous aspect of the act may, I believe, augment its moral value. Here we turn back again to criticize Kant's principle, for, if I am right, the moral worth of this sort of action may derive from its *not* having been done from duty.

We have to be careful at this point about confusing the evaluations of the act, the agent, and the agent's motive. An ethic of principles quite naturally evaluates an act by its conformity to those principles, and proper motives are the desire to act in accord with the principles and thereby do what is right. But this motive to act from duty and according to principle may not be as healthy as some deontologists would lead us to believe. Michael Stocker has addressed this point beautifully in a recent article titled, "The Schizophrenia of Modern Ethical Theories."[25] I quote one of his examples at length:

> . . . Suppose you are in a hospital, recovering from a long illness. You are very bored and restless and at loose ends when Smith comes in once again. You are now convinced more than ever that he is a fine fellow and a real friend — taking so much time to cheer you up, traveling all the way across town, and so on. You are so effusive with your praise and thanks that he protests that he always tries to do what he thinks is his duty, what he thinks will be best. You at first think he is engaging in a polite form of self-deprecation, relieving the moral burden. But the more you two speak, the more clear it becomes that he was telling you the literal truth: that it is not essentially because of you that he came to see you, not because you are friends, but because he thought it his duty, perhaps as a fellow Christian or Communist or whatever, or simply because he knows of no one more in need of cheering up and no one easier to cheer up.
>
> Surely there is something lacking here — and lacking in moral spirit or value.[26]

Acts of love, friendship, fellow-feeling, affection, and a sense of community, are beyond our basic moral duties. To carry them out dutifully is to treat the people involved impersonally, as "other persons" in the abstract. Acts done from duty reveal only that we are dutiful and moral in a narrow house-rules sense. There are other worthy virtues, of course, and these can be evinced in action that is gratuitous.

One way of summarizing this discussion is to say that neither deontological nor teleological theories account for supererogation. The basic difficulty is with all principled theories of morality. There is a category of actions which we know to exist (the supererogatory) and which we can only define within a principled ethic as "above and beyond duty." But then we have no convincing way to track the moral worth of those actions. Once one takes the perspective of an ethic of personal virtues,[27] that class of actions becomes more understandable (supererogatory actions are expressions of laudable virtues, of character — often extraordinary expressions). Perhaps at that point the term *supererogation* can be discarded. An ethic of virtue tends to see saintly and heroic actions not in relation to duty, but as manifestations of marvelous and unique characters,[28] finding fulfillment, as Grice would have it, in a distinctive mode of life.

III

Let me begin this section by setting out several features of supererogatory acts in summary form:

1. Supererogation includes acts that exceed our moral duties, meritorious nonduties, and permissions to others to fall short of their duties.
2. These acts have moral worth derived from moral values other than the requiredness of the acts.
3. Many of these acts are extraordinary, going beyond our normal expectations in being excessively dangerous or self-sacrificial. This is the heroic and saintly dimension of supererogation.
4. Some of these acts reflect ultra obligations, special duties one imposes on oneself by accepting a mode of life as fulfilling.
5. Many of these acts are freely given, neither obliged nor coerced nor done out of principle, but springing from one's sense of value.

There is yet another feature that is often associated with saintly and heroic acts — moral style. It is possible to be moral in a ponderous and graceless way in which right action calls attention to itself and is accomplished only with considerable stress and ill effect. It is also possible to act morally in a graceful, artful way, in a manner that may seem effortless to others. The Greeks certainly built something of this ideal into the concept of *arete* ("virtue"), and Aristotle applied it to his *phronimos*, the man of practical wisdom who does the right thing at the right time in the right way.[29] Glenn Gray, in *The Promise of Wisdom*, writes: "Morality without imagination is humorless, dull, and all too likely to produce immorality in those closely associated with it."[30] I suppose one might think of this matter of style as a special case of the extraordinary element — an extraordinariness of sensitivity and imagination. The impression of morality as a set of onerous constraints, a collection of rules which run contrary to the natural inclinations of human beings, a set of noble burdens to be shouldered — a view propagated since the Stoics — is not the whole story. Supererogatory actions can reveal moral springs that flow naturally within us and are not a mere attempt to follow some rule or moral duty. To elevate moral style is to celebrate our moral sensitivity and imagination; duty may prescribe a single action on a specific occasion, but there are an infinite number of supererogatory actions possible if one is sensitive to circumstance and person and imaginative about one's response.

By now the prevalence of aesthetic terms in this section is overwhelming: style, grace, sensitivity, imagination. They suggest a comparison which I shall characterize as a heuristic simile: morality as an art form.

When I say that morality is an art form, I mean that it may be engaged in more or less skillfully, that it involves an interplay between the gratuitous or spontaneous and the controlled, that it entails a sense of form, and that it permits the development of style. If being moral were simply a matter of adjusting one's behavior to conform to a set of rules and institutionalized exceptions, one could characterize the moral almost mechanically. But there is more to being moral than following the house rules. Feinberg seems well aware of this when he writes: "The better part of wisdom is a kind of knack or flair which cannot be bottled up in simple formulas."[31] Supererogatory acts of course give primary evidence that the moral spirit cannot be confined to obligations; there is room for creativity in moral action. How does one learn an art? Of course there are basic, sound rules to learn and apply faithfully. The primary mode of learning, however, is through imitation. If we would learn practical wisdom, we apply the Golden Mean, says Aristotle, as a *phronimos* would apply it. We have the benefit of many models — the saints and heroes whose supererogatory actions show us not only adherence to duty under trying circumstances, not only actions devolving from ultra obligations, but spontaneous and unselfconsciously moral deeds that exemplify character in rich and striking ways.[32]

NOTES

1. Paul Edwards, ed., *Encyclopedia of Philosophy* (New York: Macmillan & Free Press, 1967), for instance, contains no entry for *supererogation* in its index. Acts of supererogation are by definition anomalous in one sense of that word; they are deviations from the commonly expected, from the normal rule or order.

2. My summary is drawn from an account by Reinhold Seeberg in *The New Shaff-Herzog Encyclopedia of Religious Knowledge* (1911), which is quoted in Joel Feinberg, "Supererogation and Rules," *International Journal of Ethics* 71 (1961): 276–88; reprinted in *Ethics*, ed. Judith Jarvis Thomson and Gerald Dworkin (New York: Harper & Row, 1968), pp. 391–411, n. 10. Pagination in succeeding references to the Feinberg essay is from the Thomson and Dworkin volume.

Feinberg goes on to discuss the problems of distributive justice posed by these escrowed merits: should they be distributed equally, or to those that most deserve them, or to those most in need of them, or should they perhaps be distributed so as to maximize salvation?

3. This is the gist of the entries for the term in small dictionaries.

4. J. O. Urmson, "Saints and Heroes," in *Essays in Moral Philosophy*, ed. Abraham Irving Melden (Seattle, Wash.: University of Washington Press, 1958), pp. 198–216; reprinted in *Moral Concepts*, ed. Joel Feinberg (New York: Oxford University Press, 1970), pp. 60–73. The pagination in succeeding references is from the Feinberg volume.

5. Urmson, "Saints and Heroes," pp. 62, 65. Urmson says that this characterization captures "the hero or saint, heroic or saintly deed, *par excellence*."

6. Feinberg, "Supererogation and Rules," pp. 391–411.

7. Ibid., p. 393.

8. Ibid., p. 391. In the same paragraph, Feinberg elaborates: "The fundamental error . . . is to treat what are essentially *non*institutional facts as if they were some kind of *special* institutional facts."

9. Roderick M. Chisholm, "Supererogation and Offence," *Ratio* 5 (1963): 1–14; reprinted with subtitle in Thomson and Dworkin, *Ethics*, pp. 412–29. The pagination in succeeding references is from the latter volume.

10. Ibid., p. 424. Chisholm complicates and confuses his account later in the article when he notes parenthetically that there are also cases of supererogatory nonperformance. These are acts which it is good not to do and neither good nor bad to do. He says: "People not demanding their rights provide us with obvious cases of supererogatory nonperformance" (p. 425). At this point there is no basis given by Chisholm for calling both types "supererogatory." These are both acts which are not obligatory, not forbidden, and not morally neutral; but so are what Chisholm calls "offences." Moreover, I find Chisholm's example dubious: why is it obviously good not to demand one's rights?

11. David A. J. Richards, *A Theory of Reasons for Actions* (New York: Oxford University Press, 1971).

12. Ibid., pp. 103, 196ff. Richards seems to waver between saying the contractors would be *required* to follow these principles and saying they would be *encouraged* to act in accordance with them.

13. Ibid., p. 198. This particular quotation refers to the Principle of Civility, but similar remarks are made for the others. The Principle of Beneficence, however, is an exception: compliance with it justifies praise, but there is no blame for noncompliance. Richards's distinction between supererogatory and other moral principles turns on the difference between coercion and "informal criticism, rebuke, and blame." There are borderline cases: consider the practice of "shunning" used in some religious communities.

14. See Burton M. Leiser, *Custom, Law, and Morality* (Garden City, N.Y.: Doubleday, 1969), for a discussion of the differences between the moral and the customary. Whether these points of view have common sources is not at issue here, and admittedly the lines of demarcation are not always sharp.

15. Morality and custom may be hopelessly entangled in a basic social institution like marriage, but one is not likely to confuse the etiquette of placing the silverware on the table in certain positions with moral prescriptions against murder.

16. Feinberg, "Supererogation and Rules," pp. 397ff.

17. Immanuel Kant, *Fundamental Principles of the Metaphysics of Morals*, trans. Thomas Kingsmill Abbott (Indianapolis: Bobbs-Merrill, 1949), sec. 1.

18. Richards might be an exception since he regards his principles of supererogation as establishing requirements, though we have a moral liberty to violate these. On balance, Richards seems to confuse the legal and the moral.

19. Sheldon P. Peterfreund, "Supererogation and Obligation," *The Personalist* 56 (1975): 151–54.

20. Urmson, "Saints and Heroes," pp. 67ff.

21. Ibid., p. 64.

22. Ibid.

23. Geoffrey Russell Grice, *The Grounds of Moral Judgment* (Cambridge: At the University Press, 1967).

24. Ibid., p. 166.

25. Michael Stocker, "The Schizophrenia of Modern Ethical Theories," *Journal of Philosophy* 73 (1976): 453–66.

26. Ibid., p. 462.

27. See William K. Frankena, *Ethics*, 2nd ed. (Englewood Cliffs, N.J.: Prentice-Hall, 1973), pp. 63ff.

28. My wife, Karen, first pointed out the role of an ethic of virtue in my treatment of supererogation.

29. Aristotle, *Nicomachean Ethics* 2; 6.

30. J. Glenn Gray, *The Promise of Wisdom* (New York: Harper & Row, 1968), p. 109. I first saw the phrase "artistry in conduct" in Gray's book, though he does not relate it to supererogation.

31. Feinberg, "Supererogation and Rules," p. 403.

32. An earlier and briefer version of this paper was presented to the Florida Philosophical Association.

PART III

Ethics in a
World Community

9

The Ethics of the Auspicious:
Western Encounter with Hindu Values

JOHN B. CARMAN

The cortege had reached the pyre. . . . Now Shushila began to divest herself of her jewels. . . . She stripped them off quickly, almost gaily. . . . When all her ornaments had been removed except for a necklace of sacred *tulsi* seeds, Shushila held out her slender ringless hands to a priest, who poured Ganges water over them. . . .

To the sound of . . . chanting, she began to walk round the pyre, circling it three times as once, on her wedding day and wearing the same dress, she had circled the sacred fire. . . . The silent crowds stood motionless, and none stirred as the suttee mounted the pyre and seated herself in the lotus posture. She arranged the wide folds of her scarlet dress so as to show it to the best advantage, and then gently lifted the dead man's head onto her lap. . . .

The shadows had begun to lengthen and the day that had once seemed as though it would never end would soon be over — and with it, Shushila's short life. . . . She had been a wife and a queen, had miscarried two children and borne a third who had lived only a few days; and now she had been widowed, and must die. . . . "She is only sixteen —" thought Ash. "It isn't fair. It isn't *fair!*" . . . Perhaps it was the brightness of the torch, or the sound of it as the flames streamed up on the still air, that woke her from the dreamworld. . . . She stared about her, no longer calmly, but with the terrified gaze of a hunted animal. . . .

The boy's hands, guided by the priest, lowered the torch until it touched the pyre near the feet of the dead man. Bright flowers of fire sprang up from the wood and blossomed in orange and green and violet . . . the priest took the brand from him and went quickly to the other end of the pyre and touched it to the logs at the suttee's back. A brilliant tongue of flame shot skyward, and simultaneously the crowd found its voice and once again roared its homage and approval. But the goddess of their worship thrust aside the head on her lap, and now, suddenly, she was on her feet, staring at those flames and screaming—screaming. . . .[1]

Thus does a contemporary British novelist, who spent her first ten years in India and later returned there as the wife of a British military officer, describe *satī* ("suttee"), the immolation of a Hindu princess on her husband's funeral pyre. This crucial midpoint in a long historical novel, *The Far Pavilions*, is set in a princely state in Central India, long after the British had outlawed the custom in the parts of India they directly ruled. It is one example of the lingering memory in Western literature of a Western encounter with Hindu customs in the early nineteenth century. The British East India Company had slowly been building spheres of influence in India that had already started to turn into an empire, and British officials thus became the de facto rulers of India. They preserved as much of the existing law as they could, both Islamic and Hindu, and their general policy was certainly to let each religious community as far as possible continue its own customs. They were however responsible for public order, and they felt the moral outrage of Europeans for whom suttee was either socially encouraged suicide or thinly disguised murder.

In the controversy about suttee there were at least three positions advocated:

1. Conservative Hindu: a hallowed custom expressing the beautiful ideal of a wife faithful to her husband even to death and beyond. Those widows courageous enough to uphold this ideal should be allowed to do so.
2. British and Indian views affected by Protestant evangelical and Enlightenment rationalist positions: a barbaric

custom opposed to both Christian and general human decency. It should be stopped by force, if necessary.

3. Some older British administrators and some moderate Hindus: a mark of the degeneration of latter-day Hinduism, since it is a custom unsanctioned by the most authoritative Hindu scriptures. It will disappear as Hindus become more enlightened and more aware of their own ancient principles, but British officials should not try to stop it by force.

As it turned out it was the second of these alternatives, enforced suppression, that won the day. Yet — possibly for reasons given by the third position — Hindu resistance was not very strong, even though suttee undoubtedly continued occasionally for several years in some outlying areas and in the small states outside British control governed by Hindu princes.

A generation later another British encounter with Hindu customs took place, and this time there was much less dissent from the British decision to stamp out a barbaric custom: that of the *devadāsīs*. These temple dancers, called the "maidservants of God," were regarded by the British and by many educated Indians as prostitutes who compounded their offense against public decency by claiming to live in the service of religion.

In recent times only a few *devadāsīs* have managed to continue their profession in more remote temples and in places under the direct protection of Hindu rulers. By the turn of the twentieth century another issue was developing regarding Hindu women, once again centering on widows. There was growing concern with the harsh lot of child widows in high-caste Hindu homes. These were women whose much older husbands had died before the marriage was consummated or at least before any children were conceived. These young women were shorn of all their finery and compelled to live with shaved heads and plain white garments, often treated like servants at the beck and call of mothers-in-law and sisters-in-law in the joint family home of their deceased husbands. Various efforts were made to provide some form of education for them, and pleas were made that they should be allowed to remarry. Reform with respect to this practice has been gradual and still partial, right up to the present day, especially for higher-caste women most strictly adhering to traditional Hindu customs.

This cluster of customs — the practice of suttee, the role of the *devadāsīs,* the treatment of widows — is so alien to our modern Western conception of ethics and ethical behavior that we tend instinctively to reject them as simply unethical. What that characteristic Western moral judgment misses, however, is a distinctive dimension of the Hindu ethos, the value of auspiciousness. But in order to have any sense at all of how auspiciousness functions as a value in Hindu ethics, it is important to understand first two fundamental categories of Hindu philosophy, the notions of *mokṣa* and *dharma. Mokṣa* ("release") is a path for renouncing the world and attaining eternal salvation. *Dharma,* variously translated as "law," "duty," "religion," or even "truth," specifies the moral, legal, and religious duties of all the groups making up the Hindu hierarchy of castes.

Considering *mokṣa* to be the primary emphasis of Hindus led Albert Schweitzer to conclude that Indian civilization was not concerned with ethics, but was dominated by the attitude of "world and life negation." This consists in one's

> regarding existence as he experiences it in himself and as it is developed in the world as something meaningless and sorrowful, and he resolves accordingly (a) to bring life to a standstill in himself by mortifying his will to live, and (b) to renounce all activity which aims at improvement of the conditions of life in this world.[2]

This is in marked contrast to the concern for ethics, characteristic of European culture.

> Ethics demands of man that he should interest himself in the world and in what goes on in it; and, what is more, simply compels him to action.[3]

Schweitzer admitted that the contrast was not absolute, and he thought that the negative Hindu view of the world was increasingly challenged through Hindu history by its own devotional movements. Moreover, he held up the Indian ideal of spiritual perfection as an example to the West. His own ideal was to combine the monistic and mystical character of the Hindu world view with the world-affirming and ethical character of the Western world view.[4] Even so, it was Schweitzer's sharp contrast that drew upon him the ire of many Western-educated Indians, perhaps because they thought they heard in this distinction an echo of earlier Western criticisms of the Hindu character: that it passively accepted squalor or degradation, or that it actively supported a social system of tremendous inequality, or that it sanctioned expressions of unbridled and even perverse sexuality.

Schweitzer's analysis, however, is of a different kind, based on what we call Indian philosophy, which consists primarily of the metaphysical discussion related to the various ways of securing release from the present imperfect world, and thus is part of what has been called the "extraordinary" rather than the "ordinary" side of Indian culture and religious life. Unlike Buddhists, for whom the primary meaning of *dharma* was the truth leading to enlightenment and *nirvāṇa*, Hindus considered *dharma* in the first place to signify moral conduct in society or the ideal social structure in which such appropriate behavior should take place.

Both Schweitzer and his Hindu critics talked about Hindu ethics as a part of Hindu philosophy. This has made it necessary for many modern Hindu thinkers to try to demonstrate that Hindu philosophy does not have a negative view of the world and that the fundamental ethical principles related to its metaphysical insights provide a creative basis for the moral action of Hindus in the modern world. In classical Hindu thought, however, reflection on *dharma* was in a different sphere than reflection on the path to *mokṣa*. The two were generally treated by quite different groups of scholars. Many treatments of *dharma* by the Hindu jurists acknowledge *mokṣa* as the supreme goal of human life, but the pursuit of *mokṣa* requires different practices and different attitudes from that of *dharma*, which is concerned with the living out of life in the midst of society, especially discharging the responsibility of raising a family and providing for its material needs. It is true that certain common virtues were acknowledged, especially the basic five of telling the truth, refraining from injuring living beings, remaining chaste, not stealing, and non-attachment to possessions. Jains and Buddhists made an easier form of these common virtues the basis of the ethic for lay persons, just as their more severe form was the basis for living as monks and nuns.

Among Hindus, however, these common virtues were practically less important than the responsibility of each group in society and every individual in the group to practice *svadharma*, one's own specific duty reflecting one's own particular nature. Fulfillment of one's *dharma* produces merit (punyā) just as neglect of one's *dharma* produces sin (*pāpa*); and such good and bad results of action (*karma*) have consequences beyond this life, among them the bettering or worsening of one's status in subsequent lives. Sufficient bettering of one's status might bring one to the point of moving beyond societal duties altogether into the ascetic path. Alternatively, one might follow Lord Krishna's advice to Arjuna in the *Bhagavad Gītā*: doing one's own duty without desiring its karmic fruit, both emulating the Lord's free action to maintain the universe and committing oneself to the Lord's gracious love right now in the midst of this present life with its social and ritual obligations. But neither the common idea of accumulating good *karma* nor the familiar teaching of the *Gītā* to move beyond concern with karmic fruits makes it possible to deduce what people of each status and stage of social life should actually do.

The action appropriate for particular groups at particular stages in life is what is taught in the treatises on *dharma* (*dharma-śāstras*). Some of this action can be viewed from other points of view than that of its rightness. Its potential contribution to the quest for *mokṣa* we have already noted, but there are also more material ends, regarded as legitimate ends of human conduct, provided they are kept in the larger framework of *dharma*. The French student of Hindu law, scholar Robert Lingat, has expressed this connection as follows:

> Hindus contrast with *dharma* (which is the good) both *artha* ("the useful") and *kāma* ("the pleasurable"), which also motivate human behavior. Under the heading of *artha* the rule is assured by the measure of profit, the advantage one draws from it; under that of *kāma* the measure is that of the pleasure which is experienced. . . . A rule founded on *dharma* has an authority superior to that founded on *artha*, just as the latter has an authority superior to the one motivated by *kāma*. For Manu (II, 224) wisdom is to be found in a harmonious combination of the three prime motives of human nature.[5]

These treaties on *dharma* recognize that there are four goals of human action. In addition to *dharma* and *mokṣa* there are two others that are most directly connected with this world, with sustaining physical existence and promoting social well-being. One goal is *artha*, which means power and wealth; the other goal is *kāma:* the satisfaction of physical desire. There are separate books on these subjects in which everything is viewed from the standpoint of *artha* or of *kāma*. From the standpoint of *dharma*, accumulating and enjoying wealth and power and enjoying sexual satisfaction are a legitimate and necessary part of human life, but they ought to be subordinated to the requirements of *dharma*. These subordinate realms of *artha* and *kāma* are closely related to that elusive value which is our theme, the value of the auspicious.

The word *auspicious* sounds a little strange and old-fashioned in modern English. At its simplest it seems to mean simply "good luck"; and we sometimes use the expression "an auspicious occasion." The Hindus, however, go much further in their recognition of the auspicious, for every day is divided up into periods of forty-eight minutes, some of which are auspicious time-periods, and others of which are inauspicious or unlucky. Important events should be scheduled to take place at auspicious times, as determined by experts in astrology. These important events include all the life-bringing and life-fulfilling ceremonies of the life cycle. The most important of these ceremonies is the wedding, often called "the auspicious time." The equivalent of our wedding ring, the wedding chain and pendant hung around the bride's neck by the bridegroom, is called "the auspicious chain" (*mangalasūtra*).

Even more distinctive of Hindu society than lucky times and special events, however, is the location of auspiciousness or good luck in certain persons. A woman is auspicious from the time she is married as long as her husband is alive. The red mark in the center of her forehead or in the center parting of her hair is not a caste mark; it is a sign of her auspiciousness. So too are her jewelry and the beautiful colored saris that she wears. It is sometimes said that a Hindu woman *wears* her family wealth — in her jewelry. That is often true, but in a deeper sense we can say that a Hindu wife *is* her family's wealth. She does more than symbolize auspiciousness; she embodies it. The power in her body to produce the next generation and to nurture it is a share of a mysterious and a more than human power. She brings honor to her husband, and she empowers him, making it possible for him to continue his responsibility for the family line.

In earlier times there were at least two special categories of persons who embodied auspiciousness. For different reasons, both have largely disappeared. Both represented on earth the divine beings who are the source of all auspiciousness on earth: the god Vishnu and his wife Lakṣmī, goddess of wealth.

In ancient India the earthly representative of Vishnu was the king or prince, the rajah ruling the territory. He was auspicious during his entire life, and the unlucky times affecting other mortals did not affect him. He gathered wealth and power and distributed wealth with a generous hand. Through his virtue the rains fell as they should and the entire people prospered. It is true that the king's prerogatives concerned this-worldly power and wealth, and that in the social rank of the caste system he acknowledged the superior position of the Brahmins. As a practical matter, moreover, the Brahmin caste shared a near monopoly of learning with the monks of different religious persuasions including the Buddhists and Jains, so that the king was dependent on others for the learning necessary to administer the kingdom. Nevertheless, with respect to the good things of this earthly life, the king was supreme. He was auspiciousness incarnate.

I use the past tense, for the many centuries of Muslim rule over large parts of India greatly reduced both the political powers and the symbolic pomp of Hindu kings. And now in independent democratic India the rajahs and maharajahs are considered an anachronism, a mere memory of a bygone age.

The other exceptional manifestation of the auspicious was the *devadāsī*. The distinctiveness of the temple dancer is that she has no human marriage. She is symbolically married to the god represented in the temple, and as the king is an earthly representative of the god Vishnu so she is an earthly representative of the goddess Lakṣmī.

A recent study of one of the last remaining groups of temple dancers — at the great temple of Vishnu called Jagannāth in the city of Puri in Orissa — has been made by Dr. Frédérique Marglin, who now teaches anthropology at Smith College.[6] Dr. Marglin gained the confidence of the *devadāsīs* because she is herself an accomplished performer of classical Indian dance, having been a dancer before she became an anthropologist. Dr. Marglin has discovered much that is important not only in understanding the *devadāsīs* but in understanding the importance of the auspicious. Because the *devadāsīs* have a divine "husband" they can never become widows. Hence, like the king, they are permanently auspicious; and, whereas widows are thought to bring bad luck to auspicious occasions, *devadāsīs* bring good luck through their presence and especially through the songs they sing.

Most modern students of Indian society have paid little attention to the auspicious. They have either seen it as a primitive remnant of good luck signs, or they have taken it, as I did for many years, as an expression of the central principle of *dharma*, which is purity. The *devadāsīs*, however, rank low on the scale of *dharma*. As "fallen women" without husbands and families they are manifestly impure. On the scale of auspiciousness, however, they rank very high. Once Dr. Marglin had seen that in this instance purity and auspiciousness did not go together, her eyes were opened for the many other situations in traditional Hindu life where the rank of purity, which is in the realm of *dharma*, and the rank of auspiciousness, which is in the realm of *artha* and *kāma*, diverge.

In my study of some villages in South India more than twenty years ago[7] I had not seen any distinction between the impure and the inauspicious, but I had noticed that there were two opposites to this negative state: auspiciousness and caste-transcending liberation. I still think that for many Hindus the pure and the auspicious are closely related or even merged in their notion of the sacred or holy. The South Indian conception of Vishnu as the supreme Lord and ultimate Godhead closely relates the notions of pure and auspicious in listing the personal qualities of God. Good fortune in its transcendent form merges into the divine purity, and similarly the auspiciousness with which Brahmins are very much concerned tends to be included in their own notion of the pure life in accordance with *dharma*.

Nevertheless there are certain clear distinctions between the pure and the auspicious. The auspicious is concerned with fertility, renewal, and enlargement of life and wealth, while the pure is negatively the absence of organic products of the body and positively the maximum presence of the highest element of material nature: *sattva*. The negative notion certainly gives the emotional tone: the avoidance of polluting substances, things, and persons; while the positive gives the basis for a permanent hierarchy of social groups based on the relative amount of *sattva* in the nature of each group.

Ceremonies at birth and at puberty are auspicious but impure. The wedding ceremony is auspicious and pure, and is filled with royal symbolism, which agrees with the special status of the royal family as embodiments of auspiciousness and free from impurity or pollution. The funeral, on the other hand, is both inauspicious and polluting. The widow, like the ascetic, is pure but inauspicious, but her purity of life (fasting, eating only pure foods, and chastity) has been thrust upon her by bad fortune, whereas the ascetic has freely chosen to break with fertility, prosperity, and well-being in the family circle. An out-caste woman whose husband is living, on the other hand, is normally auspicious even though impure by nature and polluting by her husband's presence. The *devadāsī* is impure because of her sexual relations outside of human marriage but is extraordinarily auspicious because she is married to a divine husband who will never leave her widowed. She avoids contact with illness, death, and ancestor worship, but blesses with her auspicious presence and her singing all life-cycle ceremonies except those connected with death.

The *devadāsī* is a symbol of kingship, which draws its power from its link with the goddess of the earth. In his coronation ceremony the king symbolically marries Bhūdevī, goddess of the earth, and by symbolically uniting with the earth makes it fertile. In Puri the king is called a "walking Vishnu" (in contrast to the stationary image of Vishnu in the great temple of Jagannāth) after this coronation ceremony. He is the householder *par excellence* who supports those at other stages of life. He is inferior to his Brahmin priests on the scale of purity and must prostrate himself before them, but on the scale of auspiciousness he stands supreme. He may gratify his physical desires beyond the limit of ordinary mortals and possesses power and wealth as his due. The military side of that power he owes to the grace of Durgā, the goddess born of the gods' wrath to fight the buffalo demon. The power of fertility is linked to the earth and also to the lifegiving waters, and the power of wealth is linked to Lakṣmī, the goddess of auspiciousness.

The ancient Indian theory of the three strands of material nature once explained the Brahmins' superior purity as the predominance of *sattva* in their constitution, yet the theory may itself hint at a very early recognition of other values than purity and impurity. There are three strands, not two, and while the strand of *tamas* might seem to be the direct opposite of the pure strand of *sattva*, the middle strand of *rajas* ("passion"), dominant in the warrior caste, is not an opposite but a different kind of quality. From the Brahmin's standpoint, passion is inferior to purity and binds the passionate person to the material world. From the standpoint of the warrior caste, however, passion (*rajas*) is an essential ingredient of life and the quality it is their privilege to embody in double measure.

I have appended a diagram with three concentric boxes, representing three circles of value in Hindu life and thought. The inner circle is well-being in the present temporal world, called *saṁsāra*. This corresponds to the ancient Roman notion of the *saeculum:* it is of this world. But it is not secular in the modern Western sense, for it is filled with powers that either aid worldly well-being or threaten it. For most Hindus the most significant ritual events take place in this sphere, and the central ritual is marriage, the auspicious rite (*mangala*). Economics and politics are in this sphere, both included in the single concept of *artha*, for the power to rule and the fruit of rule are closely connected. Every householder tries to amass wealth, and as long as he lives his wife is the concrete embodiment of auspiciousness.

The middle circle represents the hierarchy of caste structure arranged according to the Brahmin's scale of values, in which the pure element of matter (*sattva*) ranks highest and may be considered a link to a higher purity that transcends material nature altogether. This is the sphere in which *dharma* takes precedence over *artha* and *kāma*, and in which *karma* may be accumulated to better one's lot on the same scale of *sattva-rajas-tamas* in the next existence. A person's purity on this scale is relatively fixed for the present lifetime, but it is possible to follow a more ritually pure (that is, more Brahmanic) lifestyle than is the norm for one's caste. Such relative purity of life will bring great karmic reward.

The outer circle is concerned with purity in a more radical sense. Purity for one who has renounced life in society goes in

Mokṣa contradicting *dharma* and excluding *artha* and *kāma*. Renunciation (*sannyāsa*) of society and pursuit of liberation (*mokṣa*).

Temporal Purity

Hierarchy of caste structure based on preponderance of pure matter (*sattva*) over passionate matter (*rajas*) and dull, heavy matter (*tamas*).

Temporal Auspiciousness

"Good luck" or well-being in the present temporal world symbolized in the wedding (*mangala*), in married women whose husbands are living, in the king or prince.

Pursuit and enjoyment of wealth and power (*artha*).

Satisfaction of physical desires (*kāma*).

The Brahmin higher than the king or the wealthy merchant. All three higher than artisans or laborers.

Dharma takes precedence over *artha* and *kāma*.

Each caste has its own specific duties (*svadharma*), fulfilling which helps one attain purer material bodies higher in the caste scale in future lives.

Seeking liberation in the midst of society through detachment from worldly goals. *Mokṣa* including *dharma* and transforming *artha* and *kāma*.

principle beyond all the strands of material nature, even its purest strand of *sattva*.

Such indeed is the theory behind the shocking reversal of worldly values dramatized by some early Hindu ascetics, who flaunted the laws of pollution by living in graveyards and using human skulls. In fact much Hindu asceticism in recent centuries has been less radical, making a more positive link with the purified lifestyle of Brahmins and others. In the devotional movements, moreover, auspiciousness as well as purity has been concerned with a transcendent dimension, which links in symbolism the well-being of the temporal world with the overflowing riches of God. In such thinking the category of *kāma* moves from the lowest human aspiration to the highest, a transformed desire, no longer for a human partner but for the Divine Spouse, and a transformed attachment, no longer to material things but to the Divine Lord.

These three distinct circles of value seem to me clearly present in the Hindu perception of social reality even though the ranking of the circles is less clear and may vary from group to group and especially from circumstance to circumstance. This multivalent perception may make it easier for the Hindu in the modern world to add another circle, the values of Western modernity, even when such values seem in conflict with traditional attitudes.

Part of our Western difficulty in understanding the various institutions related to auspiciousness comes from the subordination of auspiciousness to other categories by the intellectual representatives of the Hindu tradition: Brahmins and ascetics. Understanding auspiciousness is certainly important to our more adequate comprehension of the complex Hindu scheme of values. But does it make sense to talk about the ethics of auspiciousness if this is an area of symbolic behavior and intuitive feelings rather than of moral reasoning? We tend to give the name "ethics" not to some bundle of indistinct values but to a clearly articulated system of moral reasoning. We might go further and ask how the category of "good luck" could conceivably be part of ethics, Western or Hindu.

Such questions are important in recent efforts at developing comparative ethics, but they are far away from the specific situations with which we began. The emotional power of those controversies came in part because they spoke to a visceral level of moral values in the *Western* participants, values considered to be embodied in women even if they are not articulated by women. In fact, both Western women and Hindu women were involved in the discussion of at least the second and third controversies, and the slow reform in the social status of Hindu women has been to a considerable extent a reform *by* women. In any case, the Western reactions involved questions of taste and aesthetic appreciation (certainly on the negative pole of distaste and sickening horror). These aesthetic sensibilities may be difficult to put into any moral calculus, yet they need to be perceived by Western students in order to make substantial progress in intercultural understanding. It may be that we *can* use the Hindu category of the auspicious as a curved mirror, distorting yet illuminating, to help us discover some important things about our own implicit values, both where they are surprisingly familiar to Hindu feelings and where they are sharply different. It may be quite important to be aware of values that powerfully motivate people even though they are not consciously articulated, or at least are not incorporated into our self-conscious moral systems. For example, do business executives also worship a goddess of good fortune? Are there values in the worlds of sports and entertainment that we don't include when we think about guides to moral action? Is the accumulation of political power comprehensible on our present moral map?

All these questions presume a limited but significant goal for comparative ethics: finding a common language that can make comprehensible the diverse moral perceptions and justifications of different cultural and religious traditions. The search for such understanding is important, and it involves hard work and the hard-won recognition that human beings in different cultures live to some extent in different worlds with different systems of values.

If that is all we can any longer hope for in comparative understanding, however, our nineteenth-century forebears would certainly accuse us of timidity and obtuseness. We need to ask ourselves whether we can get close enough to people of another culture to understand them without being involved in some of their moral decisions, and they in ours. We need also to ask ourselves whether the universalism present in our quest for an understanding of all human cultures is separable from the venerable Western quest for a natural law, that is, a moral structure inherent in human nature as such.

The critical question for us, however, is whether the value of the auspicious, still concretely expressed in the lives of contemporary Hindu women, is of legitimate ethical concern for anyone outside the Hindu community. The multivalency of Hindu social ethics reflects an effort to include as many diverse values as possible within a unified system. Moreover, Hindus have not been as limited to the land of India as some of their own traditions suggest, and now in some countries outside India there are large communities of Hindus. How are the value of auspiciousness and the value of caste purity to be regarded by non-Hindu neighbors, in Boston or Birmingham as well as in Banaras or Bombay?

Both the scale of caste purity and the scale of auspiciousness mark persons with a certain rank. On a scale of zero to ten with respect to caste purity the learned Brahmin ranks ten and the untouchable ranks zero. Similarly with respect to auspiciousness the vanishing king and vanishing *devadāsī* rank ten, the normal Hindu wife about eight, and the high-caste widow without children ranks zero. I say high-caste widow, because it is one of the ironies of this framework that it most seriously involves those upholding the Brahmanic *dharma*. Widows in lower castes frequently remarry. It is true that a Brahmin widow may accept her misfortune as divine fate and devote the rest of her life to pious deeds and meditation, becoming a semi-ascetic within the family circle. She does not lose her purity when she loses her auspiciousness; indeed, she is removed from the impurities of sexual involvement and the worldly entanglements of all the emblems of auspiciousness. But such is the power and attractiveness of the auspicious state for Hindu women, including Brahmin women, that the widow's lot is frequently a pitiful one. Not only is she treated by others as being without dignity, but her own sense of worth may be destroyed, especially if she has not attained the status and dignity of being a mother.

Is this a price that must be paid in any hierarchical system? That is a question with which Hindus themselves are dealing, but we have to look critically at what seems to many in the modern West the desirable alternative: not marking persons as embodying or failing to embody values. In some ways traditional Hindu society has been more realistic: the unfair allotment of good luck and bad luck cannot be removed by legislation. Both are recognized in their concrete embodiments in persons. Less and less do

American women celebrate their status as wives and mothers with emblems of good fortune. Many reject that value altogether and see themselves as very low on the value scale of a male-dominated society. The confrontation of values is a fact in the modern world and a matter for continuing concern, not only for widows and orphans and handicapped, but also for those whose family roles are being robbed of meaning by the business and professional values of the modern world.

I confess that when I became interested in comparative ethics I thought it was a field that might admit of more rapid progress to eventual consensus than is possible in religion and theology. Alas, natural law is as hard to determine as divine law, and indeed in many cultures there is little to distinguish them. Presiding over the secular sphere of material well-being and "good luck," Hindus believe, are the same deities whose grace is requisite for progress toward final salvation. The domain of auspiciousness is a human reality that points beyond itself to a mysterious realm from which all our good fortune comes, but also to which we must turn when our good fortune fails.

For millions of Hindus the deepest meaning of *satī* is neither that of a horrific rite nor that of a romantic ideal. Satī is the name of a goddess, a wife of the great Lord Śiva who committed suicide when her father, Dakṣa, failed to invite her unkempt husband Śiva to the Vedic sacrifice. Widows who commit *satī* ("suttee") identify themselves with the goddess Satī. Both the suttee and the *devadāsī* escape the usual state of the inauspicious widow. The suttee remains auspicious by staying with her husband even in death, hoping for another lifetime of auspicious living with him in their next incarnation. The *devadāsī* remains auspicious by foregoing the security of a human husband and a normal human family. She is symbolically married to Lord Vishnu and thus is identified with the Divine Consort of Vishnu. She, too, at a heavy price escapes the usual fate of a woman: widowhood.

Both the suttee and the *devadāsī* are "limit cases" that teach us something about the value of auspiciousness for Hindu women, and for Hindu society as a whole. The nineteenth-century British reaction was to suppress both of these unusual Hindu institutions on the grounds of their immorality. For traditional Hindus both practices transcended the usual morality of caste purity and opened up a vista of an eternal divine realm in which the time-bound auspiciousness of the Hindu wife merges with the transcendent beauty and plenitude of the Divine Wife. Today most Hindus would regard such breaking of moral limits as attempted shortcuts from human society to the divine community that ignore the ordering wisdom of the Hindu tradition. Yet Hindus have thus far preserved their sense of the auspicious, a concentration of well-being in certain events and certain persons, a value that shines through but goes beyond the human realities of luck, power, wealth, and physical beauty, because it is rooted in a divine reality: the gracious form of the Divine Consort, which is also the mutual love of the Divine Couple.

NOTES

1. M. M. Kaye, *The Far Pavilions* (New York: St. Martin's Press, 1978), pp. 776–80.

2. Albert Schweitzer, *Indian Thought and Its Development*, trans. Mrs. Charles E. B. Russell (New York: H. Holt, 1936), pp. 1–2.

3. Ibid., p. 8.

4. Ibid., pp. 9–10.

5. Robert Lingat, *The Classical Law of India*, trans. J. Duncan M. Derrett (Berkeley: University of California Press, 1973), p. 5.

6. Frédérique Apffel Marglin, *Wives of the God-King: Rituals of Hindu Temple Courtesans* (Ph.D. dissertation, Brandeis, 1980).

7. John B. Carman and P. Y. Luke, *Village Christians and Hindu Culture* (London: Lutterworth Press, 1968).

10

Ethics and Mysticism

STEVEN T. KATZ

ETHICS AND MYSTICISM, we are told more often than not, are un-related, even antithetical. This common wisdom is predicated on a specific understanding of morality and a flawed, though wide-spread, conception of mysticism and mystical traditions. It is yet another manifestation of the misunderstanding that mystics are essentially arch-individualists who struggle against their traditions in order to find some sort of personal liberation or salvation. Ac-cordingly, mystics are seen as rebels and heretics, antinomians and spiritual revolutionaries, if not also political subversionists and underminers of existing social and religious structures.

Unfortunately this image is incorrectly drawn. In this essay, I cannot argue all the detailed reasons why this understanding is simply incorrect, but I will offer this: mystics share both the ontological problem and its solutions with their particular tradi-tions. They are fully situated in the metaphysical, theological, and social contexts of their traditions.[1] Essentially, they share the *Welt-anschauung* of their inherited circumstance, seeking existentially to realize the solutions proposed by the tradition; that is, they accept the general analysis of the ontic predicament of their com-munity and seek to actualize, in their own lives, the ways out of the predicament recommended by the same tradition. For exam-ple, Christian mystics seek an existential encounter with Christ as the solution to sin and alienation; kabbalists search after *deve-kuth* as the solution to the world's fragmentation; Buddhists seek nirvana as the haven from suffering (*dukkha*) and rebirth; Hin-dus look for "Ātman and Self" as the release from *saṁsāra* and transmigration. When the Christian mystics encounter Jesus or the Virgin they do not overthrow Christian tradition but confirm it. Kabbalists are staunchly conservative; Buddhists who attain nirvana and Hindus who achieve *"Brahman is Ātman"* affirm the correctness of the Buddhist and Hindu analyses of reality, respectively. The complex meditation, study, and teaching, and communal, doctrinal, metaphysical, epistemological, theological, and social structures involved in these and like mystical traditions all draw on their respective traditions and serve to reinforce them. Indeed they are shaped by these inherited circumstances in absolutely fundamental ways.

This reconsideration of what relation mystics and mystical traditions bear to their larger religious environment is necessary in order to set the stage for a more adequate understanding of the specific subject of this essay: the relationship of ethics and mysticism. For just as mystics are not religiously anarchic or theologically anomic, so too they are not morally indifferent or worse. As a simple historical observation, it is difficult to find any major mystics, or mystical traditions, that can be said to preach moral indifference; and certainly none preach immorality. (I am allowing here for the range of different understandings of morality that exist across religious traditions from Judaism and Christianity to Hinduism and Taoism, and whose variety is not in any way unique to the mystical components or practitioners of these traditions.) This in itself should be, at least, cause for caution. Hypothetical structures or convoluted analyses should be checked against the evidence, and there is little of it that would support a view like that of Arthur Danto as to the unconnectedness of the two domains.

It is, on closer inspection, not at all surprising that mysticism and morality are neither antithetical nor unrelated. In all the major mystical traditions, morality does count positively — in one way or the other, depending on the peculiar structure of the particular tradition — in achieving the mystical goal, whatever it happens to be. (Beware the illusion that they are all the same!)

One further, brief, preliminary remark is required. By *morality* in this essay I do not mean any specific moral system or moral tradition, such as Kantian or utilitarian, Christian or Buddhist. Rather, I want to allow for the varieties of the traditions to exist simultaneously, recognizing the larger context in which they operate and from which they draw their meaning. However, I deny the strong Kantian position that values actions as having moral worth only if they flow from a disinterested, autonomous, ethical will, which seems to me overly narrow as a definition and criterion of ethical behavior. I would argue that an act can be morally significant whatever its intentions. Thus, seeing moral actions as part of a theological frame of reference does not disqualify them as worthy moral acts. It should be noted in this connection that even Kant needed to introduce God as the "highest perfection" into his ethical system.[2] If "impartial rational agents"— allowing for the ambiguity and difficulty with this Kantian-Rawlsian phrase — would approve of an action as moral, regardless of the motive of the actor, the act is fairly said to be an ethical act.

I

Let us begin by considering the Buddhist case, which is usually cited as a paradigm of moral unconcern and otherworldly indifference.[3] For example, according to Arthur Danto, "Buddhism qualifies as a religion . . . because of this: . . . its moral relevance is uncertain."[4] As a consequence of this judgment, Danto feels able to conclude his discussion of Buddhist ethics or non-ethics by commenting: "This is not to say that Buddhism is lacking in moral rules. It is only that they are not internal to the theory of Buddhism."[5]

This statement, which touches upon the extrinsic character of ethics in Buddhism, is, in fact, the key to his critique. That is, the essence of his conclusion lies in his claim that the search for nirvana is one thing, while concern for one's fellows is another. But is this correct? Is this analysis even operating within the correct conceptual framework?

In the Eightfold Path which is the route out of the saṁsāra world, steps one to three are: "right speech," right action," and "right livelihood." These are, or at least clearly entail, what on any account would constitute moral action. It is true that they are the first three rather than the last three steps on the ladder (which are "right understanding," "right aspiration," and "right effort"), but they are also quite clearly not extrinsic to the attainment of nirvana. That is to say, moral action is integral to the

Buddhist quest and its attainment. Unless one crosses up and through these first three rungs, all of which deal with how we should treat one another, the higher levels of consciousness and spiritual attainment remain always distant shores. The essence of understanding this lies in appreciating that for Buddhism ethical action as intentional action reflects back upon consciousness *per se*. Thus in order to purge one's consciousness of its imprisoning ignorance one has to purge all one's actions — and certainly one's moral actions — of misunderstanding. Immoral behavior is ignorance and further binds consciousness in the chains of ignorance, a condition antithetical to liberation.

As a consequence, moral action, rather than being unconnected to the achievement of nirvana, is essential to it. It is one of the inherent modalities involved in the transformation of consciousness; without it this transformation in its completeness is unattainable. The epistemological, metaphysical, and ethical here coalesce; the achievement of any one is interconnected and interdependent with the other two. Hence ethical correctness is a form of epistemological and metaphysical awareness, while ethical action in turn encourages and reinforces the epistemic and metaphysical. One might reduce the idea to its skeleton thus: right action is wisdom and wisdom is nirvana. Or, inverted, one cannot do what is correct unless one knows what is correct; hence again the dialectic of consciousness and morality is emphasized and ineluctable.

The connection of a correct analysis of reality and morality prompts another, related, consideration. Buddhism is founded upon and grounded in what it considers the correction of an epistemological-ontological error; its most radical and basic claim is that there are no permanent selves, that the essence of Hinduism, the metaphysical doctrine of "*Ātman is Brahman*," is quite simply wrong. The Hindu metaphysical account rather than liberating only ties human beings more tightly to the wheel of rebirth and suffering. In contradistinction, the Buddha's basic truth is that there is no self, the thesis of *anattā*. The metaphysical corollary is that all attachments cause suffering because attachments are rooted in a false self-love, a false craving for the satisfaction of the desires of a self that, in reality, does not exist. False egoism is the essential epistemic-*cum*-ontic illusion. The ethical corollary is this: non-ethical behavior also derives from this mistaken analysis of the ontological situation, this desire to assert the self at the expense of others. As a consequence, ethical action is to be seen as a necessary corollary of a correct realization of "no-self"; while ignorance of "no-self" leads to and reinforces both ethical misbehavior and metaphysical entrapment. Here again, ethics is inseparably ontology and ontology is inseparably ethics.

The doctrine of *karuṇā* ("compassion") now makes sense. Whether in its Theravāda form or its more magnificent Mahāyāna version, it is a characteristic of Buddhism. One of the *brahmavihāra* ("divine abodes"), it is integral to the accomplishment of enlightenment. The Buddhist is here encouraged to reflect on the inseparability and continuity of all suffering so that there is no final or ontically real separation of my suffering from the suffering of others. The unity of all being, of all consciousness, means a unity of suffering so that true enlightenment can come only when, recognizing this metaphysical truth, one acts to overcome all suffering wherever it might occur. Therefore, we act to prevent and overcome what we would properly call injurious acts of immoral behavior to our fellow human beings as well as to other forms of sentient being, such as animals. That is to say, compassion is a corollary of the ontic doctrine of "no-self" (*anattā*), which in turn eventuates in the moral-metaphysical doctrine of nonviolence (*ahiṃsā*). *Ahiṃsā* is thus the product of enlightened consciousness and the producer of enlightenment, so that to act otherwise is to reveal one's still deluded consciousness as well as to further reinforce such delusions.

If the Theravāda tradition already teaches the importance of the doctrine of *karuṇā*,[6] it is in Mahāyāna that the doctrine reaches its full and paradigmatic status. According to Mahāyāna teaching, *karuṇā*, or, rather, *mahākaruṇā* ("great compassion"), is not only propaedeutic to enlightenment but representative of enlightenment *per se*. Enlightenment according to Mahāyāna (the "greater vehicle") means not only or primarily individual release from the wheel of suffering and rebirth but collective liberation of all sentient reality from its imprisonment. Hence the *bodhisattva*, the ideal of Mahāyāna spirituality, does not enter *parinirvāṇa*, leaving the rest of us behind to struggle on alone with our fate, but continually reenters time and history to help others achieve their redemption — which is redemption of the *bodhisattva* as well.

One can put this formally: to seek one's own release is selfishness and hence to aspire to it is the contradiction of enlightenment. Mahāyāna encourages a profound doctrine of the interdependence of all being and the concern for the release of all being from *saṁsāra*. No Kantian could ask for a more disinterested ethic. No ethicist could ask for a more universal concern. Even Danto is forced to admit: "Selflessness is a metaphysical thesis of Buddhism, not an ethical teaching, though it is transformed into something like that in Mahāyāna."[7] Alternatively, his later objection that this Mahāyāna doctrine doesn't really count as a moral system because it is so idealistic as to be impractical is hardly to be taken as a serious philosophical objection, common as it is to all moral ideals and systems.

What one can thus conclude regarding Buddhism is that, in contradistinction to those who would argue that it is otherworldly in its concerns and amoral in its this-worldly consequences, Buddhism, including Theravāda, is profoundly moral. Its practitioners — the *arhat* and especially the *bodhisattva* — are fundamentally concerned with moral action; and, very importantly, morality is an essential part of both the way and, at least in Mahāyāna, the goal.

I am well aware that many difficulties have been left untouched, and voluminous sources untreated, but in a brief review all one can do is suggest that the view being opposed is neither persuasive nor accurate.

II

Let us consider now a very different mystical tradition by way of comparison: the Christian. Again the charges of moral unconcern are widely found in the existing secondary literature, but they are false. Christian mystics are neither indifferent to morality, nor do they disconnect morality from an intrinsic relationship to their mystical quest — be it union or encounter — with Jesus, the Virgin, or the like. Augustine teaches that the story of Leah

and Rachel is an allegory in which the active life represented by
Leah is intrinsic to the contemplative life depicted by Rachel, while
Gregory the Great asserts: "We ascend to the heights of contem-
plation by the steps of the active life."[8] He defines the active life
as: "to dispense to all what they need and to provide those en-
trusted to us with the means of subsistence."[9] These samples could
be multiplied at great length and almost without exception in the
teaching of the major Christian mystics.[10] This exercise, however,
is both out of place in the present circumstances and, I hope, unnecessary. Instead, the more general issues raised by the place and
significance of morality within the Christian mystical tradition
need our attention.

To begin, the nature of morality *per se* as it is understood
in the Christian mystical tradition must be properly appreciated.
Morality is not an independent reservoir of values; rather, as must
be the case in such a theistic system, morality issues from and
leads back to a divine origination, a divine Originator. Morality
is part of God's Law, a revelation of God's will. To be moral is
to be truthful to God. To be moral is to attune one's will to God's
will. Moral behavior is simultaneously religious behavior; morality is simultaneously piety; acts of morality are simultaneously
acts of obedience. Morality not only creates a social fabric but
also operates, on the metaphysical and theological level, to bring
the individual's will into alignment with God's will, an absolute
precondition for all higher stages of Christian spiritual attainment, especially mystical encounter. The great Christian mystics
are the great Christian subordinators, subordinating themselves
to God's demands. The importance of obedience is striking in Saint
Francis, Eckhart, Tauler, Ruysbroeck, Teresa of Ávila, John of the
Cross, and all their many spiritual disciples. It is this which leads
Ruysbroeck quite typically, in Book III of his *Spiritual Espousals*,
to move from humility to purity through the following progres-
sion: "Humility as the foundation and Mother of Virtues" (chap.
19), "Humility fosters obedience" (chap. 20), "Obedience fosters
denial of our own will" (chap. 21), "Denial of our own will fosters
patience" (chap. 22), "Patience fosters meekness" (chap. 23), "Meekness fosters mercifulness" (chap. 24), "Mercifulness fosters compassion" (chap. 25), "Compassion fosters mildness" (chap. 26),
"Mildness fosters zeal for virtue" (chap. 27), "Zeal for virtue fos-

ters moderation and sobriety" (chap. 28), and finally "Sobriety fosters purity" (chap. 29). He describes purity thus:

> Now you must know that the purity of the spirit preserves man in his likeness to God, undisturbed by creatures, inclined towards God and united with Him. . . . Because a man preserves purity out of love and to the honour of God, so it is made perfect. . . . Purity of heart causes the grace of God to be renewed and increased. In the purity of the heart all virtues are inspired and revealed and contemplated. . . . Purity is . . . a lock to close the heart against earthly things and against all deception, and to open it to heavenly things and to all truth. And therefore Christ says: "Blessed are those who are pure of heart, for they shall see God." In this seeing of God consists our eternal joy and all our reward and the entrance to our blessedness.[11]

This description, of course, is still not of the final ecstasy experienced in the *unio-mystico*, but, as Eckhart in his *Tractate to Sister Katri* notes after the initial essentially moral instruction is given: "To the question: 'Sir, is this the best way?' he [the confessor] will answer, 'No, but what I am telling thee is indispensable.'"[12] That is to say, this moral practice, involving its purificatory aspect, is the common property of Christian mystics. Christian mystics all recognize that the higher stages of the mystical life come about through the channels created by the moral ordering of one's existence. Thus Eckhart, despite or perhaps more correctly because of his ultimate view on the nature of the mystical moment, can teach that union with Christ is impossible "unless the soul is first established in right conduct and cleansed of willful sin."[13] Of course he goes on to say that the disciple must "pass through virtue and transcend all virtues and only receive virtues in the ground of the soul,"[14] but this is an affirmation of morality, not its negation, avoidance, or denigration.

What Eckhart teaches out of his scholastic and neo-Platonic ideology, Teresa of Ávila and John of the Cross teach in their more emotional Spanish environment — all drawing on a common Christian tradition. In *The Way of Perfection* and *The Interior Castle* Teresa makes it plain that no spiritual progress is possible outside of the cleansing and obedience supplied by morality. "Believe me," she tells her faithful in *The Interior Castle*, "what matters is not whether or not we wear a religious habit, it is whether we practice the virtues, and make a complete surrender of our wills to God."[15] Her disciple, John of the Cross, teaches the same doctrine in his *Ascent of Mount Carmel*, especially in chapters 10–12, though it is to be liberally found elsewhere in his corpus. Virtuous action is not, to repeat, sufficient for assuring the ecstatic encounter sought by the mystic, but it is a necessary preamble. Alternatively, we can be sure of this: without strenuous moral activity and achievement no mystical transformation or encounter will ensue.[16] Here the strikingly conservative character of this equation is not to be allowed to pass unnoticed: the same moral discipline that brings salvation in Catholic doctrine also is spiritually required and creative in Catholic mystical circles. Catholic mystics act the same as the ordinary Catholic believer, with moral behavior integral to the achievement of their spiritual welfare. The ethical overcoming of the willfulness that is sin, that willfulness that breaks the bonds of God's relation to humanity, produces salvation in the more traditional sense for ordinary individuals as well as the extraordinary salvation that mystical relation entails. Note too that for both the dynamic principle is the transformation of the conative dimension rather than, as in Buddhism, for example, a transmutation of consciousness.

The reigning paradigm of the Christian life that is here all-important is the imitation of Christ. It is presently impossible to itemize in detail the all-pervasive ways this model acts in Christian life, but one feature stands out and requires comment: it is not surprising that Christian mystics should seek out and act upon moral norms insofar as they are trying to imitate Christ's behavior. Christian mystics, insofar as their entire life is an attempt to replicate the example of Christ — recall, for example, the title of Thomas à Kempis's famous Christian mystical treatise — are intent on being paradigms of morality as their model (Jesus) is a moral paradigm, as well as being, of course, a soteriological, cosmic, and ontological paradigm. "Be generous to one another, tenderhearted, forgiving one another as God in Christ forgave you" (Eph. 5:32). For Christian mystics to be either indifferent to morality or actually immoral would be to impute to their reigning model — Christ — this same indifference or perversity. In emphasizing the dialogical or absorptive aspects of the Christian mystical tradition it is often forgotten, at high cost, that this entire enterprise is propelled by the passion of imitation.[17]

This moral imperative, the high place Christian mystical tradition accords to moral behavior, also finds important instantiation in the significance placed on the moral behavior of mystics after their peak experiences. Mystical behavior, indeed, is one of the standard verificationist principles employed in the tradition to adjudge a claimed experience genuine, God-given, as compared to those that are either false or caused by demons and Satan. Mystical experience and morality here coalesce, the source as well as the guarantor of the latter being the former. It is for this reason that Eckhart can encourage the faithful to allow their mystical experiences to "shine through deeds"[18] and Teresa can advise her nuns: "Be sure of this — when a soul after receiving some of the special favors . . . does not come forth firmly to forgive others and if occasion offers does not pardon any injury . . . the graces never come from God."[19] Jacob Boehme likewise, true to his predecessors, can preach: "The true divine power in man lets itself be seen externally with good works and virtues. Otherwise, there is no faith there, unless the works follow."[20] The converse, of course, also applies. John of the Cross, for example, defines false experiences thus: "The Devil's visions produce spiritual dryness in one's communications with God and an inclination to self-esteem. . . . In no way do they cause mildness of humility and love of God. . . . The memory of them is considerably arid and unproductive of the love and humility caused by the remembrance of good visions."[21]

There is even a special moral texture to this post-mystical-event morality: it has a special quality of selflessness. Now in harmony with God's will it is fully "other-directed" and unconcerned with self. It is described by Teresa and others in ways reminiscent of the Mahāyāna description of the *bodhisattva*.[22]

Morality can thus be seen to lead toward as well as away from the Christian mystical experience *per se*. Moreover, and with some confidence, we can say that without the proper moral attitude and behavior Christian mystical adherents will remain forever mired in their nonmystical state while any claims to have truly experienced the higher mystical bliss will be judged by the mystics' moral actions rather than by their experiential claims.

III

Hinduism, like Buddhism, is a much misconceived tradition in respect of the issues with which we are concerned. Scholars from John McKenzie and Albert Schweitzer to Arthur Danto have seen it as a world-denying faith which has, among other errors, an indifference to moral endeavor.[23] Hinduism, Schweitzer wrote, is a religion in which "world and life negation occupies a predominant position; . . . mysticism of identity, whether Indian or European, is not ethical either in origin or in nature and cannot become so."[24] Before responding to this widely circulated view, I must first note that Hinduism is a "many-splendored thing," that the religion of the *Vedas* is not that of Śankara, nor the "path" of the *Gītā* that of the *Mīmāṁsā Sūtra*. Recognizing this variety we will concentrate our attention primarily on the teachings of the *Upaniṣads* and the *Gītā*.

From this perspective the locus of the essential misunderstanding of Hindu ethics lies in the analysis of the interaction of the doctrines of *karma* and *mokṣa*, that is, the problem and its overcoming in liberation with which most schools of Hinduism, and for our purposes especially the *Gītā* and *Upaniṣads*, are concerned.[25] In Hinduism, as in Buddhism—which of course is its heir and which adopts many of its concerns and approaches— morality is not a separate sphere of human activity but rather an integral part of a more general epistemological and ontological structure. However, to repeat, this stance is not the same thing as moral indifference or inactivity, as has often been suggested.[26] Moral evil is generated by ignorance and does impede the quest for liberation, but this does not reduce its significance; it heightens it. Given the impedimental value of immorality, it is imperative to overcome it in order to make progress toward *mokṣa*. "Not he who has not desisted from evil ways, not he who is not tranquil, not he who has not a concentrated mind, not even he whose mind is not composed can reach this (self) through right knowledge."[27] This is now the "categorical imperative": be ethical in order to achieve transcendence. Ethics is here grounded in knowledge: knowing the real as it truly is leads to overcoming passion and the evil fruits of misplaced passion, especially the assertion of ego, *ahaṅkāra*. Without a proper ontological understanding, morality is impossible, but this requirement in favor of a proper ontological consciousness does not negate morality or make it superfluous. Rather, morality becomes an essential channel through which the ego is harnessed and brought into a disposition which aids rather than hinders the final accomplishment of release. *Sattva suddhi* ("self-perfection") is the realization of one's own moral perfection which is grounded in the ontic identity of self and Brahman.[28] "*Dharma* is *mokṣa* in the making."[29] *Ātman*, the *Muṇḍaka Upaniṣad* teaches, "is attainable by truth, by austerity (*topas*), by right knowledge [*jñāna*], by the constant (practice) of chastity [*brahmacaryeṇa*]."[30]

The claim that the liberated self inhabits a place "beyond good and evil," a much-repeated statement in both the primary sources and the secondary literature, now can be properly understood. In truth the self, free of karmic constraints, is not good or evil, for good and evil are tied, by the rules of the system, to karmic activity. However, there is a connection between the self in *karma* and the Self who transcends it: unless one is ethical, one never acquires *jñāna*, the gnosis that saves.[31] Then again, though not rule-bound, for rules belong in another — a karmic — realm, the liberated self, much as in Western mystical traditions, now in possession of the truth of the interrelationship of all being, acts kindly toward all as a matter of the natural affection of being toward being: "The holy men whose sins are destroyed, whose doubts are cut asunder, whose minds are disciplined and who rejoice in [performing] good to all creatures attain to the beatitude of God" (*Gītā* 5:25). That which selves bound in *karma* perform out of duty, liberated selves perform out of their more correct metaphysical awareness, particularly their awareness of the unity of reality, the unity in which all selves are part of each other. This transcendent consciousness produces action which some might not, for technical reasons arising out of their own definitions and philosophical systems, want to call ethical. But all would have to agree for accuracy's sake that such action is not immoral and is parallel to that enjoined by acknowledged ethical systems. If the liberated self does not steal, hate, envy, seduce, or lie, if it displays infinite compassion, lack of destructive egoism and perfect *ahiṁsā* ("non-violence"), are we to denigrate it as do Hume, Schweitzer, Danto, and others as a negative and nonmoral path? Or rather, does it not make far more sense to see the self in the state of *sthitaprājña*, as it is called in the *Bhagavad Gītā*, or in the state of *jīvan-mukti*, as it is called in Jainism, Buddhism, and yoga systems?[32] This self is "beyond good and evil" primarily in this sense: rather than acting morally owing to external norms and constraints (what we call "good and evil" in usual discourse), the liberated self acts morally as a matter of natural inclination. For such selves being and acting are integrated; knowing the good is synonymous with doing the good. In this sense they transcend karmic morality. In the *Gītā* Kṛṣṇa pronounces: "Although there is not for me any duty to be done in the three worlds, nor anything to be obtained which has not been obtained, yet I am engaged in work" (*Gītā* 3:22).

Before taking leave of Hinduism, it is imperative to emphasize its rejection of the view that the quest for *mokṣa* is equivalent to inactivity. The words from the *Gītā* just cited indicate this fact. More generally, it can be said that to equate the quest for self-perfection with passivity is simply an error. Perfection is not inactivity; rather, it is activity perfectly informed and performed. The only school that preaches inactivity is Advaita Vedānta,[33] and even that doctrine must be qualified in this sense: Advaita advises inactivity only for those who have achieved *mokṣa*, but in order to achieve this exalted state it is necessary to perform one's *dharma* with great care. Then, again, this inactivity of the liberated is not to be confused with immorality, with *adharma*.

IV

Before offering some general conclusions, I would like to consider briefly the relation of morality to mysticism manifest in the Jewish mystical tradition. This is the tradition I know most intimately, and therefore I trust I may be allowed to review it in a few broad strokes and to speak, as it were, *ex cathedra* on kabbala.

The kabbalistic tradition gives very great weight, as one would expect, to morality as an integral part of the quest for *devekuth* ("adhesion or clinging to God"), the desired end of kabbalistic religiosity. Kabbalism presents an extraordinarily complex theo-sophical structure, encompassing the most systematic mystical teaching in existence with worlds built upon worlds, and souls upon souls. One principle which reflects the traditional halachic world view (that of the rabbinic legal system) remains in place, however, and makes the system Jewish. This is the emphasis on *mitzvoth* (prescribed religious deeds) and morality. The genius of the kabbalistic imagination is its ability to adopt essentially neo-Platonic and gnostic ideas in creative and authentic Jewish forms, never allowing the gnostic-theosophical element to overwhelm the centrality of the Torah.[34] Therefore, it avoids antinomianism and emphasizes, as does rabbinic Judaism, strict adherence to the regimen of *mitzvoth*. As the *Tikkunei Zohar* expresses it: "With-out fear and love it [the soul and its service] cannot soar upwards nor can it ascend and stand before God" (*Tikkun* 10).[35] As a gen-eral principle, the kabbalists argue that it is the performance of the *mitzvoth* that regulates the balance of good and evil in the universe, with the ultimate redemption, *tikkun ha-olam*, being the result of the victory of the *mitzvoth* which contains cosmic, mystical, unitive powers. This is related, of necessity, to their ad-ditionally held metaphysical doctrine, the interdependence of "above and below": what mortals do directly affects the "upper worlds" just as what occurs in the "upper worlds" directly affects events on the human level. Hence human action is not just hu-man, but much more. Human deeds are world-consequential. In the words of the *Zohar*: "The impulse from below calls forth that from above" (1.164,a). Human life is part of the divine life itself, inherent to the cosmos's most basic rhythm, influencing—even decisively—the fate of the unity of the divine reality. When per-sons act, the reverberations are felt, as it were, in heaven. Human moral and religious actions are of cosmic import. Thus kabbalis-tic devotion and practice are inescapably ethical in character, for the ethical is not understood, to use the modern technical idiom, deontologically.

In more precise detail the kabbalistic ontology posits *Sefi-roth* ("Divine Emanations"), all of which are given, in addition to gnostic connotations, ethical attributes. These are the source

of ethical qualities in the temporal realm; and what transpires
in the ethical realm below has an impact, in turn, on the *Sefiroth*
and their intra-Sefirothic interaction and attempted reintegration.[36]
In the sixteenth century Moses Cordovero wrote in his *Palm Tree
of Deborah*, "Until now, we have expounded the thirteen qualities by which man resembles his Maker. These are the qualities
of higher mercy and their special property is that just as man
conducts himself here below, so will he be worthy of opening
that higher quality from above. As he behaves, so will be the af-
fluence from above and he will cause that quality to shine upon
the earth."[37]

The inextricable intimacy of ethics and the deepest theosoph-
ical levels of kabbalistic thought is discussed in many classical
sources,[38] being perhaps paradigmatically expressed in the monu-
mental work of R. Schneur Zalman of Liadi, founder of *Chabad*
(Lubavitch) Hasidism. I will quote a small sample of his teaching
in place of a further, extended, analysis. In explaining the mean-
ings of the Torah and its relations to God, he writes:

> The 613 commandments of the Torah, together with the
> 7 commandments of our Rabbis, combine to total the numeri-
> cal equivalent of *keter* ("crown") which is the blessed *Ratzon
> Elyon* ("Supernal Will"), which is clothed in His blessed Wis-
> dom, and they are united with the light of the blessed *En
> Sof* in a perfect union. "The Lord by wisdom hath founded
> the earth," which refers to the Oral Law that is derived
> from the Higher Wisdom, as is written in the *Zohar*, "The
> Father [*chochmah*] begat the daughter [i.e., *Malchut*, 'the
> Oral Law']."
>
> And this is what the *Yenuka* meant when he said that
> "the Supernal light that is kindled on one's head, namely,
> the *Shekinah*, requires oil," that is, to be clothed in wisdom,
> which is called "oil from the holy anointing," as is explained
> in the *Zohar*, that "these are the good deeds," namely, the
> 613 commandments, which derive from His blessed wisdom.
> Thereby the light of the *Shekinah* can cling to the wick, i.e.,
> the vivifying soul in the body, which is metaphorically called
> a "wick." For just as in the case of a material candle, the
> light shines by virtue of the annihilation and burning of the
> wick turning to fire, so does the light of the *Shekinah* rest

on the divine soul as a result of the annihilation of the animal soul and its transformation "from darkness to light and from bitterness to sweetness" in the case of the righteous, or at least through the destruction of its garments, which are thought, speech, and action, and their transformation from the darkness of the *kelipot* to the Divine light of the blessed *En Sof*, which is clothed and united in the thought, speech, and action of the 613 commandments of the Torah.[39]

This last quotation represents the matter as directly as it can be represented. Morality, demanded as it is by the Torah, is necessarily tied up with kabbalistic thought and practice; indeed, kabbala is unthinkable without morality.

V

In conclusion, I would like to offer a few generalizations.

1. To understand the relation between morality and mysticism aright, one has to know something about both mysticism and morality.
2. To accomplish this, one has to properly situate these disciplines in their religious, historical, and philosophical contexts.
3. The issue of means and ends is as confusing as it is important. Close attention to the complexities of this issue is required, and new perspectives would be most welcome.
4. To say that "x"—whether "x" is *devekuth*, nirvana, *mokṣa*, or the *unio-mystico*, or whatever—ultimately transcends morality does not mean that morality is either unimportant or unrelated to "x."

Finally, as far as this can be observed, there seems basically no difference in the moral practices encouraged by the great mystical traditions and the moral practices enjoined by the religious systems out of which the mystical systems emerge. Therefore, the kabbalistic ethic is not fundamentally different from, and certainly does not contradict, that of halachic Judaism enjoined on every Jew. Likewise, the Christian and Hindu mystical traditions do not appear to encourage their adherents to an ethical ideal very different from that encouraged more generally by Christianity and Hinduism respectively. Another way of saying this is to note that there is no recognizable pattern that suggests that Christian mystics or Hindu mystics or any other mystics act in ways contrary to, or disapproved of by, the larger Christian or Hindu or other communities. Despite the common caricature, mystics tend to be good citizens, in nearly every sense, of the traditions out of which they emerge and on which they in turn have an impact.

NOTES

1. For more on this contextual approach see my articles: "Language, Epistemology, and Mysticism," in *Mysticism and Philosophical Analysis*, ed. Steven T. Katz (New York: Oxford University Press, 1978), pp. 22–74; and "The Conservative Character of Mystical Experience," in *Mysticism and Religious Traditions*, ed. Steven T. Katz (New York: Oxford University Press, forthcoming).

2. Immanuel Kant, *Critique of Practical Reason*, trans. Lewis White Beck (Indianapolis: Bobbs-Merrill, 1956), p. 158.

3. Most recently Richard H. Jones has made this the incorrect central thesis of his essay "Theravāda Buddhism and Morality," *Journal of the American Academy of Religion* 47 (September 1979): 371–87. Jones totally misunderstands the sources and the metaphysical character of ethics in Theravāda Buddhism. Jones's criticism has been properly responded to by Noble Ross Reat, "Theravāda Buddhism and Morality: Objections and Corrections," *Journal of the American Academy of Religion* 48 (September 1980): 433–40.

4. Arthur Coleman Danto, *Mysticism and Morality* (New York: Basic Books, 1972), p. 72.

5. Ibid., pp. 87–88.

6. See, for example, the *Dhammapada*, the *Khuddakāpatha*, the *Sutta-Nipāta*, and the *Jātaka* tales, among many other sources.

7. Danto, *Mysticism and Morality*, p. 81.

8. These early Christian examples are cited from Dom Cuthbert Butter, *Western Mysticism* (London, 1922), pp. 188, 218.

9. Ibid., p. 214.

10. In very rare instances a neo-Platonic type of mystic does not emphasize the centrality of ethics for mysticism — for example, Pseudo-Dionysius — but this very rare exception only proves the general rule. Christian neo-Platonists, such as Eckhart, do not follow Pseudo-Dionysius' lead here.

11. Jan van Ruysbroeck, *The Spiritual Espousals*, trans. Eric Colledge (London: Faber & Faber, 1952), p. 74.

12. Meister Eckhart, *Tractate to Sister Katri*, trans. C. de B. Evans (London: Watkins, 1924), p. 315.

13. Meister Eckhart, as cited by Carl Franklin Kelley, *Meister Eckhart on Divine Knowledge* (New Haven, Conn.: Yale University Press, 1977), p. 218.

14. Ibid.

15. Saint Teresa of Ávila, *The Interior Castle* 3.2., in *The Complete Works of Saint Teresa of Jesus*, trans. E. Allison Peers (London: Sheed & Ward, 1978).

16. The same doctrines are taught by nearly, if not all, Eckhart's disciples: by nearly, if not all, the Spanish and Italian Catholic mystics — both male and female — and by Protestant mystical giants like Jacob Boehme.

17. For a full discussion of the roles "models" play in mystical traditions see my essay on "The Conservative Character of Mystical Experience," in Katz, *Mysticism and Philosophical Analysis*.

18. Meister Eckhart, "This, Too, Is Meister Eckhart Who Always Taught the Truth," in *Meister Eckhart: A Modern Translation*, trans. Raymond Bernard Blakney (New York: Harper & Row, 1957), pp. 112–13.

19. Saint Teresa of Ávila, *The Way of Perfection* 36.7, in *Complete Works*, trans. Peers. See also Teresa, *Interior Castle* 6.4; 6.6.

20. Jacob Boehme, *The Way to Christ*, trans. Peter Erb (New York: Paulist Press, 1978), 3.24.

21. John of the Cross, *Ascent of Mount Carmel*, bk. 2, chap. 24.6, in *The Collected Works of Saint John of the Cross*, trans. Kieran Kavanaugh and Otilio Rodriguez (Garden City, N.Y.: Doubleday, 1964). For more on this issue see Augustin François Poulain, *Graces of Interior Prayer*, trans. Leonora L. Yorke Smith (St. Louis, Mo.: Herder, 1950), chaps. 20–22. For the philosophical issues raised by this text see Nelson Pike, "On Mystic Visions as Sources of Knowledge," in Katz, *Mysticism and Philosophical Analysis*, pp. 214–34.

22. Teresa, *Interior Castle* 7.3. See also Evelyn Underhill, *Mystics of the Church* (New York: Schocken Books, 1964), for a discussion of this issue.

23. John McKenzie, *Hindu Ethics* (Oxford: Oxford University Press, 1922), pp. 206–207; Albert Schweitzer, *Indian Thought and Its Development*, trans. Mrs. Charles E. B. Russell (New York: H. Holt, 1936); and Danto, *Mysticism and Morality*. See also Robert Ernest Hume, *The Thirteen Principal Upaniṣads* (Oxford: Oxford University Press, 1931), p. 60.

24. Schweitzer, *Indian Thought*, pp. 17, 226ff.

25. For a standard criticism see Danto, *Mysticism and Morality*, pp. 48–49.

26. For a paradigmatic example of this objection, see ibid., p. 71.

27. *Kaṭha Upaniṣad* 1.2.24, in *The Principal Upaniṣads*, ed. and trans. Radhakrishnan (London: George Allen & Unwin, 1953). All subsequent citations from the *Upaniṣads* are from this translation.

28. *Muṇḍaka Upaniṣad* 3.1.8–10; *Bṛhad-āraṇyaka Upaniṣad* 2.5.2; *Śvetāśvatara Upaniṣad* 6.4.

29. This felicitous phrase comes from D. S. Sarma, "The Nature and History of Hinduism," in *The Religion of the Hindus*, ed. Kenneth William Morgan (New York: Ronald Press, 1953), p. 21.

30. *Muṇḍaka Upaniṣad* 3.15.

31. See, for example, *Kaṭha Upaniṣad* 2.10; 3.7–8; *Muṇḍaka Upaniṣad* 3.1ff; *Bṛhad-āraṇyaka Upaniṣad* 4.4; *Taittirīya Upaniṣad* 1.4; and *Chāndogya Upaniṣad* 8.4.

32. For more on this see Ishwar Chandra Sharma, *Ethical Philosophies of India* (Lincoln, Neb.: Johnson Publishing Co., 1965), pp. 94ff.

33. Kalidas Bhattacharya, "The Status of the Individual in Indian Philosophy," *Philosophy East and West* 14 (July 1964): 141.

34. The remarkable exceptions are, of course, the pseudomessianic mystical movement of Sabbatianism and its offshoot, Frankism. For a brilliant study of this see Gershom Gerhard Scholem, *Sabbatai Sevi* (Princeton, N.J.: Princeton University Press, 1973). It should, however, be noted that it is probably the concept of messianism — misunderstood — that causes Sabbatai Sevi's antinomianism rather than his kabbalistic theosophy. The same of course is unquestionably true of Jacob Frank.

35. See the exposition of this teaching in R. Schneur Zalman of Liadi, *Tanya* (London: Kenot Publication Society by Soncino Press, 1973), chap. 39.

36. For more on this notion of the disunity of the "upper worlds" and its consequences see Gershom Gerhard Scholem, *Major Trends in Jewish Mysticism* (New York: Schocken Books, 1954), chaps. 5–7.

37. Moses Cordovero, *The Palm Tree of Deborah*, trans. Louis Jacobs (New York: Hermon Press, 1974), p. 69.

38. See, for example, Moses Hayyim Luzzato, *The Path of the Upright*, trans. Mordecai Kaplan (Philadelphia, 1966), chap. 26.

39. Zalman, *Tanya*, chap. 53.

11

Tragic Choices:
Ethics after the Holocaust

ROGER S. GOTTLIEB

THE HOLOCAUST IS A decisive event for our time, but one of which contemporary philosophers have by and large taken little notice. In this essay, I hope to show that the Holocaust has some decisive implications for both ethics and social philosophy. I will focus on four particular issues: (1) the normative question of the authentic form of remembering the Holocaust; (2) some problems raised by the Holocaust for theories of human nature; (3) the relation of the Holocaust to the positivist conception of rationality; (4) implications of the Holocaust for concerns with social justice — specifically, in regard to the creation of the state of Israel and the Israeli-Palestinian conflict.

I. REMEMBERING

The systematic and self-conscious murder of six million innocent and defenseless people is an event of such significance that our relation to it is a matter of moral concern. However, while we possess great knowledge of the factual details of the Holocaust, comparatively little attention has been paid to the distinction between authentic and inauthentic ways of remembering what we know.

Let us begin by considering a familiar form of remembering. We make a list of things we have to do over the weekend. Inscribing each potential act on paper registers, locates, and limits it. Once written, we know the tasks as things which can be handled: so many trips to the store, attics cleaned, floors washed, or phone calls made. If these are capable of being handled, they are in turn capable of being easily forgotten. In fact, we only make the list in order to forget what we have just remembered. In this remembering-in-order-to-forget, we indicate our mastery over and our unconcern with that which we remember.

Remembering the Holocaust in this way implies that we have mastered the meaning of the event for our own subjectivity. By *subjectivity* I mean that aspect of our personal identity which is formed by a confrontation with problems the solutions to which are both of crucial importance and of lifelong duration. These problems cannot be "solved" because part of their solution is our continuing response to them. Kierkegaard, whose usage of the term I have adopted, identifies two such problems: what it means to die and what it means to pray.[1]

A subjective confrontation with the Holocaust can provide serious subjects for reflection. For instance, what does it mean to have to choose — as many Jews did — between saving the life of your sister or your wife, your mother or your husband, your father or your son? What does it mean to resist Nazi power when you know that the Nazi policy of collective reprisal will lead to the torture, starvation, or murder of fellow Jews as punishment for your resistance? Under what conditions, as Simon Wiesenthal asks in "The Sunflower," would we forgive one of the killers? A study of the factual details of the Holocaust reveals moral dilemmas which demand a subjective understanding. Such an understanding requires that we "think ourselves" out of what appears to be our everyday existence and into the Holocaust, rather than try to describe it in familiar terms which would allow us to remember it in a mode of forgetfulness.

Yet the necessity for a subjective understanding of the Holocaust should not lead us to encapsulate the event in a sterile and distorting shroud of mystery. The Holocaust must not be relegated to the realm of the necessarily and ultimately incomprehensible.[2] I believe that Elie Wiesel may be doing this when he states that the victims died with the truth on their lips, a truth we can never know. This approach to the Holocaust is, paradoxically, another form of trivialization. It denies that, in relation to the Holocaust, there exists a truth *for us*. While we may in fact never know the truth which perished with the victims, we have an obligation to discover a truth which exists for those who did not perish. This truth, in turn, requires that we take the Holocaust into ourselves; and therefore that it not remain fundamentally mysterious and endlessly external, like a shrine or an idol. If the Holocaust is essentially incomprehensible, then we cannot, in the deepest sense of the word, think it. But that which cannot be thought cannot be part of ourselves and is, therefore, irrelevant to our identity.

Last in this necessarily incomplete catalog of forms of remembrance is remembering-as-obsession. Here the event is remembered but everything else, including the self, is forgotten. We become immersed in the Holocaust. The gas chambers and barbed wire, burnt buildings and burning bodies become more real than our own lives. Our life becomes the Holocaust — a Holocaust which cannot end because it has occurred already.

Obsession is inauthentic because it attempts to blot out the self who is the subject, the agent, of the act of remembering. We cannot have a relation to the Holocaust if we dissolve ourselves in it, if our own reality is negated by acts of imagination in which we seek to become the past. Further, that seeking is itself a revelation of who we are. Obsession with the Holocaust cannot eliminate the reality of the post-Holocaust self; it can only be that self's pretense at such elimination. But — and here Sartre's account of human identity comes to mind — any attempt to eliminate the self is precisely a project of the self, though one carried out in bad faith. If nothing ever happened but the Holocaust, then neither our present nor our future really exists. And if this is so, then there is need not for action, but only for remembrance. But such remembrance is itself a form of action — one whose partial goal is the obliteration of the moral reality of the self which undertakes it.

In the distorted forms of remembrance I have described, either the Holocaust becomes an event which is essentially unreal or unimportant, or the present itself becomes drained of reality. In either case the significance of the Holocaust for the present and future action of a moral agent is diminished. By contrast, what I take to be the morally appropriate relation of remembering the Holocaust is one in which we remember it as a problematic and continuing event and in which we remember ourselves as moral agents as well. Or, to put the point another way: the Holocaust must be remembered authentically partly *because* it is a problematic and continuing event for us as moral agents. Consider, for instance, the fact that we are faced with the existence of survivors of the Holocaust. What do we who did not directly experience the Holocaust owe to survivors? What does Auschwitz survivor Fanya Fenelon deserve in relation to a television production of her memoirs when someone she believes to be a publicly vocal anti-Semite is chosen to portray *her* life? What do survivors in Skokie, Illinois, deserve when the American Nazi Party proposes to march through their community? How does the reality of the Holocaust alter our usual conceptions of moral obligation and political rights in such situations?

If we have remembered the Holocaust in order to forget it, we will lack the subjectivity necessary to begin to understand that there are problems here. If the Holocaust is mystery or obsession then we will have lost the capacity to act in the present in regard to such problems. In either case, only an authentic remembering makes possible an adequate moral identity.

Finally, the continuing and problematic character of the Holocaust is not limited to our relation to the survivors of the event itself. As we shall see in section IV, the subject of the Holocaust is not simply a large number of individuals, but a single community. That community has survived the Holocaust and remains a subject of history; yet its fate and those of communities with which it comes in contact have been decisively altered by the Holocaust. The problematic character of the Holocaust thus includes its continuing historical effects on the nature of relations between Jews and other national groups. What does anti-Semitism mean to the Jews as a people as opposed to the particular Jews who might experience it? What actions taken by Jews in regard to their survival as a people make sense only when understood as actions taking place after the Holocaust? How can the Holocaust itself be used both authentically and inauthentically by Jews and non-Jews alike? And, finally, in what ways are Holocaust-like events happening or near to happening to other groups?

II. HUMAN NATURE

The vast majority of people simply did not believe that the Holocaust was possible. Even Zionist Jews, who denied the possibility of eradicating anti-Semitism within the Diaspora, found it hard to believe eyewitness accounts of the extermination camps. Jews and non-Jews initially interpreted this event in the categories of the past: as yet another pogrom or expulsion.[3] The widespread character of this mistake testifies to the fundamental newness of the Holocaust. This newness does not reside in the facts of mass murder or of the destruction of a particular national community. Such things had happened before. Rather, the newness had to do with (at least) two other facts. First, the perpetrators intended to destroy an entire community of human beings and to do so without reference to other, ulterior goals. Of course various sectors of German society benefited from the political use of Jews as scapegoats and the economic values of expropriated Jewish property and Jewish slave labor. But there was little benefit to anyone in mass murder. Rather, there is evidence that in the latter part of the war pursuing the Final Solution was at odds with Germany's military goals.[4] By this time, however, mass murder had become an end in itself.

Second, this pursuit of mass murder was no temporary aberration or crazed outburst. It was carried out in a calm, orderly, and scientific manner. Detailed records were kept of it. It was a carefully conceptualized process in which human death became an industry and human body parts served as raw materials. And it was a process conceived and executed by Germany's best administrative, political, and scientific minds.

These facts pose some problems for a number of theories of human nature; that is, theories which purport to explain, in the most general terms possible, why people do and do not act in the ways they do. To be successful, theories of human nature cannot take certain forms of human action as a given. For example, a sociological explanation which shows how German society created a tendency to submit to authority takes for granted the existence and nature of German society. A psychological explanation which explains Führer-worship by reference to German family structure is similarly limited, unless it includes an account of why families necessarily possess the structures they do. The problem I wish to examine, then, is whether encompassing theories of human nature are adequate to the particular features of the Holocaust. I will limit my treatment to two types of such theories: biological and social-environmental.

Biological deterministic theories claim that human beings have a biological structure which produces certain characteristic drives, intentions, instincts, and desires.[5] These are believed to include drives toward aggression and are seen as causing certain characteristic behavior patterns. Despite the unfortunate moral character of the aggressive behavior caused by our biology, claim these theories, such behavior is inevitable. There exist permanent motives for it. The repression of such behavior itself will lead to physiological and psychological imbalances, and thus to a return of the unfortunate behavior in a new form. For biological deterministic theories, the major evidences for the existence of aggressive impulses are the aggressive actions they are said to cause. However, these impulses are viewed as existing independently of the actions themselves. Otherwise, there would be no way to explain what happens when aggressive behavior is inhibited and aggressive impulses are in some way repressed.

Of course it might be replied that what is repressed is essentially biological in nature, without emotional or moral character, a matter of sheer energy rather than impulses. This claim, however, ignores the fact that it is doubtful that it even makes sense to talk of repressing a biological structure. We may inhibit a physical reaction (the blinking of an eye, for example). We do not, however, repress it, for the term *repression* refers to the alteration of a goal-directed energy—of, in short, an intention. But neither biochemical reactions nor physical movements are, in and of themselves, intentional in this sense. They are not goal-oriented. This can be shown by considering how strange it would sound to talk of heartbeats, the exchange of fluid between bloodstreams and cells, or the reaction of nerves to stimuli as aggressive or peaceful, hostile or loving. Likewise, even if an agent's physical movements cause the death of another person, we cannot necessarily say that the agent acted aggressively. The agent may simply have made a mistake. Biochemical processes and bodily movements have no emotional-moral character unless they express intentions. The familiar point here is that adjectives such as aggressive, hostile, and loving can be applied only to a consciousness — to an awareness and a set of intentions. Only in the presence of a consciousness do we have the kind of human action which biological deterministic theories sought, initially, to explain, such as aggressive action.

This point is of crucial relevance to the Holocaust because many of the people who planned and executed the Final Solution did not do so out of aggression or hostility. They may have disliked or been contemptuous of Jews. But this dislike and contempt did not match the scope of their behavior. For many of these people, Jews were not enemies to be annihilated. Rather, they were objects to be treated in correct administrative fashion. They were not targets of hostility any more than were coal supplies, welfare payments, ammunition, or those other things which the bureaucrats of the Nazi machine were called on to organize and dispose of. This aspect of the Holocaust is described in Arendt's account of Adolph Eichmann. Eichmann's central motivation was not aggression, but devotion to duty.[6] He took no joy in the destruction of the Jews and felt guilty for once striking a Jewish communal leader. His happiness resided in his ability to carry out his duty, to look good in the eyes of his superiors, to obey orders from higher sources effectively and thus fulfill his social role.

Similar attitudes can be found in Himmler's praise of the S.S. for resisting the temptation to spare their particular favorite Jews, thus resisting their own personal wishes. "To have carried this out and . . . to have kept our integrity . . . this is an unwritten . . . page of glory. . . ."[7] Similarly, historian Raul Hilberg cites complex bureaucratic decisions whose goal was to distinguish political from personal killings and to show that only the former were justified. The basic message was that the destruction of the Jews was in fact legitimate only insofar as it was part of a legal, rationalized, orderly procedure, and not as an expression of rash impulses on the part of individuals.[8]

It could be argued that the surface orderliness and self-control of the Eichmanns was itself a sublimation of aggression, that "duty" was a mask. Yet what evidence is there for such a claim but the existence of the aggressive actions themselves? Why should such actions necessarily counteract the evidence I have just cited? The Nazis' actions can just as well be viewed as evidence of the taking on of intersubjectively created social roles as of biologically based aggression. Or, to cut the point a little finer, a sense of social solidarity may *itself* have been the cause of aggressive impulses. Hatred of the Jews may have been caused in many cases as much by the desire to be a "good German" as by the focusing of biological drives. Also, an examination of the rise of Nazism shows how much of the Nazis' financial support — and thus their capacity to structure public opinion — derived from the self-conscious desire of Germany's ruling group to manipulate public opinion.

Forgetting the objections already described, a theory which seeks to explain human action solely on the basis of biologically caused aggression can make sense of only one part of the Holocaust. Such a theory cannot account for the heroism, self-sacrifice, cooperation, and love shown by the victims. Yet their actions require explanation as much as do those of the murderers. In the face of this point biological theories begin multiplying fundamental drives. Human life becomes a battleground between aggressive and cooperative drives, between love and death. To explain the outcome of these struggles in particular cases, however, we will be forced to look beyond the posited drives themselves. We must turn away from the motivational consequences of biology and toward theories which take as their object the social structures shaping individual identity rather than the biological structures supposedly underlying them.

To serve as theories of human nature, social-environmental theories must be theories of history. They must explain not only a particular society, but the range and development of society as such. Since I take classical liberalism and Marxism to be the most widely held theories of history of the past century, I will describe the challenge posed for them by the Holocaust.

Liberalism can be described as follows.[9] The development of rationality will lead to both increased self-knowledge and increased general happiness. As history unfolds, the growth of knowledge will lead to societies increasingly dedicated to individual fulfillment and social justice, since both of these accord with the rational pursuit of self-interest by individuals. The fundamental problems of social life are those of knowledge and democracy. The movement of history, and thus the scope of human action in any particular society, is determined by the degree to which the rational acquisition and utilization of knowledge fulfill human interest. The more human beings are awakened to the nature of their interests and the rational fulfillment of those interests, the more society as a whole will reflect the values of rationality and justice. Liberalism thus offers a view in which rationality is inherent in human beings, and progress toward increased rationality is the basic movement of history.

Such a view is challenged by the eruption of fascism after the existence of democracy; by the rise of the ideological obscurantism and brutal mysticism of Nazism in one of the most cultured and civilized of modern nations; by the substitution of pseudo-science for rational methodology, for instance, in the use of theories of racial superiority and the rewriting of history to make the Jews the source of Germany's post-World War I problems; and by the creation of a machine for mass murder in the first country to have introduced social welfare legislation.

Nazi Germany rejected rationality and destroyed democracy. For liberalism these developments must be viewed as regressions. But liberalism has little room for regressions, since regressions are caused by rejections of the accomplishments of reason. Such rejections contradict liberalism's picture of a human history structured by the sure advance of our inherent rationality. As a consequence, liberalism is reduced from a theory of history to a political ideology and a set of moral values. Without a faith in the natural human attraction to reason and its accomplishments, the classic liberal theory of historical development cannot be maintained.

For Marxism, human history is shaped by the dialectic of modes of production. Each such mode is a form of social action within a particular natural and historical setting. Within each the form of action is contradictory: actions performed in the pursuit of fulfilling socially created needs eventually lead to a fundamental transformation of the productive life, class relations, and culture of the entire society. This pattern leads in the general direction of both greater technical power and greater political freedom. The final stage of this process is the transition from capitalism to socialism and, later, communism. Socialism becomes possible because capitalism develops forces of production adequate to guarantee each human being a comfortable life beyond scarcity. Socialism is made necessary because the working class recognizes that these forces of production will not be so used within a society dominated by capitalist social relations. The working class creates various political institutions to express its interest in the overthrow of capitalism; and the inevitable social crises caused by capitalism make it, eventually, possible and necessary for those institutions to take power.[10]

This picture is contradicted by the utter failure of the working class and its organizations to resist the growth of Nazism successfully and, as a consequence, to prevent the Holocaust. The electoral and ideological success of the Nazis took place in a country with a long history of working-class political activity. Yet in the face of a social and economic crisis, the majority of the population of an advanced capitalist country turned away from socialist politics to fascism. Two highly developed Marxist-oriented parties — the Social Democrats and the Communist Party — could neither win over the majority of the population nor effectively resist the power of the Nazis.

It might be replied that Marxism has no trouble explaining the growth of Nazism by reference to the needs of German imperialism and monopoly capitalism, or accounting for the rise of fascist ideology by reference to the monopoly capitalist class's need to justify the growth of the state sector and unify an alienated German population in support of a militaristic foreign policy. Similarly, one might point out that theories of imperialism account for aggressive and dictatorial policies by the German government.[11]

Whatever their analytic force, these points do not refute the claim that Marxism, as a theory of history, cannot account for the success of fascism as a mass movement in a country with well-developed working-class institutions, political parties, and political consciousness. In traditional Marxism's vision of history, there is no room for the possibility of the ultimate failure of the socialist project. That the working class as a whole, and its political parties in particular, could be defeated by other forces in an advanced industrial society contradicts the basic historical confidence of traditional Marxism.

As a consequence, Marxism, like liberalism, has retreated from its attempts to forge a theory of history. Like liberalism with respect to rationality, Marxism has seen that an analysis of economic development is an insufficient basis for predictions concerning the future of social life in general. Simultaneously, there has developed a tradition of Western Marxism, which is marked in part by the degree of importance it accords to noneconomic social relations and processes and by its refusal to commit itself to a theory of history. Much of this work—especially that on both mass psychology and the consequences of scientistic theory—is a direct response to the rise of Nazism.[12]

The Holocaust is part of a historical regression against which both reason and the working class were helpless. As such, it constitutes a crisis for both liberalism and Marxism. In response to this crisis there has been a reworking of historical schemas into transcendental-moral ones. For example, Jürgen Habermas has recently sought to construct a developmental-logical account of human evolution based on the progressive development of norms of increasing rationality.[13] But though Habermas does show how certain past historical transformations match the developmental order of his schema, he is quite clear to stress that the future may not lead to any progress whatsoever. His schema, at least as far as the future is concerned, is normative rather than predictive. This distinguishes it from both traditional Marxism and classical liberalism, which claimed predictive as well as normative status. Similar limitations attend the recent high-water mark of liberal political theory, John Rawls's book *A Theory of Justice*. That work constitutes an attempt to provide a rational grounding for norms of justice. It in no way offers arguments to support the claim that such norms will in fact ever be put into practice.

The failure of the three theories just discussed in regard to the Holocaust make that event an intellectual problem. Or, to put it another way: it is not only for our subjectivity that the Holocaust poses a problem, but for our objectivity as well. An adequate remembering of the Holocaust requires an adequate understanding of it. Yet such an understanding cannot be predicated on theories of human nature which are incompatible with the event. One significant connection between our objectivity and our subjectivity is contained in the fact that believing that we have some general theory of why people act the way they do is central to the conduct of our individual moral and collective political life. Especially in regard to the fundamentally optimistic theories of liberalism and Marxism, the Holocaust poses a fundamental barrier to the regaining of confidence in the future course of human development. Similarly, normative ethics rests partly on the confidence that human beings will follow such principles and rules. In the face of the prospect that the human race will choose fascism and genocide over other forms of social life, however, normative ethics becomes problematic.

Thus one thing that is lost for both our moral and political lives — or at least drawn disturbingly into question — is the sense of trust that underlay much of our activity in the realms of morality and politics. The belief that the morally correct actions will necessarily create a better world for us, our children, or at least that abstraction "the human race," is lost. We may continue to will the good as moral and political agents, but our expectation that the good will be accomplished in any but the most limited way cannot be supported.

III. POSITIVISM AND RATIONALITY

Rationality was once used to refer to a faculty which enabled persons to identify the highest, most appropriate ends for humans as humans. Since the seventeenth century, however, both this usage and its philosophical underpinnings have come under attack. In the last century an antagonistic position has emerged, in the form of positivism.[14] For positivism, the choice of final ends is not susceptible to rational justification. Rationality is limited to the knowledge of the theoretical laws of the natural sciences or the practical application of such knowledge in the pursuit of arbitrarily chosen ends. For positivism, rationality becomes instrumental rationality — a form of reason to which moral values and political norms are external. These latter are considered to be the outcome of interests, choices, forces, or compromises, not rational justification.

The Holocaust may be the *reductio ad absurdum* of positivism. For positivism, it is possible to assess the rationality of the Nazis' actions independently of any evaluation of the goal to which those actions were directed. If goals are not susceptible to rational justification, then there is no reason that efficient Nazis are not rational. The only irrationality of the Nazi enterprise, on this view, would be inconsistencies or inefficiencies.

Now this conclusion does not *logically* refute positivism. It is possible for a positivist to say that one can criticize Nazism adequately by using concepts such as evil, immoral, brutal, cruel, without needing to have recourse to "irrational" as well. Yet I believe the prospect of calling people devoted to mass murder "rational" does lead partisans of positivism to reconsider the fundamental validity of their position. Being unable to label certain enterprises as irrational becomes progressively less appealing the more we see the scope of the behavior of which humans are capable — or when we become aware that the Nazis thought of themselves as, and were in the positivist sense, rational.

Designating the Nazi enterprise as rational includes the Nazis within a certain realm of discourse. It makes possible certain kinds of arguments with Nazis and rules out others. We do not argue with a person designated as insane in the same way as we do with someone who is rational but cruel or brutal. Desiring to murder an entire race of people is itself conclusive evidence of irrationality bordering on insanity. Interactions with people who have such desires must take the form of dealing with people who have not merely become morally deficient but who have lost their reason (though these two are not mutually exclusive). Of course, the use of terms such as *irrational* or *insane* in regard to whole societies is itself problematic. However, in a century of the Holocaust, understanding which is meant by "social insanity" is crucially important.

Also, we may consider how integral the concept of rationality is to a host of associated, and highly significant, descriptive and evaluative concepts such as sanity, intelligence, and adulthood. The application of these predicates depends, in part, on the use of *rationality*. For positivism, a person's commitment to mass murder as an end in itself is irrelevant to that person's sanity, intelligence, or adulthood. This implication of positivism not only drastically limits our use of these concepts, it also seems to violate our normal use of them. We do not, I think, normally assess a person's sanity, intelligence, or adulthood simply on the basis of his or her ability to engage in instrumental rationality, to fulfill the demands of scientific, technical, or administrative reason. Nor should we. For to do so would devastate our capacity to evaluate, teach, and criticize each other.

However, the philosophical problem remains: though we may continue to use the concept of rationality in traditional ways, we are no longer sure of our basis for doing so. We know that the Nazis were not simply morally hideous; they were also irrational, unbalanced, insane. Alas, however, we do not know how we know this. Our moral knowledge is both certain and ungrounded.

Habermas's ambitious attempt to overcome this dilemma is an example of how we remain trapped between a desire to transcend positivism and an inability to do so. Habermas seeks to show that the basic social norms such as truth and justice are presupposed by the use of speech.[15] For Habermas, the use of speech for mutual understanding is the model of communication. Such communication, in turn, is said to require a fundamental reciprocity between speakers, and thus to set a model for free and egalitarian reciprocity in all social relations. To violate this model, argues Habermas, is irrational, for such violation entails violating one of the fundamental features of human life as such: the use of language. The problem with Habermas's argument, as he himself notes, is that speech can be used to deceive and oppress as well as to communicate. In fact, the purpose of some communication is simply or mainly to deceive and oppress. Communication between people who are equal with respect to their mastery of a given language can be embedded in an interpersonal or political context of domination and inequality. The superior partners in such communications thus have interests in the maintenance of unequal social relations. The general interest in reciprocity identified by Habermas thus coexists with particular interests in domination and inequality.[16]

Habermas's failure is symptomatic of the difficulties which will attend any attempt to end the reign of positivism and reexpand the concept of reason. Such a move will depend on the identification of a common interest, the fulfillment of which is necessary or appropriate for humans as humans. In the prepositivist age, this interest was believed to be derived from a shared and universal metaphysical or religious reality. From Plato to the Middle Ages the ultimate reality of the universe was seen as capable of providing a foundation for identifying rationally justifiable ends for humans as humans. With the replacement of metaphysics and religion by modern science and philosophical ontology, however, such an interest can no longer be derived. Thus, antipositivist theorists are forced to seek some other commonality, as Habermas does in language. These attempts, however, founder on the fact that contemporary social life creates us as persons with significantly different interests; for example, it stratifies us by class, race, sex, and nationality. Also, the absence of a compelling and universal metaphysical or religious myth, and the lack of likelihood of one being generated in a scientific age, mitigate against a return to a pre-positivist framework. It is the claim of Marxism that the ending of the above-mentioned stratification and the creation of a classless society are possible. Such a society would found the universal rationality of ends on the shared interest in an egalitarian and free society, rather than depending on belief in a shared metaphysical or religious reality. The Marxist claim, however, remains hypothetical until such time as a truly communist society comes into existence.

IV. SOCIAL JUSTICE

The Holocaust, as the precipitating event in the formation of the state of Israel, contributed to the creation of one of the most morally perplexing social conflicts of the modern age. Without the rise of Nazism there would not have been sufficient Jewish immigration to Palestine to create even a potentially independent Jewish community there. Without the Holocaust, the world would have been even less sympathetic to the formation of a Jewish state against the will of more than half the population of Palestine (the Arab citizens) and of all the surrounding countries. Finally, the Holocaust won over the vast majority of world Jewry to the Zionist enterprise. The Holocaust thus served as motive and justification for the formation of Israel. Yet this formation caused — and, some will claim, required — the creation of a stateless mass of Palestinian Arabs. The satisfaction of the claims of justice of the Jews resulted in a great injustice done to Palestinians.[17]

Situations of this kind, I believe, are not adequately dealt

with by existing theories of justice. Such theories usually take as
their goal the rational support of norms which guarantee a just
treatment of all members of a given community. Rawls, for example, seeks to identify those procedures under which a community
can identify social norms as just, or under which injustice works
to the benefit of the group as a whole or of the least advantaged
members. He is not concerned to study the conditions under which
a group must accept an injustice from which other people benefit
and it suffers. Similarly, Marx sought a "universal class," the redress of whose wrongs would result in the ending of all forms
of oppression. Such universalism does not address a situation in
which the redress of wrongs of one group requires wrongs done
to another.

Now the notion of an ethical agent facing unavoidable moral
conflict will be familiar to readers of Kierkegaard and Sartre. However, these authors focus on individual decisions, not on the fate
of communities in history. Also, and equally important, these dilemmas are presented from the point of view of a particular agent
forced to fulfill one obligation at the expense of another. The Israeli-
Palestinian conflict, however, is defined by the competing view-
points of two adversaries, two "moral agents," the satisfaction of
each of whose claims requires the negation of the other's. Compromise is extremely difficult, perhaps impossible, here: historically, satisfaction of the minimal demands of each group excluded
satisfaction of those of the other. The Zionist movement demanded
at least a bi-national state in which they would have equal rights
and powers with Palestinians. The Palestinians sought national
independence in their homeland, with the Jews as no more than
a national minority. Similarly, noncompromise positions are taken
by the leading adversaries (the Palestine Liberation Organization
and the Israeli government) in the present.

The result has been a monstrous injustice for the natives of
Palestine. Yet this is an injustice for which they do not have, in
the usual sense of the term, the "right" to seek the full restoration
of their land and the return of the Jews to the European and Middle Eastern countries from which they came. This is so because
the injustice done to the Palestinians is itself part of the process
of redressing past, and preventing future, injustices to another
group.

The morally perplexing features of this conflict should lead us to examine its peculiar historical features. When we do so, the morally relevant agents can be seen to include both the general European tradition of anti-Semitism and the particular expression of that tradition which was Nazism. We might also include accounts of the machinations of both the imperialist powers and the Arab governments. When we situate a question of the redress of injustice within such a broad historical context, the achievement of the kind of abstract justice described in most philosophical accounts of the subject is impossible. There is no single, identifiable agent of the "necessary" injustice done to the Palestinians. How then could redress be possible?

When we see injustices as essentially historically situated, and identify general historical factors as their causes, we find ourselves confronted by morally perplexing situations. The Israeli-Palestinian conflict may be the most extreme example of this, but it is not the only one. Moral problems of the justice of affirmative action, for instance, reflect the difficulty we have in understanding how to redress the history of injustice done by whites to blacks and by men to women. The present instance is all the more striking because it might be claimed that by establishing Israel the Jews have in fact achieved some measure of recompense for the Holocaust in particular and for historical anti-Semitism in general. Such a claim, however, would suggest that it makes sense to talk of recompense for an event such as the Holocaust — a suggestion which is highly doubtful. It also leaves unsettled the question of the morality of the relation between Israeli Jews and Palestinian Arabs. To address such issues remains a task for future moral theory.

Though I cannot develop such a theory here, I can mention at least two of its features. First, we may note that our moral perplexity over issues such as the Israeli-Palestinian conflict or affirmative action derives partly from our habit of thinking about morality from the point of view of individual agents. We have given little attention to the fact that communities as well as individuals can be both the subject and the object of moral relationships. This becomes clear when we remember that what is distinctive about genocide is not that it is the murder of a large number of individuals, but that it attempts to destroy an entire, discrete community. Likewise, the identity with which we function as moral agents is not a purely individual one, but is shaped by our participation in and identification with various collectivities. Ethical theory after the Holocaust must reflect these facts.

Second, such an ethical theory will be shaped by the realization that the world in which morality exists is, in certain essential respects, evil. Ethical theory will no longer presuppose that the accomplishment of moral values is possible. In a post-Holocaust age we need a moral theory which situates human actions within a history which compels us toward evil, where (at times) the meeting of the needs of one group inevitably leads it into conflict with another. For this moral theory, tragic choices are not the exception, but the rule, of moral life. Justice is not a norm to be achieved; rather, injustice is a permanent and perennial fact to be lessened. We will no longer believe that achieving justice in a particular situation is incompatible with simultaneously creating injustice. The effects of history on communities will be seen to be such that human needs can be met only by a gradual lessening of injustice, not by the complete fulfillment of the demands of justice. This reworking of moral theory, of course, requires as a complement more traditional forms of such theory. Without those forms, there would be no independent analysis of conditions of justice, or injustice, at all. But this new form of moral theory, in situating the pursuit of abstract moral values in a historical context of evil, reflects the values and concerns of a modern age shaped by an awareness of evil. This awareness, in turn, can be derived from no historical event more than from the Holocaust.[18]

NOTES

1. Sören Kierkegaard, *Concluding Unscientific Postscript*, trans. David F. Swenson (Princeton, N.J.: Princeton University Press, 1968), pp. 125–62.

2. For a development of this point, see Miriam Greenspan, "Responses to the Holocaust," *Jewish Currents* (October 1980): 20–26.

3. "That period [of annihilation] struck Jews like a cataclysm of unparalleled proportions, a natural disaster without historical precedent or rational meaning. . . ." (Lucy Davidowicz, *The War against the Jews* [New York: Bantam, 1975], p. 466).

"Locked within their ghettos, under strict surveillance and unrefined terror . . . the Jews . . . tried to assess the possible authenticity of the reports [of extermination camps] in the light of experience and logic. The horror of an enterprise that could deliberately destroy human beings who were innocent of any wrongdoing was inconceivable. The senselessness of the undertaking further undermined the acceptance of the information. . . . These evaluations were for the most part shared by all levels of Jewish leadership and by the masses as well. The information about the death camps was rejected all over Europe, not only by the Jews . . ." (Raul Hilberg, *The Destruction of the European Jews* [New York: Harper & Row, 1961], pp. 474–75).

4. For the conflict between military objectives and the Final Solution, see Davidowicz, *War against the Jews*, pp. 191–97. For a financial cost-accounting which indicates the strain the Final Solution placed on the German economy, see Hilberg, *Destruction of the European Jews*, pp. 644–46.

5. For example, theories of Nietzsche, Freud, Lorenz, and Ardrey.

6. See Hannah Arendt, *Eichmann in Jerusalem* (New York: Viking Press, 1963).

7. Davidowicz, *War against the Jews*, p. 200.

8. Hilberg, *Destruction of the European Jews*, pp. 646–49.

9. For classic liberalism, see the works of John Stuart Mill and James Mill. For an opponent's summing up of liberalism as a theory of history, see Fyodor Mikhailovich Dostoevsky, *Notes from Underground*, trans. Serge Shishkoff, ed. Robert G. Durgy (New York: T. Y. Crowell, 1969).

10. See, for instance: Karl Marx and Friedrich Engels, *The Communist Manifesto*, trans. Samuel Moore (New York: Washington Square Press, 1964); Rosa Luxemburg, "Social Reform or Revolution," in Rosa Luxemburg, *Selected Political Writings*, ed. Dick Howard (New York: Monthly Review, 1971); and the 1891 *Erfurt* Program of the German Social Democratic Party, the most powerful and influential party of the Second International, described in Carl E. Schorske, *German Social Democracy* (New York: John Wiley Press, 1955), pp. 5–7.

11. Rudolf Hilferding, *Das Finanzkapital* (Vienna: Wiener, 1910); Vladimir Il'ich Lenin, *Imperialism, the Highest Stage of Capitalism*, vol. 19 of *Collected Works* (London: Lawrence & Wishart, 1942); Rosa Luxemburg, *The Accumulation of Capital* (London: Routledge & Kegan Paul, 1951).

12. For a survey of Western Marxism, see Dick Howard and Karl Klare, eds., *The Unknown Dimension* (New York: Basic Books, 1972).

13. Jürgen Habermas, *Communication and the Evolution of Society*, trans. Thomas McCarthy (Boston: Beacon Press, 1979), pp. 69–177.

14. The sources of positivism range from Hume's denial of the logi-

cal relations between *ought* and *is* to Karl Popper's claim that rationalism in science and social life can only be founded on a species of faith or personal decision.

15. Jürgen Habermas, *Knowledge and Human Interests*, trans. Jeremy J. Shapiro (Boston: Beacon Press, 1971); *Theory and Practice*, trans. John Viertel (Boston: Beacon Press, 1973); and *Communication and the Evolution of Society*.

16. For a development of this point, see my "Habermas and Critical Reflective Emancipation," in *Rationality Today*, ed. Theodore F. Geraets (Ottawa: University of Ottawa Press, 1979), pp. 434–40; and "The Contemporary Critical Theory of Jürgen Habermas," *Ethics* 91 (January 1981): 280–95.

17. For surveys of the history involved, see Walter Laqueur, *A History of Zionism* (New York: Schocken Books, 1976); and Maxine Rodinson, *Israel: Colonial-Settler State?* trans. David Thorstad (New York: Monad Press, 1973).

18. A slightly revised version of this essay appeared under the title "Some Implications of the Holocaust for Ethics and Social Philosophy," in *Philosophy and Social Criticism* 8, no. 3 (Fall 1981): 307–27.

12

Reflections on the
Ambiguity of Science

ROBERT S. COHEN

I SHALL OFFER MEDITATIONS on two texts, one from C. S. Lewis, the distinguished Christian theologian, and the other by Max Horkheimer, the equally well-known founder of the Frankfurt School of modern German Marxism in the 1930s.

C. S. Lewis: "What we call man's power over nature turns out to be a power exercised by some men over other men, with nature as its instrument."[1]

Max Horkheimer: "The ideological dimension of science comes to light, above all, in what science closes its eyes to."[2]

These strikingly severe judgments are, in part, judgments upon science, and also evidence that feelings for science in the present century oscillate between fear and trust. Five observations about the role of science in the modern world may help explain this ambivalence.

First, science is the only ideology with global legitimacy, cross-culturally characterizing entire societies in the world of the late twentieth century. If there is any believable global ideology, science is it, the only one.

Second, this legitimacy of science is thin and weak for most people in the world, in spite of its universality and the nearly unanimous support it receives from the ruling elites and official-doms of society.

Third, the massive tidal flows, from fear to trust and back, depend on more general swings of mood about society, and the kind of trust and prominence that those elites and rulers give to science. Science, it seems to me, is completely, inseparably, linked nowadays with what we think about our society. And this is something beyond the specific fluctuations of attitude concerning technical matters, such as nuclear power or kidney dialysis.

Fourth, support for science — whether East, West, or Third World — will continue, and will largely be unaffected by public moods. That is to say, science receives its support from the ruling powers, generously and often on a loose rein, partly because its cost is so low relative to the social budgets of other social costs. This support also depends on the fact that so few scientific leaders have threatened to become members of the ruling elite; they are no threat, they are cheap, and they pay off.

Fifth, scientists and the sciences will have a difficult time during the remainder of this century and at least the first half of the next, protecting themselves from increased, enhanced exploitation. These observations paint a gloomy picture, and we must test whether it is accurate.

Take an image from another time. Society is a great amoral beast, and science is the great sun, a fabulous source of light and warmth. Will the sun prevail, tame and master the evils of society, or will science simply nourish the beast? But, then, what determines *our* science to be what it is? The answer is both obvious and impressively diverse. Social factors, economic factors, and military needs clearly do. But so do religious needs to understand the cosmos and the microcosmos, or to find grounds for wonder; and literary needs; artistic needs; political needs; needs for enjoyment and play; the tacit needs of instincts for power, and curiosity to be satisfied. These all can be illustrated as factors which have played into, or fed into, science — posing problems, suggesting ideas, suggesting metaphors, supplying instruments, providing resources for thinking and for communicating, and even providing motivations, not to mention the need which one science creates for another. The suggestion has even been made that astronomy by itself, once it got started (and for whatever reasons, be they mystical, religious, practical — perhaps for making calendars or timing agriculture), was able, *alone*, to generate the other parts of science: the mathematics needed, the physics that came along, the instrumental developments. Surely there is a self-developing character in science, a genuine scientific dialectic, which makes science itself one of its own major cultural sources.

What then does it really signify for the science that we have, that it has been stimulated, called for, somehow caused, by all these complexities of society, themselves so interrelated? For the science *we* have, because of our sociohistorical situation, is different from the science that another civilization would have produced. We need not compare modern Europe, or even classical Greece, with hunting and gathering societies; we must refer bluntly to the science of other mature civilizations. For they have different views of nature, different ways of dealing with nature.

But then I must be using the word *nature* in different ways. The nature in which we live is, to some extent, genuinely modified by the way we live in it, and the way we perceive ourselves and nature interacting.

Polluted nature shows what I mean. If we pollute it, then there is a different nature. The vast majority of species do not change the cyclic rhythms of nature; but ours can, and at last does. Nature has been socialized; and therefore the nature we live in does actually vary with social differences of perception, imagery, and ideology.

The sciences of our nature result from the social powers which produce those sciences, which determine, influence, and pay them. The Western world imperialist culture and market system of the past three centuries therefore included our sciences, and rejected those of third-world cultures such as India and China. It comes as no surprise, then, that in the national liberation movements there has been a difficult problem: what to do with Western science? And yet, Western science is no longer Western; it is now world science. The problems selected, the material resources utilized, the particular ideas chosen for explanatory criteria, which characterize our science, play a partly pernicious role when denying or ignoring those other philosophical, theological, humanistic, literary, aesthetic characteristics which have served other societies and which constitute their historical souls. To what then have we closed our eyes?

Would science be different if it were carried out against the grain, as it were, by different forces within Western society? While looking at the history of Western religions, for example, we see subterranean forces within religions and churches. As with religion, were there different views of nature in the non-ruling parts of Western society? Was there, or might there have been, a feminine way with nature? Or might there be, or was there, a proletarian science? Would views of certain problems in the understanding of nature—not the whole problem, perhaps; not every specific bit of knowledge; not, say, whether things fall under gravitational attraction differently for women or industrial workers —follow upon differing criteria for choosing problems and different metaphors for explaining? Different models, different tests, different verifications? If we had selected different problems, perhaps there would have been a different kind of science, or perhaps, to use a mechanical image, a different weight, a different center of gravity, in a feminist or proletarian or a differently class-based science.

We may be skeptical, even cynical, about such might-have-been speculation. But we know very well that science in our times —in practice since the early nineteenth century and in self-conscious intention since its beginnings in the seventeenth—has been the servant of power. From the seventeenth to the nineteenth centuries, the subjective morality of the creative scientist and the external, utilitarian dimension of science were parallel. The two went together fairly well. It was the age of Little Science, in Derek Price's apt words. With the swing to twentieth-century industrialized Big Science, however, there was a shift in the moral life of scientists. At this point the servants had become soldiers, with assigned tasks to be carried out.

The military domination of science and technology after the First World War forms a new industrial revolution more striking even than the nineteenth-century industrialization of science. These contemporary scientific technicians are soldiers on a moral escalator, wondering when to get off. It was one step to enlist in the development and production of atomic bombs, say, in 1941, but another to get off that escalator as the nuclear military momentum increased after 1945.

The moral issue may be stated another way. A soldier has a particular moral responsibility: to obey. And the main moral quality of scientists, exhibited even within the formalisms of theories and surely in the communicative behavior of scientists as they debate and publish, is: question! Let us say it more boldly: rebel! Indeed, we might as well stress the blunt and genuinely opposing term: disobey! Why so firm? Because scientists are supposed to find out, and when they are individually free from problems of professional advancement, of careerism, they recognize what their role is: to know. The scientist's job is to be responsible for the scientist's own judgments — in turn, then, not to obey. Scientists should obey their own inner need, and should not obey the external command authority. So, responsibility works both for soldiers and for scientists, but each has a different moral story. We need deplore neither the morality nor the courage of the soldier. But what a different sort of morality, what a different sort of courage it is from that of the scientist!

Where then is the scientific obedience to power? Knowledge itself has become a commodity, and its production part of the industrial society. From the Solomon's House of Francis Bacon to the great industrial and national laboratories and think-tanks of today, the purpose was the same: society needs wise people and must pay them to give answers to society's questions, not their own. The linkage in our years between science and social problems is tighter because we live within a continuity of science with technology and material production. Science has proceeded all the way into the production of its new inventions, not limited any longer to training engineers; we recognize, in every modern society, the linked process of science-technology-production. We have, then, the "knowledge business." And, with Big Science, we have "knowledge factories," whose workers often do not know what the entire enterprise is accomplishing, or seeking. Research papers are published with a multitude of authors, in institutions with dozens, even hundreds of workers; where the collaborations of the glass blower, the instrument maker, the electrician, and the civil engineer, are far down the production line, producing knowledge; where the manager in the central office is far from the machinery of knowledge production, either of experiment or of design. Science is not only a part of the creation of goods but a new kind of commodity producer, a manufacturer of new knowledge. The deepest invention of the scientific revolution was how to discover laws of nature: scientists discovered how to discover.

The method is philosophically sophisticated since we have a curious way of trial and error. There is no algorithm which instructs us to plug things in — data, algebras, symmetries — and out comes the new theory. Yet we do have a renovated ideal of automatic intelligence, of machines which think, artificially, thoroughly, rapidly, for all the world as though *we*, with *our* artificial intelligences, will soon be able to try all possible and relevant ideas in the solution of a given problem. Then what might *all possible* mean? Perhaps all that we, and our artificial memories, know about. But this is truly a great advance, because by such high-speed artificial trial and error of all possible known ideas, we set our natural minds free, even free to invent new ways of thinking.

We must not criticize these massive achievements unfairly; but what we have is a technology for producing ideas in novel combinations. Is it a technology for the production of imagination? Think of Jackson Pollack, producing paintings by random technique. Think of the deliberate use of random connections, as in Dada, to break through all established and routinized connections, all authority; but is not Dada also mechanized even as it artificially breaks apart the rigid limitations of cultural and social dogma?

Perhaps we simply do not know what we have in science, now that it is a force of production; we have before us a new social reality, with values which clearly enough are not the values of the previous Little Science. So science now would have to be described as itself dominated by those who have power in society, by interest groups, tugging, conflicting, but dominating. And yet this domination itself is of two sorts: domination *over* science, but also domination *within* science, with a quality of irrationality within science due to those who dominate.

As an example of the internalized ways of thinking within science that reflect the criteria of the outer society, consider the criteria for a successful factory: simplicity; precision; analysis into simple components; impersonal objective standards of quality and control; economy of tools and materials; efficiency without surplus effort; unified, consistent, and complete development from raw materials to finished product; determinate relations between inputs and outputs. Are not these criteria for a successful factory also the criteria for a successful theory?

We may try another sociological analysis of science: scientific theories, we notice, should be well ordered, with as few assumptions as possible, resistant to change. Is this not the peculiar character of anality in Freud's characterology: order, parsimony, obstinacy?

Or, to pursue another social analysis: what are the characteristics of a money economy? Indeed what is money? It is abstract, impersonal, objective, quantitative, rational. This briefly
summarized view of the sociologist Simmel seems to state the characteristics of scientific theories, and of science itself as it exists
in our industrial society with its money economy.

And what about the transformation of human nature as understood through differing stances toward the natural environment? What sort of difference does this society, with *its* science
understanding *its* nature, make to nature itself? Again the word
pollution comes to mind. Marcuse named two human qualities
which have been transformed during the past two centuries in our
Western society: aggression and sexuality. They have been transformed in the ways by which they show themselves in human
character and behavior, a historical mutation of earlier modes
of aggression and sexuality with less guilt. The influence of science upon modern conceptions of human nature, and upon the reality of that human nature, are just as suggestive as the pollution
of lakes and the atmosphere of our biochemical environment.

Happily, however, science also gives pleasure to our society,
as nature did to traditional China and India. There is no blinking
the record of pleasures that scientists have received and enjoyed
in their scientific labors — though surely not all scientists, at all
times. With careerist scientists about us, we recognize that there
are not just fashions in the way of experiencing, experimenting,
and explaining, but also genuine sociological transformations in
the class of scientists. Was my generation the last to feel a pleasure-
oriented goal in becoming a pure scientist, or would each generation say so, looking at their successor young ones on the go? And
yet other scientists of our mid-century have also lamented this
lapse, in their different countries: Rutherford and Hardy in England, Kapitza in the Soviet Union, our Oppenheimer, Langevin
in France, come to mind. It would seem that riding that moral
escalator in the atomic bomb project and its subsequent silicon
valleys here and abroad may actually have transformed the role,
and with it the pleasures, of creative work in science. I should
like to think not.

At any rate, we do know that science, in its creative stages
and moments, has given pleasures which seem similar to those
artists receive. Aesthetics seems to supply the criteria to enable

scientists to talk about their standards and their satisfactions. But aesthetics is not values as such and is surely not morality. There is no moral criterion at work when a scientist says that a certain theory is beautiful, or when we say that a particularly profound theory is deep. Einstein was wise to say that moral questions and scientific questions are not joined as such, and surely neither in the behavior, nor the language, nor the thinking of scientists.

There is beauty *within* science, whether it be seen in symmetries and simplicities, or in structural complexities and nested relationships. But just as surely there is a denial of beauty *without*, in the applications of science. Here is a description of modern scientifically engineered society:

> Enjoyment was separated from labor, means from ends, effort from reward. Eternally chained to only one single little fragment of the whole, man himself grew to be only a fragment; with the monotonous noise of the wheel he drives, everlastingly in his ears, he never develops the harmony of his being, and instead of imprinting humanity upon his nature, he becomes merely the imprint of his occupation, *the imprint of his science.*[3]

This was Friedrich Schiller, 1810, before Marx, before Engels in Manchester, before our "modern times," before Charlie Chaplin. It does seem that the denial of whatever beauty there is within science has been a part of society's application of science, part of "the imprint of their science" upon industrial humanity. And how distressing Schiller's figure of the imprint, so different from what is its source.

There is yet another aspect to the analogy between pure science and the arts: a reaching beyond the self. To the classical scientist, science transcends the individual, going beyond the self. There is an impersonal factor, which to some may be religious, which seems inescapable; it is to be seen, curiously, in the *impersonalism* of science, of the scientist finding out and thinking through. We think of Newton who talked about playing with pebbles on the shore, like a child, gathering insights while the whole ocean of knowledge and reality lay before him; or of Einstein and Schrödinger and Mach with their own descriptions of modesty combined with an access to universality. Is there a Buddhist flavor

to these statements of great scientists about reaching beyond themselves, musing that the moments of their discoveries and their con-
templations are part of something beyond the self by losing their
consciousness of self? Even in the scientist's speculation about the
role of the subject in knowing the object, measurement depends
on the fusion of the known with a larger principle and potential
of knowing, rather than on a petty private subjectivity.

We speak about nature in culturally relative terms. Nature
as seen by modern science has been distorted and mechanized;
we flourish by the domination of nature. What if we were no longer
to dominate nature but to go forward, beyond domination? What
would it mean to speak of the "liberation of nature"? We must
consider two types of science: liberating science, and repressive
science.

It may be that science, subordinated to different centers of
social power, is thereby just another example of the anarchic character of the modern world society, since these dominating centers
of power are not rationally integrated, and instead are themselves
in an anarchic conflictual relationship. If so, science has failed;
or the scientists have failed to come to terms with their social roles
and their human responsibilities. If they are in fact the instruments
of a dominating social will, then their science, and ours, is guided
by those dominating social interests; and then Brecht will be judged
right in his *Galileo*.

For Brecht, Galileo set the pace of science: do not stand up
to power. He was frightened, no doubt, and we may think of Bruno's
fate. He was also prudent; but the point remains that he did what
he did in fright. Who can doubt that it is better to live, and run
away to fight another day; but he did not fight another day, although he did sneak out some manuscripts. Galileo taught the
moral lesson for subsequent science: to bow to authority, to lie,
perhaps to mutter to oneself, to wriggle about morally, to earn
a peculiar and justified right to some self-righteousness. The lesson
was quickly learned; look at the behavior of Descartes after Galileo was so badly treated.

So we do not find a record of much moral strength in the
history of Western science. There is no scientific Socrates, no Prometheus. We find some cowardice, much acceptance and assimilation to the way things are, some private moral independence, a

few heroes, and many retreats from social conflicts. We have, to be sure, a fine code of morality *within* the scientific community, combined with complete subservience to authority. Perhaps we scientists are soldiers, not instruments.

Is there an alternative? For one thing, there is hope in the single important and invariant value of all scientists, no matter what society they work in, something that transcends historical situations. The hope rests with the little word which states the responsibility of scientists: to know. And without much sophistication, we ask, What do we know *now*? The answer requires neither major propaganda nor scholarly demonstration: we know now that there are species-wide problems which transcend all interests and all ruling powers. True, not everyone knows it, or is willing to act on such knowledge, and some are willing to gamble with it even if they know it. But it remains the case that we do know, wherever our other values may be located, that there are some problems that are inexorably human-species-wide. Our species' problems are clear enough: elimination of the relevant resources of the earth, possibly within a century; overpopulation of the whole earth, related to those finite resources; mass suicidal, totally destructive war, whether nuclear or biological. Such a list is the result of knowledge, not moral judgment or mere opinion.

The lesson to be drawn is that scientists of all sorts offer a slight but existing hope because of their one responsibility, which is to know. Scientists, in whatever society, must come to that knowledge of doom which threatens.

But beyond knowing, there is also morality in the scientific community. It is a morality of an ideal mutuality within the fold. Resonating with that ideal, there is also a practicality in science. We know that we have imperfect knowledge. We know that we must make our decisions within science on the basis of our understanding of probabilities. We know certainities are beyond us. We know that we must have contexts for knowing, testing, validating, acting—we may call them boundary conditions, or laws of nature, or by other phrases, but we know that we need to understand contexts in order to make judgments. This may be only an instrumental insight, but it is a tremendous moral lesson: that there are no abstract truths for concrete lives, no absolutes— unless reconstructed as truths for the human species. The dialectic of understanding contexts may reach to the whole human race, but as such, moral judgments and policy judgments have to be made within the historical specificity of the times within which we act.

To be sure, science has the values of mutual respect. We have authorities but always they are properly subject to rebellion. Scientific life is a kind of democracy, although the citizen voters are subjected to some severe literacy qualification tests. Science is ideally a life of mutual tolerance. This Jeffersonian democracy is a communal morality built into science.

And yet, ideal though the scientific morality is, there are three essential moral qualities of human beings to which science has no direct relation. The first is tenderness. The second is kindliness — with which science may coexist or not, willy-nilly. The third is human intimacy and love.

What science seeks, and uses, is understanding, in whose light justice and injustice might then be seen in a fearful sharpness of outline. Science understands, but without making judgments. It understands the order in the world, through the so-called laws of nature; but also it understands disorders in the world, breakdowns, volcanic eruptions, psychic disturbances, catastrophes; order or disorder does not matter to science. But science also understands potentialities and options.

What then is it to be a scientist of *our* science, today, in the light of what science now knows? If it is no longer historically possible to be servants of power for a nineteenth-century Little Science, and no longer morally acceptable to be soldiers of power for a twentieth-century Big Science, then what? Bluntly, what we now know requires a liberating science, mindful of the critical human-species-wide problem, the possible doom of nature. Because science is the only species-wide ideology, if there is to be any nature to have a science of, that science must include a new value: nature itself as context for the human species.

Little Science's servants of power and Big Science's soldiers of power both regarded nature as fact, not value, because its doom was inconceivable. Our science now knows differently; hence fact becomes value, and a new dimension is added to the morality of science and the vocation of the scientist. It is still true that science understands, without making judgments; and that tenderness, kindliness, and love are only indirectly related to the scientific venture as such. But our only species-wide ideology now gradually, awkwardly, but inevitably becomes both a new humanism and a new naturalism. No longer either servant or soldier, the responsible scientist as natural humanist has been forced, often unwillingly, to speak for the values of a species-wide community, perhaps most notably at Pugwash, but now also increasingly elsewhere. The scientist has been forced out of a passive role subservient to the ruling elite because in threatening nature the ruling elite threatens science. C. S. Lewis and Max Horkheimer were in fact setting a new agenda for the morality of science. To master human power over nature will to be to master human power over humanity; and to overcome the ideology in science will be to open our eyes.

NOTES

1. C. S. Lewis, *The Abolition of Man* (New York: Macmillan, 1947), p. 40.

2. Max Horkheimer, adapted from "Notes on Science and the Crises," trans. Matthew J. O'Connell, in *Critical Theory* (New York: Herder & Herder, 1972), p. 8.

3. Friedrich Schiller, *On the Aesthetic Education of Man*, trans. Reginald Snell (London: Routledge & Kegan Paul, 1954), p. 40.

Author Index

Subject Index

Auspicious, 9, 167ff.
Authenticity, 204–6 .

Buddhist mysticism, 186ff.

Christian mysticism, 189ff.
Christianity, 61, 89ff.
Communitarian personalism, 5, 76ff.
Community, 3, 38ff., 53

Devadāsīs, 9, 169ff.
Dharma, 9, 170ff.
Discourse, 48–50

Ecumenical ethics, 5, 95–96
Ecumenism, 94–96
Education, 26ff., 30–31
Enlightenment, 15ff.

Hindu mysticism, 194ff.
Holocaust, 10, 203ff.
Human nature, 207ff.

Ideals, 6, 125ff.

Jewish mysticism, 196ff.
Judaism, 65ff.

Liberalism, 6, 10

Marxism, 122–25
Metaethics, 37
Metaxy, 43–45

Mokṣa, 9, 170ff.
Moral agent, 2, 76ff.
Morality, 37, 39ff., 185
Morality as art, 161–62
Mysticism, 9–10, 184ff.
Mythic roots, 2–4, 32ff.

Nature, 11
New Testament, 61ff.
Noesis, 42ff.

Palestine, 217ff.
Person, 80–81
Personalism, 4–5, 87ff.
Pietism, 2, 15, 21, 32
Pluralism, 58–59
Privacy, 115ff.

Rational ethics, 2, 4, 21, 38
Rationality, 214–15
Reason, 39ff.
Relativism, 58–59

Satī, 9, 168ff.
Science, 11–12, 30, 90–93, 223ff.
Speech act, 48–50
Subjectivity, 204–6
Supererogation, 8, 149ff.

Utilitarianism, 5, 101ff.

Will, 18ff.
Wille, 22–23, 25
Willkür, 23, 25